CHERISHED BY
JESUS

A Daily
Devotional
for
Women

Other Books by Mary Kathleen Glavich, SND

The Fisherman's Wife: The Gospel According to St. Peter's Wife

Heart to Heart with Mary: A Yearly Devotional

The Book of Ruth: A Tale of Great Loves

A Love Affair with God: Twelve Traits

The Holy Spirit: Font of Love, Life, and Power

I Am Going: Reflections on the Last Words of Saints

Praying on Empty: Toward a Richer Prayer Life

The Catholic Companion to Mary

The Catholic Companion to Jesus

The Catholic Companion to the Psalms

Praying with Scripture: The Bible: You've Got Mail

The Walking Love of God: St. Julie Billiart

The Heartbeat of Faith: 59 Poems, Fingerplays, and Prayers

Totally Catholic! A Catechism for Kids and Their Parents and Teachers

The Essential Guide to Catholic Terms

Handbook for Catholics

A Child's Bible

A Child's Book of Miracles

A Child's Book of Parables

A Child's Book of Psalms

St. Teresa of Kolkata: Missionary of Charity

Voices: God Speaking in Creation

Why Is Jesus in the Microwave? Funny Stories from Catholic Classrooms

Weekday Liturgies for Children

Time to Say Goodbye: A Grief Workbook for Children

The Gift of Holy Communion for Parents

500 Plus Ways to Teach Prayer

Jumbo Book of Art Ideas

Leading Young People to Mary

CHERISHED BY
JESUS

A Daily
Devotional
for
Women

Mary Kathleen Glavich, SND

LOYOLAPRESS.
A JESUIT MINISTRY

LOYOLA PRESS.
A JESUIT MINISTRY

www.loyolapress.com

Copyright © 2024 Mary Kathleen Glavich
All rights reserved.

Cover image: Joern Siegroth/Moment/Getty Images

ISBN: 978-0-8294-6040-7
Library of Congress Control Number: 2024945933

Published in Chicago, IL
Printed in the United States of America
24 25 26 27 28 29 30 31 32 33 LSC 10 9 8 7 6 5 4 3 2 1

Introduction

Jesus cherished the women in his life: his mother Mary, the disciple Mary Magdalene, and his friends Martha and Mary of Bethany. He worked miracles for women like the widow of Nain, the daughter of Jairus, the Canaanite woman, and the woman who touched the fringe on his robe. He saved the life of an adulterous woman and defended the repentant woman whose tears fell on his feet. To care for women, he was not afraid to flout Jewish laws concerning them.

Jesus cherishes you too. You are the apple of his eye, and he longs for an intimate relationship with you. Jesus speaks personally to you through the Bible, a book drenched in love. But he especially speaks to you through his words when he walked on earth as preserved in the Gospels. Through them he teaches you, comforts you, strengthens you, and above all, assures you of his love.

At the top of each page of *Cherished by Jesus: A Daily Devotional for Women* is something Jesus said. Read the verse as a love note from him. Ponder this gem, relish it, and let it touch your heart. Think of what it might mean for you at this point in your life.

The reflection on the page is geared toward women and may act as a catalyst for your own thoughts. The day's devotion ends with a short response to Jesus.

As you spend time each day using this book to listen to Jesus, your Savior, let him touch your heart. Aim to imitate Mary of Bethany who sat at his feet drinking in his every word. Know that Jesus is always with you, cheering you on and loving you. Then no matter what your life's journey holds, you will face it with courage, hope, and joy.

JANUARY

January 1

LISTEN: *"One does not live by bread alone, but by every word that comes from the mouth of God."*

MATTHEW 4:4

Just as bread keeps our body alive and strong, God's words invigorate our spirits. Once when I was devastated by what was happening at work, my eyes fell on the encouraging Scripture passage: "When you pass through the waters, I will be with you . . . when you walk through fire you shall not be burned" (Isaiah 43:2). Perhaps you have experienced a Scripture verse comforting you when you were sad or distressed, spurring you on to action when you were apathetic, or advising you when you were confused. That is God speaking to you, assuring you that he is with you, caring for you and loving you.

At every Eucharist you are fed at the table of the bread and of the Word. Make an effort to pay attention to the readings and take home a message to chew on during the week. Do you like to read, maybe on a Kindle or Nook? The most popular book in the world is the Bible. Keep it on your pillow and each night read a verse or two. You might join a Bible study or even launch one. Nourish the children in your family by having them memorize verses and sing hymns based on Scripture.

St. Jerome said, "Ignorance of Scripture is ignorance of Christ." Jesus is your reason for living and your ultimate destiny. Get to know him better by reading God's Word.

RESPOND: *Jesus, you are the Word of God in the flesh. Keep my ears open to Sacred Scripture. Help me to listen with the ear of my heart, as St. Benedict advised.*

January 2

LISTEN: *"Do not put the Lord your God to the test."*
MATTHEW 4:7

Jesus quoted that line from Scripture when the devil told him to throw himself down from the temple and the angels would catch him. I can't imagine that anyone likes tests, whether in school or in a hospital. God doesn't want to be tested either. To test God is to demand that he do something to demonstrate his power, trustworthiness, or love. It's having the audacity and presumption to ask God to meet one's expectations. Testing God shows a lack of faith.

Here are some bad prayers that test God: If you really exist, let me see a rainbow. If you love me, let my daughter recover. If you care about me, don't let me get in an accident even though I drank too much. If you are God, make my team win. We also test God by trying to make him direct us, for example, by saying things such as, "If I am supposed to work at the food kitchen tomorrow, make me get a phone call in the next hour." These are all attempts to force God's hand.

A humble, faith-filled Christian accepts God's will whatever it is and trusts that, like a lovely piece of needlework, all things work together for good.

RESPOND: *Jesus, especially when I don't understand what is happening, let me rest in the knowledge that God is God and that he loves and cares for me. When I'm afflicted, never let me think that it is because God doesn't love me.*

January 3

LISTEN: *"Worship the Lord your God, and serve only him."*

MATTHEW 4:10

The word *worship* is derived from the word *worthy*. God is the worthiest of praise. As a Sister of Notre Dame, I was taught to pray as I roll out of bed in the morning, "O my God, I awake to praise you." The chief reason you exist is to adore and glorify God, your awesome creator. St. Irenaeus said that the glory of God is a human being fully alive. If that is true, then everything you do, barring sinful deeds, can be an act of praise.

You do not need to be in church to worship God. You worship God in the kitchen as you prepare dinner, in the backyard as you plant tulips, and at your computer as you answer emails. You worship God as you sing lullabies as well as hymns. You praise God as you kneel to comfort a crying child as well as kneeling to pray in a pew. And you glorify God as you party with friends as well as celebrate the Eucharist with the community.

Just as hummingbirds, pansies, and stars give glory to God by simply being what they are, you praise God by being the godly woman you were created to be.

RESPOND: *Jesus, may all my actions be pleasing to you and give you honor. May I serve you with my whole heart and may I serve others for your sake.*

January 4

LISTEN: *"Blessed are the poor in spirit, for theirs is the kingdom of heaven."*

MATTHEW 5:3

Babies are helpless and totally dependent on others for their life. Parents feed, wash, and clothe them; change their diapers; and carry them about. You are poor in spirit when you recognize that you are like a baby in that you are completely dependent on God. Everything you are and have comes from your heavenly Father: your very life, your world, your friends, your achievements, and your possessions. All is sheer gift.

You needn't be proud of your good deeds either, because God provides the grace for you to perform them. As a daughter of Adam and Eve, you were spiritually bankrupt. Thanks to God's boundless mercy, your hope of life with him was restored. Every time you repent a failing, that is due to God's grace.

When you are poor in spirit, you trust God to supply all you need. Also, you are not greedy nor attached to what you own. If you were to lose a great deal of money to a scam or if your jewelry were stolen, it would not be the end of the world. You know that happiness doesn't lie in accumulating money or stuff. In the end, it is spiritual prosperity that matters. This attitude leaves you free to share your goods.

RESPOND: *Jesus, keep me humble and honest by realizing my utter dependence on God. In God's loving care, I have all I need.*

January 5

LISTEN: *"Blessed are those who mourn, for they will be comforted."*
MATTHEW 5:4

When the daily news hits you with a barrage of bad news—wars in various countries, violence on our streets, natural disasters, and global warming—you cannot help but mourn. Evil is rampant, and civilization is far from the good world God originally had in mind.

When sorrow overtakes you upon learning of terrible events, you show you have a heart for others. In this, you resemble God, a loving, caring Father, who surely would cry over his wayward creation if he could. You are also like Jesus who mourned over Jerusalem for not having faith and wept when his friend Lazarus died.

You also might mourn over some past actions or omissions in your own life. Maybe you stole something or did not step up to care for an ailing family member as much as you could have. When you regret your sins and failings and wish you could relive and redo certain episodes, that is a good thing. You are blessed for ruing that you had not made your life a perfect return gift to your creator. Remember, God loves you just as you are, even when you feel unlovable.

RESPOND: *Jesus, may my sorrow over the sins of the world compel me to pray for it. And may I be truly sorry for my sins that grieve you.*

January 6

LISTEN: *"Blessed are the meek, for they will inherit the earth."*
MATTHEW 5:5

People who have inflated egos naturally repulse us. They are bossy, conceited, arrogant, loud, and always think they are right. Jesus advocates for the opposite: being meek, or in other words, humble. The meek are gentle and kind, aptly symbolized by a lamb.

Contrary to popular opinion, the meek are not weak. It takes strength to control your temper when someone criticizes you or your children. If you are a big person, you step aside and let someone go ahead in line at the checkout counter or choose the carpet or paint for a room. When you have spiritual muscles, you can admit making a mistake. You can engage in self-deprecating humor, like telling how you found your lost keys in the refrigerator. When you are meek, after hurting a person, you are quick to ask forgiveness. You exercise self-control. By not lashing out at a personal grievance, you maintain your dignity and diffuse conflicts.

Being meek doesn't mean tolerating injustice. Like Jesus who overturned the temple tables and chastised hypocritical Pharisees, sometimes you must take a stand. As a meek person, you may not be popular, but you will probably be liked.

RESPOND: *Jesus, give me the strength and courage to be meek. By not promoting myself I will be a greater person in your eyes. Your opinion means more to me than what the world thinks of me.*

January 7

LISTEN: *"Blessed are those who hunger and thirst for righteousness,*
for they will be filled."

MATTHEW 5:6

If you have ever fasted or dieted, you know what it is to be hungry. If the sun or a marathon race has dehydrated you, you know what it is to thirst. Food and water are essential for life.

Being right before God, that is, being free from anything that would separate you from him, is also a matter of life—spiritual life. That is why Jesus teaches that you must long for holiness as though you were starving for it, thirsting for it. Why? Because the holier you are, the closer you are to enjoying union with God. And that is what ultimately will satisfy your hungry heart. That is the reason God created you, to be one with him in a bond of love. Nothing else people strive for is more important than living a good life. Possessions, money, power, and fame are only transitory. They are akin to food and drink loaded with empty calories.

As conscientiously as you feed your plants with fertilizer and water them regularly, you need to tend to your soul. Nourish it with prayer and acts of mercy. Refresh it with the company of good friends and uplifting reading. Make up your mind to be the best woman you can be. These steps will make you blessed, happy. They will put an end to your craving, and in the future you will find yourself enjoying an everlasting feast.

RESPOND: *Jesus, may pleasing you always be my top priority*
and chief goal. Remind me that nothing else is as healthy or
as lifegiving.

January 8

LISTEN: *"Blessed are the merciful, for they will receive mercy."*
MATTHEW 5:7

Pope Francis said, "Mercy is the true power that can save humanity and the world from sin and evil." Mercy is compassion toward those in need. The word "compassion" is a combination of the Latin words for "to suffer" and "with." So mercy is "suffering with," entering into the misery of others and acting to relieve it.

The Hebrew word for mercy, *rahamim*, comes from the word for a mother's womb. Mercy is like the love of a mother: unconditional, intimate, and nurturing. When you are merciful, you treat others as a mother does her children: with tenderness and care. You are quick to make excuses for them.

Some theologians claim that mercy is God's greatest attribute. You could say that God's name is Mercy. Jesus taught that God is merciful by his parables of the prodigal son, the lost coin, and the lost sheep. Most dramatically, Jesus was the walking mercy of God, a Son sent to save the human race from perdition. As a daughter of God, you demonstrate the divine "mercy gene" by aiding those in trouble, reaching out to the destitute, the lonely, the ill, and the marginalized, and forgiving people who hurt you.

RESPOND: *Jesus, you beautifully showed mercy to the sick and sinners. Today your mercy toward me is a bottomless ocean. I thank you.*

January 9

LISTEN: *"Blessed are the pure in heart, for they will see God."*
MATTHEW 5:8

You like to keep things sparkling clean. You are dismayed when spaghetti sauce or coffee spots your white clothes. When guests are due, you work to make your kitchen immaculate, scrubbing the counters, the appliances, and the floor. Things that are pure are unmixed with or untainted by foreign matter. We value pure water, pure gold, pure air, pure silk, purebred dogs.

Mother Mary is called most pure and the Immaculate Conception because sin never marred her soul, not even original sin. Her whole life was dedicated to pleasing God and doing his will, even though it involved danger and sacrifice. A pure heart like Mary's, one free from sin and guilt, is something for you to aspire to. At your baptism you wore a white gown, a symbol of your new, redeemed life in Christ. Whenever sin spoils your soul, aim to restore your baptismal innocence.

In another sense, a pure heart is someone honest and transparent, not hypocritical. Such a person does not have hidden motives. For instance, offering to drive a neighbor to the doctor in hopes of impressing others is a flawed act of charity.

You cannot become pure in heart through your efforts alone. It requires God's grace and perhaps a helping hand from your all-holy Mother Mary. Pray to be pure, and someday you will be rewarded with pure joy.

RESPOND: *Jesus, create in me a clean heart. I wish to be as pure as possible when I finally stand before you and behold your eternal holiness.*

January 10

LISTEN: *"Blessed are the peacemakers, for they will be called children of God."*

MATTHEW 5:9

St. Elizabeth of Portugal (1271–1336) was a consummate peacemaker. Several times when family members were poised for war, she intervened. When her husband and son were at odds, she stationed herself, seated upon a mule, between both armies and prevented the battle. When she was sixty-five years old, her son and son-in-law, both kings, were set to fight. Elizabeth again rushed to the battlefield and persuaded the armies to set down their weapons.

Your attempts to broker peace won't be as spectacular as Elizabeth's. Still, you act as a peacemaker when you silence children who are squabbling, when you settle disputes between friends or relatives, and when you reach out to an estranged family member. If you participate in an intervention for someone who is tormented by drugs or alcohol, you promote peace. You also keep the peace when you give in during an argument, don't insist on your own opinion, and ask forgiveness after you hurt someone.

Although you are not in a position to halt the wars raging in the world today, you can pray and do penance for peace and give support to organizations that work for it. Dousing the flames of conflict whether near or far is what a follower of the King of Peace does.

RESPOND: *Jesus, thank you for making peace between God and us humans. Now make me an instrument of peace by prayer and penance, as Our Lady of Fatima and the Angel of Peace asked.*

January 11

LISTEN: *"Blessed are those who are persecuted for righteousness'*
sake, for theirs is the kingdom of heaven."
MATTHEW 5:10

As you walk the path of holiness, intent on carrying out God's will, you encounter stumbling blocks. You may be persecuted by people who resent your choices that don't align with their unenlightened opinions. If you refuse to join a group planning some evil deed, you might be labeled a goody-goody and mocked. If you stand up for a just cause that is unpopular, you may be shunned. If you dare to tell someone you don't appreciate their profane or vulgar language or point out that someone is prejudiced, so-called friends may abandon you. When you introduce religion or Jesus into a conversation, people may sneer.

Being a Christian is challenging and sometimes dangerous. Seven early women martyrs are named in Eucharistic Prayer I: Felicity, Perpetua, Agatha, Lucy, Agnes, Cecilia, and Anastasia. In 1980, Ursuline Sister Dorothy Kazel, lay missionary Jean Donovan, and Maryknoll Sisters Maura Clarke and Ita Ford were martyred in El Salvador. Believers in Jesus are still being tortured and martyred.

You probably won't be killed or physically harmed for the faith, but doing what you know in your heart is right can invite painful attacks and leave you wounded. Keep your eyes on the prize: God's kingdom. After all, what matters far more than what people think of you is what you think of yourself.

RESPOND: *Jesus, make me strong enough to withstand the*
temptations to go along with wrongdoers or be swayed by
misguided people. I want to be a staunch Christian woman who
keeps her eyes on the prize.

13

January 12

LISTEN: *"Blessed are you when people revile you and persecute you and utter all kinds of evil against you falsely on my account. Rejoice and be glad, for your reward is great in heaven . . ."*
MATTHEW 5:11–12

St. Elizabeth Ann Seton (1774–1821) is the first American-born person to be canonized. When she became a Catholic, this woman from a socially prominent Episcopalian family experienced the prejudice Jesus described. Friends and relatives deserted her, parents pulled their students out of her boarding home and school, and legislation was proposed to evict her from the state. Anti-Catholic laws had just been revoked, but Catholics were still suspect. Now two centuries later bias against Catholics is still in the air.

As the current culture becomes increasingly more secular and materialistic, believing in Jesus Christ is deemed by some to be outdated and irrelevant, if not silly. You could be at a cocktail party where you are criticized because of your faith. You may hear people speak maliciously about the pope. You may be mocked for going to Mass, wearing ashes, and supporting the countercultural stands on issues that your faith demands.

Never fear. Jesus wasn't popular either. He predicted happiness for those who suffer for his sake. You might not be canonized, but your place in heaven is assured.

RESPOND: *Jesus, I want to be your loyal follower though people may make me suffer for it. I understand that enduring persecution for your sake is sharing your cross.*

January 13

LISTEN: *"You are the salt of the earth; but if salt has lost its taste, how can its saltiness be restored?"*

MATTHEW 5:13

In Leonardo de Vinci's painting *The Last Supper*, Judas has knocked over a saltshaker. Supposedly this is the origin of spilled salt's bad reputation and why people toss a pinch of salt over their left shoulder to fend off evil. Although salt is not really a weapon against Satan, it does have positive uses, and so Jesus was clever to compare his disciples to salt.

Imagine hardboiled eggs, potato chips, pretzels, and margaritas without salt. How bland! Most recipes call for you to add salt. This ubiquitous condiment not only has its own pleasing taste, but it enhances the flavor of foods and adds zest. Likewise, Christians like you make life on earth worth living. They imbue it with meaning, hope, and joy. By handing on the teachings of Jesus, they bring out the best in people.

Salt is an apt metaphor for another reason. In Jesus's day refrigeration was unknown, so people relied on salt to preserve their food. It was a precious commodity and at one time was even used as currency. Today companies add salt to canned foods and frozen meals as a preservative. Similarly, disciples of Jesus preserve the faith. For twenty centuries they have modeled it, celebrated it, handed it down to their children, written about it, and taught it to others.

How have you seasoned someone's life lately?

RESPOND: *Jesus, make me true salt for the world. Keep me zealous in living your way and inviting others to follow you.*

January 14

LISTEN: *"You are the light of the world. . . . Let your light shine before others, so that they may see your good works and give glory to your Father in heaven."*

MATTHEW 5:14,16

A nightlight helps children who are afraid of the dark to fall asleep. When the power goes off and leaves you blind in the dark, you search for your flashlight or light a candle. You need light to see so you don't stumble over a shoe or bruise your leg on a desk corner. Light is not only practical and necessary but also cozy and comforting. It is so important that in Genesis it was God's first creation.

The sun is the major source of light; without it life would not exist. The Son is your source of spiritual life. He has shared his light with you by coming to our world and teaching by word and actions. Jesus expects you to pay this light forward. Whenever you give a good example, such as by not retaliating when someone insults you, by refusing to join in gossip, and by saying, "Let's pray over this," you edify others and influence them to do likewise. One woman confided in her daughter-in-law that she was battling a fault. Sharing this endeavor inspired the younger woman to work at eliminating one of her faults too.

Your good deeds that make the world a better place give others a reason to praise and thank God. So sing, "This little light of mine, I'm gonna let it shine," at least in your heart.

RESPOND: *Jesus, thank you for shedding your light on the world. May I glorify God by radiating your love to others by acts of kindness.*

January 15

LISTEN: *"Whoever does [the Commandments] and teaches them will be called great in the kingdom of heaven."*

MATTHEW 5:19

As a child I owned a charm bracelet with the Ten Commandments. More important than wearing the commandments though is obeying them because they spell out your Creator's will that leads to your happiness on earth and in heaven. You could call them manufacturer's instructions.

Jesus summed up the Ten Commandments in two terse laws: love God and love your neighbor. You strive to please people you love. Well, you prove that you love God by abiding by his laws, or at least trying to! "Neighbor" is a synecdoche in which a part stands for the whole. God demands that you love all his sons and daughters—people from other countries (even so-called enemies), those of a different skin color or religion, the crusty old man who lives down the street, the unkempt homeless woman, a bossy mother-in-law, and a fair-weather friend.

St. John of the Cross said, "At the evening of life, we will be judged on love alone." A parable in Fyodor Dostoevsky's *The Brothers Karamazov* illustrates this: Because a wicked woman in hell once gave a beggar an onion, God handed her an onion and began pulling her up to heaven by it. As she rose, other people grabbed onto her. Fearing that the onion wouldn't hold the weight, the woman kicked them off. As they plunged back into hell, the onion fell apart, sending the woman to hell too.

RESPOND: *Jesus, your laws are a saving gift. Grant me the wisdom to live by them and teach them to others.*

January 16

LISTEN: *"If you are angry with a brother or sister, you will be liable to judgement; and if you insult a brother or sister, you will be liable to the council."*

MATTHEW 5:22

Once a woman with a short fuse began arguing with me. I didn't even know why she was upset. Abruptly, she said, "Let's start over," and immediately the fire was quenched. Our conversation returned to normal.

Anger is a natural emotion. It takes a great deal of self-control not to lash out with harsh words that may cause irreparable damage to another person. Biting your tongue in certain situations preserves relationships and your reputation. In some cases though, just anger is called for, such as when Jesus cleared out the temple when it was being desecrated.

Horace wrote, "Anger is a short madness." Besides harming another person, anger takes a toll on your own body. It raises blood pressure, increases heart rate, and deprives you of sleep. It impairs judgment so that you do and say things you later regret. For good reason, people enlist in anger management programs.

Jesus warned against anger. If it escalates, it can lead to violence and homicide, as the daily news shows. Anger is cause for censure because it does not show love. Neither does calling another person names, insulting them, or hurtfully pointing out their defects. When you feel like exploding with rage, it's wise to count to ten and take slow, deep breaths. People tend to stay clear of those who are prone to anger.

RESPOND: *Jesus, keep me calm in the face of aggravations and problems. I want to have the patience of a saint.*

January 17

LISTEN: *"So when you are offering your gift at the altar, if you remember that your brother or sister has something against you, leave your gift there before the altar and go; first be reconciled to your brother or sister . . ."*

MATTHEW 5:23–24

Some wit noted that the three hardest things to say are "I'm sorry," "I was wrong," and "Worcestershire sauce." In Jesus's eyes, asking forgiveness of a person you harmed outweighs an act of worship. Making things right with a brother or sister must precede making things right with God.

A stunning reconciliation story is the account of Joseph in the Bible. After his eleven jealous brothers beat him and sold him to strangers, he rose to power in Egypt. Prepared for famine by warnings in dreams, he was able to distribute food to the world. When his brothers came from Canaan to buy grain, you probably wouldn't blame him if he said, "Go starve. Serves you right." But Joseph forgave them even though they didn't ask for forgiveness then.

Everyone makes mistakes. Accepting another person's "I'm sorry" and not carrying a grudge afterward requires humility, love, and God's grace. So does admitting you are wrong. It takes a big person to apologize without making excuses and mend a rift.

To preserve a relationship that is precious to you, be quick to show regret after you hurt your spouse, children, sibling, or friend and ask them to forgive you. Your heart will be freed from a burden and so will theirs.

RESPOND: *Jesus, give me the humility to own up to my faults in dealing with others and ask their pardon. And give me a heart big enough to forgive anyone who has harmed me.*

January 18

LISTEN: *"It is better for you to lose one of your members than for your whole body to go into hell."*

MATTHEW 5:30

A ron Ralston was descending a canyon when an 800-pound boulder fell and pinned his arm. After several days with no help in sight, Ralston cut off that arm with his pocketknife. His harrowing experience is recounted in the movie *127 Hours*.

Ralston took that drastic measure to save his natural life. Jesus recommended a similar action to save your spiritual life. His shocking statement is hyperbolical, a way to make people sit up and pay attention. Jesus was speaking about lust, but his words apply to any sin. His point is that nothing is more valuable than spending eternity in heaven. You must sacrifice anything, escape any boulder that would weigh you down and keep you from it.

If an intimate relationship endangers your soul, sever it. If social media lures you to watch pornography, pull the plug. If a party will lead to drinking or drugs, throw away the invitation. If a friend encourages you to shoplift, cheat on taxes, or hurt someone, drop them. Disassociating yourself from sin and occasions of sin can be difficult and painful. But this kind of amputation is called for so that you can live free and in peace—not to mention escape the fires of hell.

RESPOND: *Jesus, the idea of being apart from you for all eternity is terrifying. Give me the courage to separate myself from anything or anyone holding me back from you.*

January 19

LISTEN: *"Let your word be 'Yes, Yes' or 'No, No'; anything more than this comes from the evil one."*

MATTHEW 5:37

In our contemporary culture, fake news and lies are rampant. Not knowing what to believe leads to a precarious situation. Wouldn't it be wonderful if everyone spoke the truth?

As a child, to emphasize that you were telling the truth or would keep a promise, you may have said, "Cross my heart and hope to die." Similarly, it's been a long practice to call on God or something else to witness the honesty of words. For example, the chorus of the song "I Swear" begins, "I swear by the moon and the stars in the sky." A man might swear on his mother's grave.

Jesus teaches that his followers should not swear at all. The reason is that we are meant to be people of integrity who would never lie or break a promise. An oath then would be superfluous. And besides, an oath calling on God is a form of profanity in that it disrespects God's sacred name.

If you always speak the truth, you will build the reputation of being a trustworthy person. It is tempting to outright lie or at least bend the truth in order to impress people or to cover up a mistake. It is easy to exaggerate how many awards you won at fairs, the problems you overcame, or your aches and pains. Doing so aligns you with the devil, whom Jesus called "a liar and the father of lies" (John 8:44). It is better to be known as the daughter of Jesus, who called himself the "Truth."

RESPOND: *Jesus, make me a woman who is known for being truthful. I want to be someone whom others admire and like to be with.*

January 20

LISTEN: *"Give to everyone who begs from you, and do not refuse anyone who wants to borrow from you."*

MATTHEW 5:42

At times your mailbox overflows with appeals for a donation. People invite you to support their GoFundMe projects. Solicitors come ringing your doorbell. Firemen stand in traffic asking you to help fill their boot. Salvation Army red kettle bellringers appear around Christmas, hoping for contributions. If you responded to all these pleas for financial assistance, you yourself would become a beggar!

You are also approached by people requesting a favor: Can you drive me to the store? Would you watch my children this afternoon? Can you make something for our bake sale? Jesus advocates having a generous heart and sharing your treasure, time, and talent with others—within reason.

In Shakespeare's play *Hamlet*, Polonius advises his son, "Neither a borrower nor a lender be . . ." When someone asks to borrow something of yours—a scarf, a book, a crock pot—it is risky to comply. The borrower might damage the item, lose it, or forget to return it. Nevertheless, Jesus expects you to take that risk. Not only will you please him, but you will know the satisfaction of making someone happy.

RESPOND: *Jesus, you were patient and kind when people begged you for healing. Grant me a heart like yours so I do what I can for those who appeal to me for help.*

January 21

LISTEN: *"Beware of practicing your piety before others in order to be seen by them; for then you have no reward from your Father in heaven."*

MATTHEW 6:1

Piety here, also translated as "righteousness," comprises prayer, religious practices, and good works. Motive is everything when it comes to rightly judging a deed in God's eyes. When a virtuous action is tainted by flaunting it in front of others, it's like an exquisite vase that has a crack in it.

Some examples: a woman may sing at Mass to impress others with her voice rather than to glorify God; a job seeker may do volunteer work to bolster her resume and not out of love for neighbor; a donor may give to an organization to see her name on the list of donors or to receive a free T-shirt instead of being moved to share her blessings with others. These persons already obtained a reward in this life in the form of admiration, applause, or gratitude given to them by others. It's not likely they will win a reward from God in the next life for their deeds.

Doing a holy thing in order to look good to others is narcissistic and spoils the act. It is a common temptation. You may hope that you are observed kneeling before the Blessed Sacrament, giving up your seat, picking up someone's spilled groceries, or consoling someone who is crying. You may even secretly desire that word about your good deed spreads. Ostentatious holiness is only a sham.

RESPOND: *Jesus, may the intentions of my actions always be upright and pure. May I keep my good deeds hidden and for you alone.*

January 22

LISTEN: *"But whenever you pray, go into your room and shut the door and pray to your Father who is in secret; and your Father who sees in secret will reward you."*

MATTHEW 6:6

You relish being alone with a loved one like your spouse or dear friend. Then no one else is present to distract you from focusing on that special person. You are free to be yourself and can share secrets. The Father, who longs for a loving relationship with you, likes a similar experience with you—to be the center of your attention. Praying gathered with other believers at Mass or prayer services is praiseworthy, but God also enjoys a private conversation with you once in a while.

Give God and yourself the gift of being alone together. Withdraw from the hustle and bustle of daily life, mute the cell phone, turn off the television, and cocoon yourself in a quiet space where no one will disturb you. This may be your bedroom, a church or chapel, your car, a secluded park, or a forest. Jesus modeled this personal prayer time with his Father by taking a break from his ministry and going apart from the apostles, his huge audiences, and needy people.

Besides pleasing your heavenly Father, minutes spent praying in solitude and silence benefit you. God may shower special graces on you and give you insights into your life. Your body will calm down, and your heart will be filled with peace. Such prayer also promotes mental health. As some wit remarked, "Come apart so you don't come apart!"

RESPOND: *Jesus, I wish to deepen my relationship with the Father. Help me find the time and place to pray alone to him.*

January 23

LISTEN: *"Pray then in this way: Our Father in heaven,*
hallowed be your name."

MATTHEW 6:9

God's name is equivalent to God. More than a label like your name, the divine name stands for God's very being. "Hallowed be your name" has two interpretations. First, "hallowed" means holy. Of course, God, the transcendent One, is holy, that is, perfect in every way, which you acknowledge in the Our Father. The words are a prayer of praise and adoration. In voicing it, you echo the angels in Isaiah's vision who were calling, "Holy, holy, holy is the Lord of hosts" (Isaiah 6:3). You are also like those angels in Bethlehem who proclaimed, "Glory to God in the highest heaven."

Alternately, you can view the words as a petition. You ask that all people hallow, or revere, God. How? By worshiping our Creator, by obeying his commands, and by treating his name with respect and love.

The saints, the hallowed ones, continually hallow God. When you pray the Our Father, or any other prayer, you join them. You also hallow God when you offer up actions as a gift, such as sweeping the floor, drying someone's tears, or sending a supportive card or email. In these two ways you fulfill your purpose, which St. Ignatius defined thusly: "The human person is created to praise, reverence, and serve God . . ." With God's grace, someday you will be praising God as a saint in heaven too.

RESPOND: *Jesus, not everyone fulfills their reason for existing.*
Please bring back my relatives and friends who appear to be
estranged from God. Enlighten those who worship idols such as
material goods, money, fame, and power.

January 24

LISTEN: *"Your kingdom come. Your will be done,
on earth as it is in heaven."*
MATTHEW 6:10

As a child I had a large doll with lovely blond curls. One day I asked my mother if I could wash the doll's hair. She said no, but stubbornly I proceeded to wash it anyway. To my horror, the hair and scalp came off into my hand! Fortunately, the bald doll was repaired at a doll hospital and returned to me at Christmas. My mother was wiser than I was; disobeying her led to what to me was a tragedy.

Many of the calamities in today's world are the result of people disobeying their heavenly Father/Mother. God, who is all-knowing and wants only the best for you, graciously gave you directions for living well in the Ten Commandments and the teachings of Jesus. They are God's will for you. Flouting it brings about sadness, tension, sickness, danger, and death. Complying with it helps bring forth God's kingdom of peace, love, and joy in the world and in your heart.

If you are a mother, teacher, nurse, or beautician, you are pleased when your advice is taken. You know you have made someone happier and maybe kept them from harm. In the same way, God smiles when you follow his instructions, as he surely smiled when Jesus carried out the will of his Father. And although it was extremely difficult for Jesus, a world was saved. The angels and saints also obey God. If we people here did too, there would be heaven on earth.

RESPOND: *Jesus, help me do my part to establish your kingdom by
following your laws of love.*

January 25

LISTEN: *"Give us this day our daily bread."*

MATTHEW 6:11

Bread comes in many varieties: wheat, multigrain, rye, pumpernickel, challah, naan, and my favorite, cinnamon raisin. I grew up eating white Wonder Bread at home. But there was no match for the tantalizing, mouthwatering aroma of my mother's freshly baked bread, both loaves and buns. Bread is a staple at most meals all over the world.

Asking the Father for daily bread may mean food in general. You probably don't worry about where your next meal is coming from. But it's estimated that more than 800 million people, including children, do. You can pray this petition in the name of those starving families. Then maybe wealthy people will be moved to share their assets with their brothers and sisters in need.

"Our daily bread" also refers to the Eucharist, the bread from heaven that you may be privileged to consume at least once a week, if not daily. It is the living bread, Christ, and the bread of life. Where regular bread strengthens your body, this sacred bread strengthens your soul; where bread on your table becomes part of you, the consecrated bread on the altar enables you to share in divinity and gradually transforms you into Christ. It is spiritual nourishment, the true Wonder Bread.

RESPOND: *Jesus, may I always hunger for you in the Eucharist.*
I pray that you call more men to the priesthood to help ensure that
this sacred meal is available to all.

January 26

LISTEN: *"And forgive us our debts, as we also have forgiven our debtors."*
MATTHEW 6:12

What a relief for those who have their student loans forgiven! A burden that they might need to carry for most of their adult life was lifted from them.

A sin means you owe God something. In some way you deprived the Almighty of the love and obedience he deserves. It is a debt. With overflowing mercy, God will forgive you. However, in this prayer you place a risky condition at his mercy. You ask that it be in proportion to your forgiveness for those who offend you.

It's easy to carry a grudge against a person who made fun of you, criticized you unjustly, or spread gossip or lies about you. How do you forgive a husband who has an affair, a business partner who swindles you, or a man who takes credit for your work? Your first impulse is probably to retaliate or at least to wish your "enemy" bad luck. But praying the Our Father puts you in a bind. If God answers your prayer, when you refuse to extend mercy to someone, God will limit the mercy he shows you.

Here are a few thoughts to awaken mercy in your heart. People who hurt you are loved by God. Jesus died for them. Possibly they had a traumatic childhood, or they have a weak character that acts as a catalyst for poor behavior. Besides, you are not an innocent lamb; at times you too have wounded another person either intentionally or not. And the most persuasive thought: you want God to forgive you your trespasses fully!

RESPOND: *Jesus, give me a heart so loving that I will forgive people who wrong me. Only then will I be free and at peace.*

January 27

LISTEN: *"And do not bring us to the time of trial,*
but rescue us from the evil one."
MATTHEW 6:13

The evil one is none other than Satan, who "like a roaring lion . . . prowls around, looking for someone to devour" (1 Peter 5:8). Because Satan is an angel, though a fallen one, he is powerful and extremely intelligent. He is intent on luring people away from God, whom he hates. His first human prey was a woman, mother Eve, and he successfully tricked her into defying God. You, her daughter, can also succumb to Satan's temptations if you are not vigilant and strong. Fortunately, you have a good angel on your side, a guardian angel to protect you from Satan's wiles. You also have a pure heavenly Mother praying for you and shielding you from attacks. Mary is sometimes depicted crushing Satan, in the form of a serpent, underfoot.

In addition, you can look to your heavenly Father to defend you against his archenemy. Satan is no match for God, who cast him out from heaven. During a desert retreat Jesus fended off Satan's three temptations. He freed multiple people who were under Satan's control, including Mary Magdalene, who was said to be possessed by seven demons, as well as the ostracized man who was inhabited by a legion (hundreds) of devils.

Don't play with temptations. They are like fire, and no one is made of asbestos. God can be as effective in putting out temptations as a fire extinguisher is in dousing kitchen fires. That is why it is smart to appeal to him for help by praying the Our Father.

RESPOND: *Jesus, keep me steadfast in withstanding temptations.*
I want to spend eternity with you, not Satan.

January 28

LISTEN: *"So do not worry about tomorrow, for tomorrow will bring worries of its own. Today's trouble is enough for today."*
MATTHEW 6:34

An early memory is my first-grade teacher calling me a worrywart, an ugly word to me, associated with warthog. I admit I'm an inveterate worrier. It could be that you too are plagued by thoughts like: What if my flight is canceled? What if my physical exam reveals cancer? What if my baby is born too early? What if there is a nuclear war?

Jesus understands that every day you face problems, from a broken fingernail to a broken heart. He teaches that we should focus on the immediate trouble instead of imagined ones that might not occur. He would agree with these wise words attributed to author Corrie ten Boom: "Worry is carrying tomorrow's load with today's strength—carrying two days at once. It is moving into tomorrow ahead of time. Worrying doesn't empty tomorrow of its sorrow, it empties today of its strength."

Looking back on how you survived past difficulties encourages you to regard the uncharted future without fear. Think too of God's love for you that assures he is with you in good times and bad. St. Francis de Sales elaborated on that fact: "The same everlasting Father who cares for you today will care for you tomorrow and every day. Either He will shield you from suffering or He will give you unfailing strength to bear it. Be at peace, then, put aside all anxious thoughts and imaginations . . ."

Worry affects your body. It harms you physically and mentally. Stay healthy!

RESPOND: *Jesus, some days I seem to attract problems like a magnet attracts metals. May my steadfast trust in God's love for me keep me free from worry.*

January 29

LISTEN: *"For the gate is narrow and the road is hard that leads to life, and there are few who find it."*

MATTHEW 7:14

My sister and I once hiked the trail up Diamond Head in Hawaii. We tramped along the dirt path's switchbacks under a hot sun. We climbed two staircases, one with seventy-four steep stairs, the other with ninety-nine, and walked through a long, narrow, dim tunnel. At one rest stop a few people turned back, but we two forged ahead. At the top of the old volcano, the fantastic, panoramic view of the Pacific Ocean, Honolulu, Waikiki, and Oahu's south shore was worth the arduous trek.

At times you must choose between two courses of action, two paths such as the ones that diverge in Robert Frost's poem "The Road Not Taken." One route may be smooth and easy and the other rough and challenging. You can watch a "chick flick" for two hours or visit a lonely person. At the end of a contest, you can snub the fellow competitor who won or congratulate her. After a late Saturday party, you can sleep in on Sunday or go to church.

If you are a true follower of Jesus, you will muster your courage and take the way of the cross, which is the way of love and self-denial. You will avoid the road of egotism and creature comforts, which the current culture tends to promote. Yes, taking the harder path makes all the difference. It leads to heaven, a place even more awesome than Hawaii.

RESPOND: *Jesus, during my life's journey I often come to a fork in the road. When I must choose between good and evil or between good and better, my conscience directs me to the safe route. Give me the grace to follow the paths that end with you.*

January 30

LISTEN: *"I do choose. Be made clean!"*

MATTHEW 8:3

During my pre-op for neck surgery to repair a painful herniated disk, a nurse told me that Jesus cured her husband of epilepsy after the parish prayed for him. I said, "I've been praying for weeks, but Jesus hasn't cured me." She replied, "Oh, but he is healing you . . . through the doctors." And Jesus did.

Jesus was known as a healer. About twenty percent of the Gospels deal with healing. Sick and disabled people longing to be well thronged around Jesus. One leper showed remarkable faith by asserting that Jesus could heal him if he chose. The result was a miracle.

Jesus always desires the greatest good for you. When you are suffering physically, mentally, spiritually, or emotionally, he cares. Turn to this Divine Physician with confidence if you are in pain, if you have self-doubt, if you think you are not good enough, if you are nursing a grievance, and if you have regrets.

Leprosy is a metaphor for sin, which mars your beautiful soul. Jesus is elated when you come to him to be cleansed of wrongdoing and the guilt that accompanies it. Trust that no sin is too grave for him to forgive, even one that wounds you repeatedly, like a painful corn that keeps growing back. Jesus chooses to make you whole and happy. After all, he chose to die for you.

RESPOND: *Jesus, whenever I am sick, remind me to ask you for help. Also, give me the wisdom to ask other believers to pray for me.*

January 31

LISTEN: *"Do you believe that I am able to do this?"*
MATTHEW 9:28

One Thanksgiving Day my mother was in pain after cataract surgery. I tracked down her doctor on the phone. He said he would meet us at his office if I could get her there before the building closed at 3:30. After a wild ride (usually over the speed limit), my mother met him and was treated. The kind doctor had left twenty-eight dinner guests at home in order to care for her.

Two blind men received their sight because they believed in Jesus, another compassionate ophthalmologist. You too can appeal to this expert physician for improved sight. You can also ask to be cured or preserved from nonphysical kinds of blindness, for example:

- Pray that you can see people for who they really are, not blurred or darkened by your imagination, jealousy, or what others say about them.
- Pray to discern clearly to make right decisions, those that are in line with God's will.
- Pray to see yourself with 20/20 vision so you have neither a poor self-image nor a magnified one.
- Pray to focus on what is truly important in life.
- Pray, too, for the grace to have insights about God, faith, and Scripture.

After your life has run its course, may you be rewarded with the Beatific Vision, beholding God face-to-face.

RESPOND: *Jesus, thank you for the gift of sight. Bless my eyes so that they function as they were meant to. Help me to see others and myself as you see us. And give me the grace to trust you blindly.*

FEBRUARY

February 1

LISTEN: *"See, I am sending you out like sheep into the midst of wolves; so be wise as serpents and innocent as doves."*
MATTHEW 10:16

In an Aesop fable, wolves persuade sheep to dismiss their guard dogs. The sheep then become a feast for the wolves. Jesus warned his disciples, his sheep, that their mission was dangerous. This proved true, for many were prey to wolves, tortured and killed for preaching about him. Jesus's advice for his followers was to be shrewd and not commit sins that would give others reason to reject their message and attack them.

Among your family members, friends, and acquaintances are probably "nones," or those who have left the Church, non-Christians, and atheists. As you carry out your mission to draw these people to Jesus, be smart. Invite them to attend a prayer group or Bible study with you. Involve them in a volunteer activity sponsored by your church. Give them a spiritual book to read. Recommend media like *The Chosen* or a YouTube video on an aspect of the faith. Avoid criticizing their beliefs, which could antagonize them. Listen with interest to their explanations. Invite questions. And in your enthusiasm, be careful not to be too aggressive.

Your strongest "argument" for Jesus is your own goodness. By being generous, cheerful, patient, and positive, you will attract people. They will wonder what your secret is. When they learn it is your relationship with Jesus, they may decide to join you in following him.

RESPOND: *Jesus, make me bold in carrying out my baptismal commitment to evangelize. Inspire me with ways to bring others to know and love you.*

February 2

LISTEN: *"Come to me, all you that are weary and are carrying heavy burdens, and I will give you rest."*

MATTHEW 11:28

St. Martha was preparing a superb dinner for Jesus, her two siblings, and who knows how many hungry disciples. Jesus rebuked her for being worried and distracted about many things. He wanted her to relax and enjoy the present moment for her own good.

On some days you can identify with Martha. Responsibilities weigh on you, making you feel as though you are being crushed by rocks. Some tasks are unavoidable. Your mother is sick and you are her caretaker. You have a work deadline to meet. A friend needs help with a project. Bills are mounting up. To complicate matters, you are in a tizzy because of things that are none of your business or because of unnecessary jobs you took on. Carrying these burdens makes you bone-tired and you want to scream.

Just as Jesus preferred that Martha sit as his feet like her sister Mary, he invites you to come to him for rest and recharging. He would like you to be calm, at peace, and happy, not frustrated, discouraged, and depressed. Go to him. He will enlighten you to set priorities and give you the stamina to do what you really need to do. He might work a miracle or send helpers. Your part will be to eliminate unimportant jobs and accept the help of others.

Martin Luther is credited with saying that he prayed two hours a day unless he was busy. Then he would pray for three hours.

RESPOND: *Jesus, when I am overcome with work and worries, give me the sense to stop a while and breathe. Remind me to find rest with you.*

February 3

LISTEN: *"My yoke is easy, and my burden is light."*
MATTHEW 11:30

Some religious groups have strict rules. The Pharisees enforced 613 Jewish regulations. For example, walking more than about two-thirds of a mile on the Sabbath and various activities like sewing and kindling a fire were forbidden. Today certain religious traditions ban dancing, drinking, and playing cards. Amish women must sew their own clothes by hand, wear a hair covering when outside, and travel by buggy instead of by car or bicycle. You won't see televisions, radios, or computers in their homes.

Jesus said his yoke, meaning his laws, was easy. The Greek word translated as "easy" means "fitted." The wooden yoke made by Jesus the carpenter is fitted just right to your shoulders. His laws do not lay heavy burdens on you.

Your life as a follower of Jesus is not complicated by hundreds of rules controlling your actions and happiness. You are free to hike on Sundays, participate in Zoom meetings, and wear high heels, make-up, and colorful outfits. Jesus asks only that you love God and others. That is enough to let you pass through heaven's gates.

Loving, though, can be a challenge. At times loving those you live with can be like hugging a porcupine. Don't worry. You have a yoke partner—Jesus himself. He walks alongside you, and his shoulders are broad and strong.

RESPOND: *Jesus, thank you for being my constant companion. With you by my side I can successfully carry out the work of right living.*

February 4

LISTEN: *"The Son of Man is lord of the sabbath."*
MATTHEW 12:8

"Remember the sabbath day, and keep it holy" is the Third Commandment. Jesus is the Lord, and his day is Sunday. Your Sundays are days to be devoted to him. You consecrate these twenty-four hours by making them special, different from your other 144 hours of life each week.

How do you keep Sunday holy? Chiefly by celebrating the Lord's Supper either on Sunday or on its vigil. That is the high point of your week. You come to the banquet dressed up for the occasion and join in the liturgy with attention, vigor, and love. During the day you steel yourself against temptations to catch up on chores and work, like emptying the overflowing hamper, or typing the report that is due at the office. Instead, you rejuvenate your body and soul by engaging in fun activities.

Sunday is the day to rest and enjoy the gift of life. So play family games, visit relatives, carry out a hobby, go swimming or hiking, play pickleball, work a jigsaw puzzle, attend a play or a concert, take a nap, or maybe even have a girls' night out. Make yourself happy by making someone else happy this day. Make God happy by spending time with him in extra prayer.

Christians moved the Lord's Day from Sabbath to Sunday because Jesus rose from the dead that day. Each Sunday is a little Easter. After observing it well, on Monday morning you arise from sleep, a little death, fresh and full of life.

RESPOND: *Jesus, your Resurrection changed the course of my life. May I make my Sundays the most joyous day of the week. Help me spend them in ways that honor and glorify you, and recharge myself.*

February 5

LISTEN: *"For just as Jonah was for three days and three nights in the belly of the sea monster, so for three days and three nights the Son of Man will be in the heart of the earth."*

MATTHEW 12:40

Burying family members and close friends rends your heart. You will never again see them or hear their voice on earth, and you will miss them sorely. But your hope is in Jesus, who also was buried for a time. When he burst out of his tomb, he made it clear that, yes, there is life after death. All your deceased loved ones still exist in another realm and await your arrival.

You can honor these people by visiting their grave and by adopting one of their admirable traits. Although Aunt Arline was born with cerebral palsy, she lived a normal life. Her blue eyes were usually alight with joy. As a seventh grader, I wrote a composition about her entitled "The Abused Handicap." My aunt inspired me to imitate her by plowing through adversities with a positive attitude.

People who pass from this world most likely have a stay in purgatory. Our Lady of Fatima assured us that this place of purification exists. If your loved ones are among the Holy Souls, you can shorten their time there by offering prayers, especially the Rosary, or fasting, alms, sacrifices, penance, and having Mass said for them.

You needn't fear dying. Jesus has vanquished the monster death for all of us.

RESPOND: *Jesus, I believe that because of you, death is merely a door we pass through to enjoy eternal life. I pray that the people in purgatory, especially those I know, will someday soon enjoy the Beatific Vision.*

February 6

LISTEN: *"The kingdom of heaven is like treasure hidden in a field, which someone found and hid; then in his joy he goes and sells all that he has and buys that field."*

MATTHEW 13:44

Think of three things you treasure, like your home, a friend, your talent, your health, a precious piece of jewelry. These are valuable to you, but nothing compares to God's kingdom of peace, justice, and love. Obtaining it is worth surrendering everything, even your life.

For heaven's sake, you may leave a high-paying job to work for a nonprofit that benefits the poor. You may cut ties with a likeable friend who tempts you to shoplift or do drugs. You may stop spending hours on the computer or binging television shows so you can devote more time to family or prayer. You may refuse to go along with the crowd even though it makes you a social pariah.

By growing to be the person God created you to be, by practicing virtues, and by aligning your priorities with those Jesus prized, you will become more worthy of God's kingdom. You can look forward to be forever with the One whose love for you is beyond words. What's more, you will have a clear conscience, peace, and joy.

RESPOND: *Jesus, I want to deepen my attachment to you. That will impel me to detach myself from anything that prevents me from becoming a citizen of heaven.*

February 7

LISTEN: *"Again, the kingdom of heaven is like a merchant in search of fine pearls; on finding one pearl of great value, he went and sold all that he had and bought it."*

MATTHEW 13:45

St. Katharine Drexel (1858–1955) is the second American-born saint. (The first is St. Elizabeth Ann Seton.) Born into a wealthy family in Philadelphia, Katharine could have married well. Instead she became a Sister and took a vow of poverty. She founded the Sisters of the Blessed Sacrament to minister to Indigenous Americans and African Americans. Katharine inherited 7 million dollars, which she could have spent on herself. She gave it all away, financing schools and missions in service of the poor. Some might say this incredible act was foolish, but by it she purchased a priceless pearl—heaven.

You needn't be a consecrated woman or an heiress who divests herself of a fortune to enter God's kingdom. The people in your life, circumstances, career, education, experiences, and every ordinary and extraordinary thing you do are all threads in the rich tapestry of your unique life. Doing your utmost to live well ensures future glory in the afterlife.

You can also help establish God's kingdom here on planet Earth. God's reign is one of justice, peace, and love. When you spend your God-given gifts of talents, possessions, time, and money to promote the well-being and dignity of others, you participate in making God's kingdom come. You do not have to be a millionaire to acquire a ticket to heaven.

RESPOND: *Jesus, give me the grace to trade what I am and have for everlasting life with you.*

February 8

LISTEN: *"The angels will come out and separate the evil from the righteous and throw them into the furnace of fire . . ."*
MATTHEW 13:49–50

During the first Great Awakening, in Connecticut in 1741, Protestant theologian Jonathan Edwards preached his famous "Sinners in the Hands of an Angry God" sermon. Fire and brimstone sermons woke people up into realizing that hell exists and God may send them there to deliver justice! In contrast, today, people are persuaded in a positive manner to live moral lives. The emphasis is on loving God because he loves us.

Both Jesus and the *Catechism of the Catholic Church* confirm that there is a place of eternal punishment. The greatest pain there, however, will not be physical fire, but the searing knowledge that one is forever separated from God.

A recently married woman once declined to accompany students on a weekend field trip to Washington because she couldn't bear being apart from her husband. You may have experienced the ache of being separated from a child at college or a spouse in the armed forces. Imagine being eternally apart from the all-good One who gave you life, who showered countless blessings on you, and who loves you passionately.

In a prayer attributed to St. Francis Xavier, we tell Jesus that we love him "not for the sake of winning heaven, or of escaping hell," but because he loves us and is our God. Love, not fear, is the strongest motivation to be good.

RESPOND: *Jesus, thank you for dying to save me from the hell of being separated from you forever. Now please give me the graces I need to ensure that heaven is my final destination.*

February 9

LISTEN: *"Therefore every scribe who has been trained for the kingdom of heaven is like the master of a household who brings out of his treasure what is new and what is old."*

MATTHEW 13:52

I smile when someone compliments me on a sweater or skirt that is at least twenty years old. You too probably have favorite items of clothing that are no longer in stores. Old things can still be valuable, like antiques and art masterpieces.

Jesus instructed his disciples that they were to present the "breaking news" of his life and teachings, but they were also to share his backstory—God's dealings with their ancestors, his chosen people. In other words, both the New Testament and the Old Testament are significant.

You might prefer to read and pray with the Gospels, but don't ignore the Old Testament. Granted, some of it is obscure and meaningless to you. But then there are those beautiful prayer-songs, the Psalms, and fascinating stories like Noah's flood, Samson's fall from grace, and David and Goliath's combat. You meet heroines like Ruth, the ancestor of Jesus who gave up her country and religion for love of her mother-in-law Naomi. You read how God saved the Israelites from death by the blood of a lamb and how he rescued them from slavery and led them to Canaan. The entire exodus event foreshadows the great saving acts of Jesus.

All Scripture is God's Word. Through it, God speaks to you personally. To deepen your relationship with Jesus, read the Bible daily, even just one verse. Let God touch your heart.

RESPOND: *Jesus, fill me with gratitude and love for your gift of Scripture. May I thirst for your Word and be open to what you say to me.*

45

February 10

LISTEN: *"You of little faith, why did you doubt?"*

MATTHEW 14:31

An elderly woman was asked what would she do differently if she could live her life over again. She replied, "I would take more risks." I love John Ortberg's book title *You Can't Walk on Water if You Don't Get Out of the Boat.* It dares you to attempt what seems impossible. Peter did get out of the boat and stepped onto the Sea of Galilee when Jesus invited, "Come." But when the apostle realized he was walking on water, buffeted by a strong wind, he became frightened, even though Jesus was right in front of him. Lacking faith, Peter began to sink. When he cried out for help, however, Jesus grasped his hand, rebuked him, and walked him to the safety of the boat.

When you face a daunting undertaking like changing jobs, flying over the ocean, or giving a witness talk or eulogy, do not fear. Jesus is right beside you, holding your hand. You can trust him to care for you and instill in you the courage and perseverance to follow through. If difficulties and doubt assail you and you feel like you are drowning, send an SOS to Jesus. The Gospel writer noted that Jesus answered Peter's plea "immediately." He will do the same for you if in view of the big picture it is for your good.

So when in your heart you hear Jesus whisper, "Come," urging you to do something brave, don't hesitate. By leaving your comfort zone you may experience a miracle.

RESPOND: *Jesus, may I never doubt your love for me. I hope that whenever I am in trouble, I remember to call out to you for help.*

February 11

LISTEN: *"It is not what goes into the mouth that defiles a person, but it is what comes out of the mouth that defiles."*
MATTHEW 15:10

After Jewish leaders criticized Jesus for not requiring handwashing rituals before eating, he taught that what you eat is not sinful.

Foul language can ally you with the devil. That is why children are taught not to swear, bully, or sass. Bad language could result in a time-out. Sins of the mouth comprise bragging to impress people, spewing insults in a spate of anger, and lying. You are exposed to crude, vulgar, and profanity on television, in movies, and in songs. How easy it is to adopt them! These habits are contrary to human dignity.

James wrote that the tongue is "a restless evil, full of deadly poison" (James 3:8). Often you must bite your tongue. When a woman you dislike is praised, it's tempting to point out a flaw she has. When you burn your finger on a hot pan, you may feel like cursing. When you come across a juicy piece of gossip, you might have the urge to spread it. Scripture says, "Anyone who makes no mistakes in speaking is perfect" (James 3:2). Before words pass your lips, ask yourself, "Is it kind, is it true, is it necessary?"

Your words can offer balm instead of poison, as, for example, when you comfort a crying child, console a grieving widow, say "let me help," "thank you," "I forgive you," and "I'm sorry" to the people in your life. You please God when you share your faith and when you praise him, the One who gave you the power to speak.

RESPOND: *Jesus, help me guard my tongue against offending you and hurting others. May my words show respect for you and them. May they always prove me a person of integrity and dignity.*

February 12

LISTEN: *"Do you still not perceive? Do you not remember the five loaves for the five thousand, and how many baskets you gathered?"*
MATTHEW 16:9

When my classroom's small bulletin board needed new material posted, I asked a sophomore boy serving detention to take it down. Unfamiliar with teacher talk, instead of removing the posted papers, the lad began pulling the board off the wall! Jesus was frustrated when his students, the disciples, misunderstood him. For example, he told them to beware of yeast, meaning false teachings, but they assumed he meant they had no bread with them.

Sometimes you may not understand Jesus or his plan for you. You wonder why he seems deaf to your petitions, you can't decipher his word in Scripture, or you don't know why your life takes such a zigzag path. Besides praying for enlightenment, you can draw on other people's expertise. Talk over your questions with your parents, good friend, priest, counselor, or spiritual director. Read spiritual books about prayer, Scripture, and discernment. Take courses or attend talks on these topics.

Ponder Jesus and his teachings. St. Isidore of Seville said, "The more you devote yourself to the study of the sacred utterances, the richer will be your understanding of them, just as the more the soil is tilled, the richer the harvest."

A good student always works to expand knowledge. You don't have to be another St. Thomas Aquinas. Still, with the help of the Holy Spirit, you can increase your understanding of our faith and the meaning of life. Don't frustrate Jesus, who only wants the best for you.

RESPOND: *Jesus, increase my understanding of your words and works. They are the key to life's mysteries as well as my happiness.*

February 13

LISTEN: *"For flesh and blood has not revealed this to you,*
but my Father in heaven."

MATTHEW 16:17

Peter had the grace to realize that Jesus was the Messiah and God's Son. You may have grown up knowing that Jesus is God in the flesh. It's something you take for granted. For others, this knowledge comes like a bolt of lightning. Atheist C. S. Lewis became a Christian through speaking with his friend J. R. R. Tolkien and reading G. K. Chesterton's book *The Everlasting Man.* I read that a woman turned from atheism to belief in Jesus as she held her firstborn baby.

Knowing about Jesus and his Paschal Mystery has consequences. You yearn to learn more and more about him. You can't help but love him, and your heart is filled with gratitude for his coming as man and saving you. Convinced that Jesus is the supreme ruler, the Alpha and Omega, you strive to do as he taught. Like the Samaritan woman who met him, you are compelled to spread the word about the Savior to other people.

At Peter's profession of faith, Jesus appointed him head of the Church. His role is symbolized by the wooden chair of Peter in St. Peter's Basilica in Rome. Your profession of faith in Jesus reserves you a seat at the table in heaven.

RESPOND: *Jesus, I believe in you, I hope in you, I trust in you.*
May each day bring me closer to you.

February 14

LISTEN: *"You are Peter, and on this rock I will build my church,
and the gates of Hades will not prevail against it."*

MATTHEW 16:18

The annals of Church history include several wicked popes like Pope John XII (papal reign: 955–964), who had several mistresses, and Pope Benedict IX (papal reign: 1032–1044; 1045; 1047–1048), who sold the papacy. The Church has adopted shameful policies like the Inquisition and has made mistakes, such as silencing Karl Rahner, SJ, before declaring him an orthodox theologian. The modern Church too has its share of sexual and financial scandals that can shake your faith. Church members are at odds. You might wonder if this mystical building is on the verge of collapsing.

The Greek word "rock" used for Peter means "pebble." Peter was only human. But the Church is both human and divine. The large rock it is solidly built on is Jesus. He is the cornerstone, its foundation. Despite the problems the Church faces, you can rely on Jesus to safeguard it to the end. Evil will not win.

You too are a living stone of the Church. By being a strong, faithful member, you contribute to its success on earth. How? You pray for it; read the Holy Father's encyclicals, other documents, and homilies; teach others about it; and live in such a way that your goodness and your devotion to the Church attract new followers to Jesus.

RESPOND: *Jesus, keep your mystical body healthy. Protect it from
sin and make it listen to your Spirit guiding it through these
challenging times.*

February 15

LISTEN: *"Get up and do not be afraid."*
MATTHEW 17:7

The apostles Peter, James, and John were privileged to witness the glory of Jesus at the Transfiguration. On hearing God's voice, they were terrified and fell to the ground. Jesus touched them and told them not to fear. Whenever you are in a scary situation—giving birth, waiting for results from an MRI or mammogram, driving at night through a rainstorm or blizzard, trembling before public speaking—you are not alone. The same powerful Jesus who allayed the fears of his three best friends is your friend too. He is with you. You can feel his gentle touch on your shoulder and hear him whisper, "Do not be afraid."

The apostles beheld Jesus for who he was, the Son of God and Savior of the world. They were emboldened to convey this news to others even when it incurred punishment and certain death. Out of billions of human beings, you are privileged to know Jesus. He also depends on you to speak boldly about him. Think of ways to introduce him to others. Slip his name into conversations.

Live as Jesus taught. Be confident that when you speak out against injustice, correct a friend who is sinning, or reconcile with an enemy, your Father in heaven is pleased and smiles down on you. You can almost hear him say, "This is my daughter, my beloved."

RESPOND: *Jesus, you are my dear Lord and Savior. May a firm conviction that you are always with me cast out all fear from my heart.*

February 16

LISTEN: *"If you have faith the size of a mustard seed, you will say to this mountain, 'Move from here to there,' and it will move; and nothing will be impossible for you."*

MATTHEW 17:20

A mustard seed is round and about as minute as a poppy seed. With care it becomes a large tree or bush. It is the fastest growing garden tree. No wonder Jesus made it a metaphor for faith. Even a smidgen of faith is efficacious in producing miracles. God listens to people who believe in him and trust him. He pleases them by answering their prayers, even in mountain-moving ways. Still, you must aim to make the faith planted in your heart grow. A seed needs sun, water, and fertilizer. Tend to your faith by giving it what it needs to thrive.

Associate with people who believe in and love Jesus. Join a parish women's group like the Legion of Mary, prayer-shawl makers, or rosary makers. Participate in organizations that work for homeless women or unwed mothers. Read biographies of strong women of faith like Dorothy Day and St. Elizabeth Ann Seton and be inspired by them. Learn more about your religion through lectures, courses, spiritual books, and Catholic podcasts, magazines, and newspapers. Read the Bible often and focus on the marvels God did for women of faith like Judith, Esther, Mary, the persistent Canaanite woman, and the woman who touched the fringe of Jesus's garment.

The most powerful way to grow your faith is by prayer, for then you encounter God personally and nurture your relationship with him. This includes celebrating the sacraments. You received faith, hope, and charity at Baptism. It's up to you to cultivate them.

RESPOND: *Jesus, I hope my faith grows a million times larger than a mustard seed. With the help of your grace, it will.*

February 17

LISTEN: *"So that we do not give offense to them, go to the lake and cast a hook; take the first fish that comes up; and when you open its mouth, you will find a coin; take that and give it to them for you and me."*

MATTHEW 17:27

Jesus had a divine sense of humor. He was not above playing a prank on Peter, the future leader of his Church. He directed this fisherman to find money to pay the temple tax in a fish's mouth of all things!

Did a strange thing ever happen that puzzled you? You wondered why God would allow it, but then it all turned out for the best. Maybe you had a flat tire on the way to work, and the stranger who fixed it became your spouse. You had minor surgery, and at the hospital it was discovered you had cancer, which you wouldn't have known otherwise. When you ordered something, the wrong item came, but you kept it and later you needed it.

In my retirement village, every Sunday I played a grand piano for the residents. One day the piano was missing. No longer could I accompany my friends as they sang golden oldies. I felt sorry for them and for me. However, two men offered to donate pianos to our community. The piano with a lid was chosen. The owner of the other piano desperately wanted to dispose of his, and I dreaded breaking the news to him that we would not be taking it off his hands. Then I was inspired to ask if he would give it to me. He gladly delivered it to my apartment!

God is all-knowing and all-wise. Sometimes he tests and teases us and then surprises us.

RESPOND: *Jesus, may I always depend on you to bring good out of mysterious circumstances. You see things that I don't. I'm in awe at how you design my life.*

February 18

LISTEN: *"Take care that you do not despise one of these little ones;*
for, I tell you, in heaven their angels continually see the
face of my Father in heaven."

MATTHEW 18:10

The cited verse shows that Jesus accepted the existence of angels, and in particular guardian angels. The gospels further reveal that angels ministered to Jesus after his temptation in the desert and after his agony in the garden.

Artists have done angels a disservice by portraying them as cute, chubby toddlers with wings. In actuality, these sublime creatures are pure spirits who have no bodies, let alone wings. They may, however, assume bodies. Majestic angels at Jesus's tomb terrified women and sent Roman soldiers standing guard into a dead faint.

St. Pio of Pietrelcina was one of several saints who was able to see angels. He encouraged a woman to treat her angel not as a friend but as family. People sent their guardian angels to him with the message that they needed his prayers.

How comforting to know that God assigned a powerful angel to protect and guide you! Take advantage of your spiritual companion. Before going on a journey, ask your guardian angel to keep you safe. When you are besieged with temptations, beg your angel to help you to resist them. If you are suffering a hardship, pray to your angel for the strength to endure it gracefully. And pray the Angel of God prayer, which is not only a child's prayer but also yours. And when people are in trouble, ask their guardian angels to rescue them.

RESPOND: *Jesus, thank you for assigning me a powerful personal*
bodyguard. When I am in need, inspire me to have recourse to my
guardian angel for assistance.

February 19

LISTEN: *"So it is not the will of your Father in heaven that one of these little ones should be lost."*
MATTHEW 18:14

Some days you might feel like the one sheep that went astray. You've detoured from the safe route to heaven and so maybe fell off a cliff or got ensnared in thorny bushes! Your temper got the better of you at home or at work. You skipped going to Sunday Masses. You cheated when you filed your taxes. You failed to break off a dangerous relationship. When you review your life, shameful incidents stand out like black blots that you wish you could bleach away. Don't worry. God knows you haven't been preserved from original sin, as was the Blessed Virgin. He understands your weakness.

Your heavenly Father regards you lovingly as his "little one." He already made the ultimate sacrifice to save you by sending his Son to atone for your sins. You can look to God, whose mercy knows no bounds, to forgive you over and over. What's more, God will shepherd you to stay the course and be enfolded in his arms at the end of your journey. Your part is to pray and take advantage of the sacraments, especially Reconciliation, where you hear the words of absolution and are fortified with grace to sin no more. God loves you as his precious child. He says to you, "I have loved you with an everlasting love" (Jeremiah 31:3). You can lean on him as you follow in the footsteps of his Son.

RESPOND: *Jesus, keep me mindful that no matter how many or how grievous my sins, I can always be forgiven. Give me the grace to regret my failings and resolve to live as God's good daughter.*

February 20

LISTEN: *"If another member of the church sins against you, go and point out the fault when the two of you are alone."*
MATTHEW 18:15

When someone spreads a lie about you, passes off your idea or work as their own, or steals from you, of course it hurts and angers you. We women like everyone to like us. Jesus does not expect you to ignore ill-treatment. That would not be holiness but spiritualized masochism! Rather, he advises you to confront the offender about the matter. Why? Because standing up for yourself is a way to love yourself. Pointing out the other person's sin also expresses love for them. Speaking up may cause them to change their behavior and become a better person. At the very least it will give them a chance to apologize.

Notice though, that Jesus advises keeping the offense a private matter. Often injured parties complain in public and may sue. The news races across the Internet and is fodder for newspapers and magazines. It is tempting to air your grievances and share your troubles with others. Doing so, though, mars the reputation of the person who hurt you and turns others against him or her. It fuels gossip. Only if your offender turns a deaf ear to you does Jesus recommend involving other people.

Keep in mind that praying for people, especially "enemies," softens your heart toward them.

RESPOND: *Jesus, help me to do what you would like me to do, especially when I don't feel like it. Use me to be a light to others by correcting them when necessary and with Christlike kindness.*

February 21

LISTEN: *"For where two or three are gathered in my name,*
I am there among them."

MATTHEW 18:20

When a Jewish family celebrates the Seder, they leave an empty chair at the table for the prophet Elijah and open the door for him. This ritual expresses their hope that he will join them and herald in peace for a world in turmoil.

As you set the table for a family celebration of a Christian feast like Christmas or Easter, or a First Communion, Confirmation, or marriage, you needn't provide a seat for Jesus and wait for him. He is already there! Being the omnipresent God, Jesus is everywhere though as invisible as your breath. As someone once put it, God is a circle whose center is everywhere and whose circumference is nowhere. No need to wait for Elijah's return; Jesus, the Messiah, is the Prince of Peace.

Jesus is present at all Christian gatherings. He is watching as you engage in church activities like a Bible study or a prayer service. He is there even if only one other person shows up! He is there as his followers come together for an event like a Eucharistic Congress or a Catholic Youth Rally. He is at hand at Catholic institutions and at your side if you teach at a parish school of religion. When you pray with friends or with your spouse and children in family prayer, Jesus is with you.

Most dramatically, Jesus is present when the people of God are gathered to celebrate the Eucharistic feast.

As Jesus promised, he is with us always.

RESPOND: *Jesus, I believe you are with your Church today just as you were with your disciples in Israel. I long for the day when I will praise you face-to-face.*

February 22

LISTEN: *"[Forgive] not seven times, but, I tell you,*
seventy-seven times."
MATTHEW 18:22

The most extraordinary forgiveness (other than the forgiveness of Jesus for us) has to be that which the Old Testament Joseph extended to his jealous brothers. At first they had intended to kill him, but then relented, threw him in a well, and sold him to traders who were en route to Egypt. The Pharoah appointed Joseph to rule the country. During a world famine, Joseph distributed grain to all who came. When his treacherous brothers arrived for a share, rather than retaliating, Joseph graciously gave them grain and then the most fertile land in Egypt!

Jesus expects radical forgiveness from you. He wants you to forgive not three times as the Jewish law required, but seventy-seven times, in other words, always.

Has a friend betrayed you? Did your coworker insult you? Did a child or grandchild disobey you? Forgiveness is called for even if there is no apology. It benefits you as well as the other person. Relationships are restored, stress is removed from your heart, you sleep better, and you feel good about yourself.

Look to Jesus and Old Testament Joseph as models. Resist holding a grudge. It's been said that resentment is like drinking poison and waiting for the other person to die. On the other hand, to quote Mark Twain, "Forgiveness is the fragrance that the violet sheds on the heel that has crushed it."

RESPOND: *Jesus, let me recognize forgiveness as a tool to live fully and freely. May I offer others the mercy I would like to receive. And give me the sense to forgive myself for past mistakes and failings.*

February 23

LISTEN: *"For mortals it [being saved] is impossible,*
but for God all things are possible."
MATTHEW 19:26

After the first humans offended almighty God, things looked hopeless. No way could these pitiable creatures doomed to die regain the right to heavenly bliss on their own. God, though, had the power and fortunately the will to reset their fate. He did more than he had to. Out of compassion, God the Son stood in for men and women and atoned for their sins, not just the original one, but the ones committed every day.

Do you ever fear that on Judgment Day you will not make it through heaven's gates? That the scales of justice will not be in your favor? Do you think that you haven't done enough to assist the poor, preserve the earth, or work to alleviate human suffering? Do you regret the sinful habits that you haven't been able to overcome or a grievous sin you committed long ago? Don't worry.

Despite your flaws, God is your champion, number one cheerleader, and best friend. He loves you every moment of the day and wishes the best for you, and so he will gladly provide the graces you need for salvation. Still, it is wise to take the advice of an often-quoted saying: pray as though everything depends on God, but work as though everything depends on you.

RESPOND: *Jesus, thank you for your sacrifice that set me free. May*
I live in such a way that it has not been in vain. Help me to make
decisions that are in line with your teachings.

February 24

LISTEN: *"And everyone who has left houses or brothers or sisters or father or mother or children or fields, for my name's sake, will receive a hundredfold, and will inherit eternal life."*

MATTHEW 19:29

A friend moved to Abu Dhabi when her husband's work was transferred there. This entailed leaving behind her mother, sister, home, and country. Love does such things. The apostles gave up much to follow Jesus, most of them even their lives. Today consecrated religious leave behind family and sometimes country as they live their vocation.

You are not exempt from having to shed what you are attached to. For love of Jesus you may need to give up people and possessions that are incompatible with living as he requires. If a friend or relative endangers your soul, you must cut ties. If a workplace or neighborhood is spiritually unhealthy, you need to move. If you come into a large amount of money, you must share it instead of using it to upgrade your wardrobe and your jewelry collection. Yes, and if you love baked goods, candy, or alcohol to the detriment of your health, you must give them up.

Following Jesus is demanding and involves sacrifice. Like Peter you might ask, "What is my recompense?" Jesus said it would be a hundredfold. In this life the hundredfold is peace, a clean conscience, and joy. And Jesus promised that in the next life you will come into your inheritance as God's daughter: the kingdom of heaven.

If Jesus is the love of your life, prove it.

RESPOND: *Jesus, on Calvary you gave up everything for love of me. I hope to have the courage to surrender anything that weighs me down and prevents me from following you wholeheartedly.*

February 25

LISTEN: *"For many are called, but few are chosen."*
MATTHEW 22:14

I once attended a First Communion party where only half of the invited guests showed up. Understandably, the mother, who had prepared food for everyone, was disheartened and upset. Maybe you can identify with her. God can. Our creator "desires everyone to be saved" (1 Timothy 2:4). God calls not just "many" but "all." But according to Jesus, sadly, few respond. Preceding this verse is the parable about a king who planned his son's wedding banquet. The people he invited refused to come.

You have an open invitation to come to God's heavenly banquet. Thanks to your free will, you can choose not to come to it. The prerequisite for entry is merely to do as God says: love him and love others. As you are busy paying bills, driving children to games, keeping the house clean, and preparing presentations for work, you may forget about prayer and going to Mass. While you focus on keeping yourself and your family healthy and successful, you may neglect the dire straits of your brothers and sisters on the margins. Your road to heaven may have pitfalls and detours. You may have to choose over and over to stay the course.

While on earth, make your RSVP a "yes" for another sacred banquet, the Eucharist. There you will receive the grace needed to be God's guest in the next world.

RESPOND: *Jesus, thank you for clearing the way for me to arrive at heaven. May all my daily decisions culminate in a place at your table there.*

February 26

LISTEN: *"If David thus calls him Lord, how can he be his son?"*

MATTHEW 22:45

All Jews knew that the Messiah would come from the line of David, their greatest king. But as Jesus pointed out, David called his son Lord, meaning God. This puzzled the Pharisees. From your vantage point after the Resurrection and Pentecost, you know that the Messiah, namely Jesus, is both human and divine. In Philippians 2:10–11 you read, "At the name of Jesus every knee should bend . . . and every tongue should confess that Jesus Christ is Lord." You confess in the Apostles' Creed that Jesus is seated at the right hand of the Father. At Christmas you sing, "Come let us adore him."

Although you might exclaim, "I adore those shoes," adoration is worship given to God alone. The honor we show toward Mother Mary is not adoration but hyperdulia, veneration. Adoration is acknowledging God's supreme perfection and authority. In Scripture people and angels expressed this physically by falling on their face before God. Today you bow, kneel, and genuflect in the presence of Jesus.

How else do you adore God? You pray, "I adore you," and sing worship songs. You adore Jesus present in the Blessed Sacrament during exposition. You offer Jesus yourself and serve him to the best of your ability. You keep Jesus number one above all people and things. In doing so, you fulfill your reason for existing: to glorify God.

RESPOND: *Jesus, I adore you with all my heart. I want to give you glory by the way I live and how I use my talents. My greatest hope is to adore you forever in heaven.*

February 27

LISTEN: *"And because of the increase of lawlessness,
the love of many will grow cold. But anyone who endures
to the end will be saved."*

MATTHEW 24:12

Violence, crime, hatred, cheating, and lies are prevalent today. Many people succumb to the temptation to join perpetrators and imitate their wrongdoing. Sometimes you too might think, "Why not? Everyone's doing it." My mother often said, "If everyone jumps into Lake Erie, will you jump too?" Seeing as I couldn't swim, that would have been disastrous! Equally dangerous is going along with the wrong crowd.

So your neighbor cheats on taxes and isn't caught, a friend coaxes you to try a drug, a coworker explains how to steal from your company. Relatives who went to Catholic school for twelve years give up the faith. So what? If you follow these weak people, you are apt to hear God's words to the church of Ephesus, "I have this against you, that you have abandoned the love you had at first" (Revelation 2:4).

The plight of today's world can be disheartening. Where is God in all this mess? Why doesn't he do something? It's easy to become bitter and turn your back on God, to forget his past favors and lose hope. Staying steadfast in the race despite the hurdles, hardships, and mysteries will win you salvation. You will know what it is to be engulfed in God's love forever.

RESPOND: *Jesus, help me not to grow weary in always doing
what is right. I know that when I grasp your hand tightly without
letting go, I can walk safely, even on stormy seas.*

February 28

LISTEN: *"[T]hey will see 'the Son of Man coming on the clouds of heaven' with power and great glory."*

MATTHEW 24:30

People perceive you in different, sometimes even opposite ways. Your children and friends may think of you as sweet and gentle, even a pushover. Your employees, however, may regard you as a strict and demanding taskmaster.

Jesus has two natures; he is both God and man. Therefore, he can be viewed in two ways. Nowadays, like the majority of people, you probably focus on his humanity: his lowly birth, his emotions of grief and anger, his persecution and suffering. This is a comfortable Jesus. But stressing the humanity of Jesus may obscure his divinity, his identity as God the Son. Jesus's description of his second coming corrects this. It reminds us that he is awesome, inspiring holy fear.

On the last day Jesus will appear in all his majesty and omnipotence. He will command angels and judge justly all the men and women who ever lived. Michelangelo's painting *The Last Judgment* seen above the altar in the Sistine Chapel expresses well the formidable power of Jesus. It depicts him with the muscular body of a superhero in the center of the scene and making a commanding gesture. He is not smiling.

By all means, pray, "I love you, sweet Jesus," but also pray, "I adore you, my King and my God."

RESPOND: *Jesus, open my eyes to see you as you are: my loving brother and friend, but also almighty God who created the cosmos. May you always be the Lord of my life.*

February 29 (Leap year)

LISTEN: *"Keep awake therefore, for you know neither the day nor the hour."*
MATTHEW 25:13

When do you think the world will end, when Christ will come again? Maybe during Advent. Maybe as the Doomsday Clock edges closer to midnight. Or maybe when evil is so rampant that you wonder if God regrets making humankind, as when he washed our planet with the great flood.

Usually you are so wrapped up in the business of daily life that the apocalypse is far from your mind. So too the hour of your death. The time of both major events is a mystery. Jesus cautions that you need to be awake, not dozing through life or complacent. So how do you prepare for the hour when according to Greek mythology the Fate Atropos cuts the thread of your life?

Strive to live by the greatest commandments, love of God and neighbor. Keep your soul pure. When sin sullies it, wipe it clean through the Sacrament of Reconciliation. Ask forgiveness of anyone you have hurt. Reconcile with an estranged family member or friend. As your spouse or children go out the door, tell them you love them.

Emily Dickinson acknowledged death's inevitability when she penned, "Because I could not stop for Death—he kindly stopped for me—. . ." We mortal beings can die any day, any minute. Heed the advice of Marcus Aurelius: "While you live, while it is in your power, be good."

RESPOND: *Jesus, grant that I approach the end of my days with joy, knowing that I have lived well. May your Mother be at my side the hour of my death as she was with you when you died.*

MARCH

March 1

LISTEN: *"Come, you that are blessed by my Father, inherit the kingdom prepared for you from the foundation of the world."*

MATTHEW 25:34

Certain sites have power to fill us with profound peace and joy. You may have experienced this on a seashore while the sun is setting, in a sunlit park surrounded by scampering squirrels and chirping birds, or in your backyard amid the butterflies visiting the roses, irises, and daisies you planted.

When God created the world, he placed your first parents in the Garden of Eden, a delightful home where he walked with them. A bad choice caused their eviction. Because Jesus redeemed you, it is possible for you to live in God's kingdom. This present natural world with its waterfalls, mountains, forests, and endless variety of flora and fauna is amazing. It promises that the next world will be beyond your imagination. There, your heavenly Father is waiting to welcome you; there, you will see, hear, taste, feel, and smell wonderful things. There will be no more wars, death, or weeping. You will be in the company of your Blessed Mother, other saints, and the angels, including your guardian angel.

Best of all, you will be in the presence of God, the one who created you, the one you yearn for with all your heart. Your heavenly Father will envelop you in love. Your joy will be complete and everlasting.

Right now God blesses you with grace that can serve as your passport into his kingdom. All you have to do is cooperate with it.

RESPOND: *Jesus, thank you for another chance to join you in your kingdom. May I benefit from your invitation by always doing the next right thing.*

March 2

LISTEN: *"For I was hungry and you gave me food, I was thirsty and you gave me something to drink, I was a stranger and you welcomed me, I was naked and you gave me clothing, I was sick and you took care of me, I was in prison and you visited me."*
MATTHEW 25:35–36

K eeping the first and greatest commandment, to love God, means also keeping the second one, to love your brothers and sisters. Jesus identifies in particular with those in need. When you assist them, you assist him. He spelled out ways to love others. And like a good teacher, he also demonstrated these: he fed the hungry with miraculous bread, gave drink to the thirsty at a wedding, welcomed strangers like the Samaritan woman, saw that the Gerasene demoniac was clothed, healed the bleeding woman, and came to earth when we were Satan's prisoners.

If you are a mother, you carried out for your family members the acts Jesus enumerated. Consider how many meals you prepared, how many glasses of water you brought to children at night, how many new little infants you welcomed, how many articles of clothing you brought or made, how many times you soothed a hurting child or spouse, and possibly how many you visited a family member in prison, a psychiatric ward, or rehab facility.

You also ministered to Jesus when you loved people outside of your nuclear family: when you donated to charitable organizations, volunteered at food kitchens, hospitals, or second-hand stores, assisted immigrants, or wrote to prisoners. Jesus desires your empathy.

RESPOND: *Jesus, I believe that the good I do for others I do for you. May I follow in your footsteps by serving those in my circle and in the world at large who most hunger for love and care.*

March 3

LISTEN: *"Truly I tell you, just as you did it to one of the least of these who are members of my family, you did it to me."*

MATTHEW 25:40

St. Teresa of Calcutta was known for being called to serve the poorest of the poor. She is one of a long line of women saints who served the underserved. For example, St. Frances of Rome (1384–1440) distributed food, clothing, and money to the needy and visited prisoners. During a famine she opened a hospital and a shelter for the homeless on her family estate. She founded the Olivetan Oblates of Mary, women who served the poor. A legend holds that when she walked to the sick and the poor at night, her guardian angel showed the way with a lantern that shone like a headlight, which explains why St. Frances is the patron of motorists!

St. Augustine described this kind of love in action: "What does love look like? It has the hands to help others. It has the feet to hasten to the poor and needy. It has eyes to see misery and want. It has the ears to hear the sighs and sorrows of men [and women]."

Author François Mauriac warned, "When your heart no longer burns with love, then others will die of the cold."

Jesus regards all persons as his brothers or sisters. Harming them harms him. Neglecting them is neglecting him. But promoting their well-being is ministering to him. It pleases him, gives you joy, and will reap you a great reward someday.

RESPOND: *Jesus, awaken me to those hurting people who could use my time, kind words, donations, and love. Give me the determination and strength to do what you urge me to do for them.*

March 4

LISTEN: *"Where is your faith?"*

LUKE 8:25

An often-told story about faith describes a man who falls off a cliff. Part way down he grabs hold of a tree branch and yells, "Help!" He hears, "This is God. Let go." The man asks, "Is there anyone else there?" The disciples in a boat during a storm were terrified even though Jesus, asleep, was with them. He chided them, "Where is your faith?"

Your faith is tested sometimes too. Suppose your plans fall apart, you lose your job, you must undergo an unexpected surgery, you're caught in a maelstrom of things to do, or a dear friend dies. Distressed and afraid, you might shed copious tears and spend sleepless nights. If you doubt that God cares about you, he could justifiably be asking you, "Where is your faith?"

God loves you more than you love yourself. He only acts for your good. In the face of dire circumstances, you need not fear. The same loving God who led the Israelites out of slavery, saved Daniel from the lion's den, healed the Canaanite woman's daughter, and calmed storms on the Sea of Galilee is at your side. You may think he is asleep, but he will either rescue you or oversee the situation as a means of strengthening you or teaching you. Confident in his loving care, you can stay serene no matter what happens. Remember, our loving God draws good out of evil. Look at what he achieved on Calvary.

RESPOND: *Jesus, I believe that you are always with me, working for my greater good.*

March 5

LISTEN: *"The spirit is willing, but the flesh is weak."*
MATTHEW 26:41

St. Paul exemplified Jesus's observation, for he confessed, "For I do not do the good I want, but the evil I do not want is what I do." (Romans 7:19). You can probably echo the sentiments of this saintly sinner. You make New Year's resolutions and then Lenten resolutions, firmly intending to keep them. But sooner or later, as Maxine said in a cartoon: "If you are very, very quiet, you can just hear the resolutions breaking all over the world." That includes yours.

You cut down on sweets for your health, but then you hear a chocolate chip cookie calling your name. You aim to exercise for many reasons, but you can't make yourself get up from the recliner and move. You promise to break the habit of watching X-rated movies, flirting with a certain man, or talking too much about yourself, but you might as well promise to climb Mount Everest. You resolve to be more positive, support a nonprofit, or reconcile with a relative, but you never get around to it. You know that absolution in the Sacrament of Reconciliation depends on a firm purpose of amendment. Still, you are a repeat offender.

You inherited this weakness from your first parents whose original sin infected the human race. But there is hope. After doing something wrong, a Christian can turn 180 degrees. Jesus understands your situation. He forgives seventy times seven; in other words, always. You can appeal to him to be your ally in overcoming your weaknesses. He offers abundant grace freely and ceaselessly.

RESPOND: *Jesus, strengthen me to be the person you designed me to be. I want to be more like you: compassionate, selfless, loving.*

March 6

LISTEN: *"Put your sword back into its place; for all who take the sword will perish by the sword."*

MATTHEW 26:52

The truth of this statement is played out daily. Countries attack each other and their soldiers die, and criminals who harm others are killed. After Peter cut off the ear of the high priest's servant, Jesus healed it. He knows that violence and conflict are not the best means of establishing justice. Like him, Mahatma Gandhi and Martin Luther King Jr. taught nonviolence to achieve their aims. You practice nonviolence when someone offends you and you stay calm and make peace. This might be difficult, for it may go against your instinct.

That the pen is mightier than the sword is a true proverb. Words, written or spoken, can be effective in disarming someone—words like, "I'm sorry you feel that way" and "What can I do to help?"

On the other hand, words can wound people. You are not likely to pierce people with a sword or stab them with a butcher knife. But cutting remarks like, "You act so childish," "You eat too much," and "Your singing is always off-key" cause irreparable damage and leave scars. You probably cringe as you recall stinging comments that were hurled at you. Hopefully you didn't retaliate but kissed the pain up to God.

RESPOND: *Jesus, keep my words kind and helpful. May I put out the fires of conflict with the waters of soothing words.*

March 7

LISTEN: *"Do you think that I cannot appeal to my Father, and he will at once send me more than twelve legions of angels?"*

MATTHEW 26:53

A Roman legion comprises three to six thousand soldiers, so Jesus claimed at least 360,000 angels—majestic spirits—could come to his defense. Because Jesus is God, angels worship him and are at his service. Most people believe that angels exist.

I once was invited to give a talk about angels. I thought, *Why angels when there are more significant Church topics?* Shortly after, Bob, a sales rep, took my assistant and me out to dinner, proudly driving his new car. During the meal the waiter urged us women to have dessert, but we declined. Back in the parking lot, we discovered that Bob's car lights had been left on; his car wouldn't start. The manager came out and moved his truck to jumpstart the car. But his cables didn't fit the battery's post. Repeatedly Bob tried to start the car but in vain. Inspired to appeal to his guardian angel, I prayed, "Bob is such a kind gentleman. This is embarrassing for him. Please help." Instantly the engine started. The manager teased, "Next time have dessert."

Besides praying to your guardian angel, call on others' angels for assistance like I did. For example, when you are worried about the safety of a family member, when a friend is being sued, or when a reader or speaker has a frog in their throat, pray to their angels for help.

The Father of Jesus is your loving Father who has sent angels to protect you and your loved ones. Take advantage of them.

RESPOND: *Jesus, I praise you, the Lord of all angels. Whenever I, or people I care for, are in trouble, let me remember to call on the powerful invisible friends sent to care for us.*

March 8

LISTEN: *"All authority in heaven and on earth*
has been given to me."

MATTHEW 28:18

Roman soldiers mocked Jesus as king, giving him a crown of thorns and a purple robe, and the crime posted on his cross was "King of the Jews." How ironic, for Jesus truly is a king, King of Kings and Lord of Lords! After rising from the dead and ascending to heaven, he received all authority. He was given the right and the power to rule supremely over everything in heaven and on earth—angels and saints, devils, and all humankind, including you. His authority is absolute. We celebrate this fact at the end of each liturgical year on the Solemnity of Our Lord Jesus Christ, King of the Universe.

What do you owe Jesus as your king? The same things you expect of children under your authority and the same things you owe your parents: obedience, gratitude, and love. Keep Jesus as king of your heart by doing what pleases him. Abide by his laws, think of him as you go about mundane tasks, adore him in the Blessed Sacrament, join in the Eucharist, converse with him, and do not permit anyone or anything to usurp his role.

At the end of the world, Jesus will exercise his authority by judging all men and women. Blessed will you be if you are worthy to enter his kingdom of peace. There he is seated on a throne at the Father's right hand, and all saints and angels pay him homage. He reigns forever. And Scripture gives you this Good News: "If we endure, we will also reign with him" (2 Timothy 2:12). So someday you could be a princess!

RESPOND: *Jesus, may I never forget that I belong to you, the king*
of heaven and earth. Grant that all my words and deeds reflect my
privileged identity as your daughter.

March 9

LISTEN: *"Go therefore and make disciples of all nations, baptizing them in the name of the Father and of the Son and of the Holy Spirit, and teaching them to obey everything that I have commanded you."*

MATTHEW 28:19–20

Before taking leave of his eleven disciples, Jesus gave them this command known as the Great Commission. Some people facetiously call it the Great Omission. Why? Because instead of zealously spreading the word about Jesus and his teachings, many Christians have become complacent.

The original disciples were on fire for Christ. They managed to bring multitudes of people to him. Take St. Paul, for instance. After meeting Jesus, he roared through the known world telling others about him. Beatings, whippings, shipwrecks, arrests, prison—nothing could dissuade him from missionary activity.

Jesus counts on you to let others know about him. You like to introduce those who mean a lot to you to other people. You enjoy saying, "I'd like you to meet my husband . . . my oldest daughter . . . my friend." Jesus is someone you should be eager to share with others. A relationship with him can result in eternal life. Don't you wish everyone would become acquainted with Jesus and have the opportunity to live the best life here and hereafter?

You can draw others to Jesus by speaking about him in conversations, writing about him, and inviting others to church with you, and by being a shining example of living as he taught.

RESPOND: *Jesus, may I take seriously your command to bring others to you. Bless with success my efforts to be a missionary disciple.*

March 10

LISTEN: *"And remember, I am with you always,*
to the end of the age."

MATTHEW 28:20

Although Jesus would no longer be with his friends in a perceivable form, as he departed, he assured them he would be with them. You are not able to see or hear Jesus either, but he is always with you. That is the point of this adapted story: A woman in a dream saw scenes from her life in the sky. In the sand were two sets of footprints, hers and Jesus's. She asked him, "Why during the roughest times in my life did your footprints disappear?" Jesus replied, "Those were the times I carried you."

Jesus does more than walk alongside you; he lives within you. As a baptized believer, you have the Trinity dwelling in the depths of your being. During the day, speak to Jesus freely, no need for fancy words. When you hear depressing news or are worried about the future, confide in him. Nothing is too small to share with him: a spat with someone, your failure to do a favor, a sleepless night. When you are happy or achieved a goal, talk about it with Jesus. He is interested when you are promoted at work, renovate your bathroom, have a child graduate with honors, or successfully prepare a new recipe.

You can totally rely on Jesus to give you comfort when you are hurting, strength when you face an ordeal, and peace when you are in turmoil. No one loves you as much as he does.

RESPOND: *Jesus, thank you for being my constant companion and*
listening to my every word. May I occasionally take time just to be
quiet and soak in your presence.

March 11

LISTEN: *"Follow me and I will make you fish for people."*
MARK 1:17

Even if you've never gone fishing, you know that it requires bait, a hook, and loads of patience. Jesus depends on you to catch people for him. This key responsibility of Christians is called evangelization. You can bring others to Jesus by luring them with your words and example, sometimes not even deliberately. St. Catherine of Siena said, "Be who God meant you to be and you will set the world on fire."

While one of our elderly Sisters was in the hospital, her roommate noticed her praying the Rosary. One day the woman asked Sister to teach her how to pray it. Then she asked, "How can I be a Sister too?" Sister replied with a smile, "Well, first you have to become Catholic. Then you have to leave your husband." Surprisingly, the roommate did join a Rite of Catholic Initiation for Adults (RCIA) program!

There are various lakes for you to fish in: your extended family, your neighborhood, your workplace, and your clubs. Your hook should not be glaring and obnoxious. Catch people by quiet words of kindness, sympathy, encouragement, and support. Let your faith show gently by mentioning Jesus, offering to pray for someone, wearing ashes on Ash Wednesday, and reading the Bible or a devotional. You might include a Scripture verse in letters and emails, or invite someone to your parish for a service or other activity.

Jesus helped the apostles, who were seasoned fishermen, locate large schools of fish when their nets were coming up empty. Today he will be your invisible assistant as you carry out his work.

RESPOND: *Jesus, use me to lure more people into the saving ark of your Church. Inspire me with ways I could influence others to be your followers. I thank you that I have been caught.*

March 12

Listen: *"Follow me . . ."*

Mark 1:17

A friend from out of town was following my car from a restaurant to my mother's house. Vehicles intervened, blocking the sight of her car in my rearview mirror. She did not have my mom's address or a cell phone. I pulled into a gas station, and, after a few frantic minutes, my friend drove up.

In the Gospels, Jesus says, "Follow me," thirteen times. He invites you to follow him, a privilege but no easy task. When you are so overwhelmed by work, doctor's appointments, social commitments, and household chores that you don't spare Jesus a thought or a prayer, you might lose sight of him. Or you might deem the way he chooses to go too risky, too uncomfortable, or too unpopular, and so you turn around. Instead of following the One who is the way, the truth, and the life, you might follow the promptings of your lesser self, the devil, a charismatic but heretical priest, or a persuasive friend who, like the Pied Piper, lures you away from Jesus and his community. If so, Jesus probably feels as frustrated as I felt when I lost my friend.

Although Jesus's way involves crosses, keep in mind the final destination it leads to, which is his Father's house. How closely are you following him so that nothing manages to squeeze between you or make you lose sight of him?

Respond: *Jesus, at my Baptism I became your follower. Give me the courage, energy, and love to keep my eyes fixed on you and persevere—no matter how hilly, twisting, or full of potholes the road becomes. If I do take a detour, set me quickly on the right path again.*

March 13

LISTEN: *"Be silent, and come out of him!"*

MARK 1:25

The Gospels record several instances of Jesus casting devils out of people. Today some think that cases of demonic possession are really misdiagnosed illnesses. Nevertheless, the Catholic Church still trains priests to be exorcists. Who can deny that there is a power struggle between good and evil in the world?

You are not likely to be possessed by the devil or persecuted by him as was St. Don Bosco. However, like all human beings, you probably harbor a bad spirit or two. Maybe it's a spirit of jealousy. You resent your sister's talent that surpasses your own; you begrudge your neighbor's good luck or new car; or you are secretly rankled by a friend's success. Maybe a spirit of low self-esteem dwells in you to the point where you don't like yourself. Or maybe a spirit of addiction has hold of you. Try as you may, you just can't quit smoking, drinking, overeating, or shopping.

Our human race is no longer held captive by Satan and facing a destiny of eternal hell. Jesus vanquished Satan for good by his sacrificial death that unlocked heaven's gates. Jesus can be your personal hero too by banishing any bad spirits within you. You need only ask Jesus for help, and he will command, "Be silent, and come out of her." Let the Savior heal you so you can be free and whole.

RESPOND: *Jesus, you who are all good wish only goodness in me and for me. I trust in your power and your love for me. Cast out any evil inclination or habit that possesses me. Then I will be a better reflection of you and more deserving of your love.*

March 14

LISTEN: *"I do choose. Be made clean!"*

MARK 1:41

When you make a doctor's appointment for yourself or a loved one, to your dismay it might not be scheduled until many weeks or months later. How you wish you had the power to cure your family members and friends who are sick! One thing you can do is to turn to Jesus, the Divine Physician, for help. During his public ministry, he compassionately healed multitudes of people suffering from various diseases and conditions. His ministry of healing culminated on Calvary when he cured the whole world of sin by his Death on the Cross—an extreme antidote.

Jesus chose to cure many lepers instantaneously. This will probably not happen in your case; years may roll by without signs of improvement. Instead of performing a miraculous cure, Jesus might heal through the ministry of a doctor. Or in his omniscient view of things, he may know it is better not to cure at all.

Besides physical diseases like leprosy, multiple sclerosis, and COVID, there are diseases of the soul. Perhaps you are afflicted with lethargy, depression, addiction, an obsession, or jealousy. Never assume that Jesus is reluctant to cure you. When you are hurting, go before him and say, "If you choose, you can heal me." The results may surprise you.

RESPOND: *Jesus, increase my faith in you as the great healer. I want to trust you to cure whatever ailments I suffer from physically and spiritually.*

March 15

LISTEN: *"Son, your sins are forgiven."*

MARK 2:5

Because you are human, you can't help hurting people at times. When your "I'm sorry" evokes "I forgive you" from a spouse, child, or friend, relief and gratitude wash over you. You are freed from the burden of guilt, and your relationship is repaired.

Each of your sins offends your heavenly Father who loves you and more than anything craves your love in return. You owe God an apology. You can rest assured that compassionately he will gladly forgive any failing that makes you ashamed: white lies, little unkind acts, pettiness, and other peccadillos as well as major offenses.

True, you can ask forgiveness privately in prayer. You can always pray an act of contrition. Venial sins are forgiven when you receive Holy Communion. The most gratifying and convincing reception of God's forgiveness, however, occurs in the context of the Sacrament of Reconciliation. There, through the priest, who is Christ's representative, you hear the words that absolve you from your sins. Then, like the paralytic who was healed body and soul, you can rejoice. As Pope Francis observed, "To be forgiven is to experience here and now, that which comes closest to being resurrected." In other words, when you are forgiven, you rise from a kind of death to a new, joy-filled life.

RESPOND: *Jesus, may true sorrow for my sins stir me to ask forgiveness of those I have hurt, especially you and our heavenly Father.*

March 16

LISTEN: *"Those who are well have no need of a physician, but those who are sick; I have come to call not the righteous but sinners."*

MARK 2:17

Mothers, teachers, and nurses pay most attention to the neediest child in their care. They hope that the extra time and energy devoted to this little one will nurture growth and wellness. Similarly, Jesus loves all people, but admitted that he focuses on those who are wounded by sin. He is eager to rescue the lost and the sick. This was his mission when he walked the earth. He forgave Mary Magdalene, Peter, the paralytic brought by his friends, the paralytic by the pool in Bethesda, and the good thief. Even as he was in his death agony, he implored forgiveness for his tormentors. Extending mercy is still his mission today.

When you find yourself in the category of sinner, don't put off making an appointment with Jesus. He has no office hours but is available night and day, 24/7. Trust him to provide the remedy for your soul's illness and restore you to health. He offers salvation for all who seek it.

Sin is like a virus. If someone you know has fallen ill from it, dare to suggest that they turn to Jesus to clear their conscience. The Holy Spirit will help you.

RESPOND: *Jesus, when I'm sick with sin, give me the humility to admit it and the courage to come to you for healing.*

March 17

LISTEN: *"No one sews a piece of unshrunk cloth on an old cloak; otherwise, the patch pulls away from it, the new from the old, and a worse tear is made."*

MARK 2:21

This metaphor suggests that Jesus was familiar with sewing and laundry. You too probably know that patching an old pair of jeans or a shirt with new material is a mistake. In the wash, the patch might shrink and tear away from the old material. The message in this comparison is that Jesus was initiating something entirely new. Some religious practices that the Jewish leaders required were outdated. Enforcing them was a mistake.

Jesus's metaphor also has meaning for the Church, which is a living institution that continually evolves with the times. Clinging to customs that were formed by the cultures of past eras is also a mistake. It would thwart the actions of the Holy Spirit, who always guides the Church toward new and fresh futures. A Church in tune with this Spirit will be relevant and attractive.

Similarly, Jesus calls you to become a new creation. Some of your habits might need to be discarded and new ones adopted. These may include how you pray, your relationship with certain people, and the way you spend your money. Today might be a good time to listen to the Holy Spirit and be open to change. Doing so can be as exciting and satisfying as assembling a new, more modern wardrobe!

RESPOND: *Jesus, keep me from the fear of incorporating new and better habits. I want to grow spiritually.*

March 18

LISTEN: *"The Sabbath was made for humankind, and not humankind for the Sabbath."*

MARK 2:27

We Christians observe the Lord's Day on Sundays. It is a gift: a chance to recoup from a busy week, a time to rest, play, and enjoy family and friends. If you participate in vigil Masses on Saturday, some of the sparkle of Sundays may have faded. You might take steps to preserve this day as the highlight of the week.

If you do celebrate the Eucharist on Sunday, dress up and put on makeup for the occasion. It conveys respect for the Lord and makes you feel good. Prepare a special meal, or at least a special dessert, and eat together. Using plates, silverware, or a tablecloth reserved for Sundays will lend an air of festivity to the meal. Strengthen your bonds with family members by having fun together: go on a picnic, play a board game, visit a park or museum. Spend extra time in prayer with the God who blesses you with these twenty-four hours each week. You might pray the Rosary, read a spiritual book, or reflect on a Scripture passage.

When your Sunday is free from ordinary work, you can take the opportunity to practice works of mercy. You might visit the sick, write a letter to a prisoner, or call a friend who needs support or advice. Two of God's greatest works of mercy occurred on Sundays: the Resurrection and Pentecost.

RESPOND: *Jesus, thank you for arranging time off each week for me. May I never squander my Sundays.*

March 19

LISTEN: *"Whoever does the will of God is my brother and sister and mother."*

MARK 3:35

Perhaps no one is dearer to you than your family members: parents, siblings, spouse, children. You share life, food, and home with them. You love them and will do almost anything to promote their wellbeing and happiness. Jesus longs for you to be an intimate member of his family. While your blood relatives and spouse have an earthly relationship with you, Jesus invites you to a spiritual relationship with him. This occurs, he said, when you obey his heavenly Father. Then, Jesus will love, esteem, and care for you as your elder brother.

How do you do the will of God? It can be summed up in one word: love. You are to love God and other people. The way to love is spelled out in the Ten Commandments, the Beatitudes, and the works of mercy. By loving, you become related to Jesus. He adopts you. What's more, you become an heir to heaven, his family home.

A corollary to this statement of Jesus is that you are bonded with all the other members of his family, both living and deceased. All those who do the Father's will form one body, the Communion of Saints. The members included in these spiritual family ties care for and support one another with love and devotion, most practically, in the parish community.

RESPOND: *Jesus, I want you to regard me as a close family member. Let me develop the strength to do what pleases God the way you did.*

March 20

LISTEN: *"Other seed fell into good soil and brought forth grain, growing up and increasing and yielding thirty and sixty and a hundredfold."*

MARK 4:8

If you are a gardener, you know from experience how essential good soil is for flowers and vegetables to grow and flourish. In a parable, Jesus compared his words to seeds falling onto hearts. When your heart is rich soil, his words take root and grow. You are able to spread them to other people.

Pollution and pesticides ruin soil. Temptations from the world, the flesh, and the devil assail hearts. Sin hardens them. Dry, rock-like hearts are impervious to God's saving words. But just as water and nutrient-rich fertilizer added to soil make it life-giving, God's grace can infuse unresponsive hearts and open them to the Gospel.

You can keep your heart tender, healthy, and receptive to God's words and actions by frequent prayer, celebrating the sacraments of Reconciliation and Eucharist, reflecting on Scripture, and cultivating positive friendships. When you till the soil of your soul in these ways, you will be a blessing for other people. Your life will yield much good fruit.

RESPOND: *Jesus, like a gardener with a green thumb, plant your words in my heart. Help me keep it free from the weeds of sin.*

March 21

LISTEN: *"Pay attention to what you hear; the measure you give will be the measure you get, and still more will be given you."*

MARK 4:24

As teachers instruct others, their own knowledge of a subject expands. For example, teaching a friend Spanish increased my Spanish vocabulary. Jesus exhorts his followers to listen well to his wise words. Then he obliges them to share a measure of this knowledge with others. They were not to keep it to themselves like a secret for a privileged few. The more they imparted spiritual truths to others, the greater understanding they would have of these truths. In fact, they will be blessed with further insights into the mysteries of the faith.

If you wish to have a firmer grasp of the faith, teach it to children, teenagers, or adults. Explain facets of what you believe to relatives and acquaintances when the opportunity arises. By teaching, you will come to an even greater understanding of the faith.

Some saints possessed an uncanny knowledge of theology. As a young woman, St. Julie Billiart astounded her bishop and priests when they questioned her about the faith. St. Thomas Aquinas filled tomes with his teachings on what Catholics believe. God will instill in you, too, a keener understanding of him, the Gospel, and life as you generously convey what you know to others.

RESPOND: *Jesus, I want to know more and more about you and your teachings. Make me bold and ablaze with enthusiasm in sharing the Good News with others.*

March 22

LISTEN: *"Peace! Be still!"*

MARK 4:39

At times you might be distressed, besieged by problems and concerns that leave you tossing and turning at night. Any number of things can disturb your peace: your computer seems possessed, a relationship is shaken, difficulties at work arise, a family member is in trouble, regrets at your past failings unsettle you, worries about the future plague you. You feel like screaming or banging your head against a wall.

When the apostles were caught in a storm at sea and in danger of drowning, they woke Jesus who was asleep in their boat. He calmed the wind and subdued the waves. Jesus has the power to free you from the storms raging in your life, too. Call on him with confidence. Realize that it might seem as though he is asleep. Your urgent plea might not elicit a quick response. If that happens, you must be patient and trust in Jesus's wisdom and his desire to do what is best for you.

Just as you might cradle a frightened, sobbing child in your arms and dispel their fears, Jesus longs to soothe you and save you. When you cry out to him for help, you are likely to hear him say, "Peace! Be still!" He loves you and cares about you.

RESPOND: *Jesus, strengthen my faith so that you are always with me. I know that no storm in my life is too terrible for me to weather with you near.*

March 23

LISTEN: *"Why are you afraid? Have you still no faith?"*
MARK 4:40

After Jesus calmed the storm at sea, he chided the apostles for being fearful when he was with them. True, he was asleep and seemingly unconscious. But his very presence should have assured them that no harm would come to them.

Because Jesus is God, like the air, he is constantly present all around you. He is also within your innermost being, sharing his divine life with you and keeping you breathing 20,000 times a day and your heart beating 100,000 times a day. However, you are not always aware of him. You do not see his holy face, hear his voice, or feel his touch, but when you firmly believe that Jesus is with you, loving you, there is no need to be afraid of anything.

Having a family member or friend accompany you to an intimidating situation like a visit to the doctor, a court appearance, or an interview gives you courage. Jesus is your best friend. He walks with you everywhere, even "through the darkest valley" (Psalm 23:4). Knowing that Jesus is at your side is bound to lessen your fears, if not banish them. You can face trials, difficulties, and unexpected setbacks with confidence and hope. You can walk through life with holy boldness.

RESPOND: *Jesus, I place all my hope and trust in you. I'm convinced that you will never abandon me.*

March 24

LISTEN: *"Go home to your friends, and tell them how much the Lord has done for you, and what mercy he has shown you."*

MARK 5:19

The man Jesus cured from being possessed by many demons wanted to stay with him. But Jesus sent him home instead to spread the word about his healing. When you are blessed with good fortune such as becoming engaged, passing a test, or getting a promotion, you can't wait to announce the news to others. Excitedly you inform them face-to-face, or you call, write, email, or text.

Your greatest blessing, indeed a miraculous healing, is that God saved you from Satan's clutches and filled you with his divine life. This news isn't something to keep to yourself. Jesus bids you to share the fantastic news of salvation not only with friends but also with strangers. How? Give someone a Bible, invite a neighbor to church, become a missionary.

God has granted you countless other favors. Some of these are unexpected and take your breath away. On the observation deck of the Washington Monument, you encounter a friend you haven't seen in decades. In a full parking lot, a car moves out, leaving a space for you. A book falls open to a page with just the information you need. These lesser or greater miracles are called Godwinks or God-incidences (not coincidences). Record these in a journal or special book so you can remember them and thereby refresh your love for God. Tell others about them, giving our good God credit.

RESPOND: *Jesus, open my eyes to recognize the countless ways you have blessed me. May I not be shy about telling others about them.*

March 25

Listen: *"Daughter, your faith has made you well."*
Mark 5:34

The woman who unobtrusively touched Jesus's cloak to steal a healing is a good model for you. She had heard about Jesus, this radical preacher and miracle worker who cured people. Believing that he could help her too, she quietly tapped into his power.

You may not have suffered for twelve years like that anonymous woman, but surely you endure some illness. This may be a physical ailment like arthritis, multiple sclerosis, impaired hearing, or headaches. It could also be an obsession, a fear, a character flaw, a secret sin, or scruples.

You became acquainted with Jesus through the Gospels and what others told you about him. Believe in his supernatural power and, more than that, believe in his love for you. No matter what others may think of you, reach out to Jesus for healing. In the Eucharist you touch more than his clothing. You consume his entire life-giving self—a perfect opportunity to beg for a cure.

Jesus is eager to address you tenderly as someone he cherishes and bring you wholeness and peace. When you exercise strong faith, you just might hear him say, "Daughter, your faith has made you well."

Respond: *Jesus, flood me with the faith that makes me realize that with you nothing is impossible. Then with confidence I will pray, "Jesus heal me."*

March 26

When Jairus heard that his daughter had died, Jesus told him not to be afraid but to believe. Jairus probably wondered what he was to believe. Yes, Jesus had cured diseases. But because Jairus's daughter was dead, the situation appeared as hopeless to him as traveling to the moon.

The death of a loved one shakes you to the core whether it is unexpected or a relief following a long stretch of suffering. Time for conversing with them has come to an end. No longer will you behold their dear faces alight with joy. No more will you feel their arms around you in a tight hug. You wonder where they are. Do they still exist? Are they aware of you now? Will you ever see them again? Sorrow overwhelms you.

Take heart! Jesus speaks words of comfort to you: "Do not fear, only believe." By dying and rising, he has conquered death in a remarkable way. Bringing people back to life during his public ministry was a foreshadowing of our resurrection at the end of time. So was his own Resurrection. Because of Jesus, you can believe in eternal life for your loved ones. Death is only a doorway into the next world. This belief destroys your fear of death, removes its sting. Someday your tears of grief will give way to tears of joy as you reunite with your dear departed ones.

Concerning death, Jesus told us that what we had hoped for was true.

RESPOND: *Jesus, I do believe in the resurrection of the body and life everlasting. I look forward to seeing you.*

March 27

LISTEN: *"Little girl, get up!"*

MARK 5:41

At Jesus's command, Jairus's dead daughter instantly came back to life, got up, and walked around. Then she ate something, which proved that she wasn't a ghost.

At times you might be "dead," not physically but emotionally or spiritually. You might be drained of energy due to illness, overwork, or stress, making a small task like sweeping the floor or sewing on a button seem monumental. Ennui may cloud your mind so that nothing interests you, not even your favorite television program. Depression can rob you of vitality, energy, and life. You just want to stay in bed. You can't pray. Worst of all, sin and bad habits can invade your life and deaden your soul.

Jesus is master over death and life. Whenever you feel more dead than alive, he is always there, ready to take you by the hand and say, "Little girl, get up!" Hopefully with the help of grace and by dint of your own efforts, your normal life will be restored.

Jairus, a devoted father, was a bridge leading to the girl's resuscitation. Jesus may rouse you to life through another person too: a family member, a therapist, a doctor, or a priest. His compassion is unfailing. He desires your well-being more than anyone, even you. Trust that he can wake you from your sleep.

RESPOND: *Jesus, when I pass through dark days, be my strength and my comfort. I look to you to revive my spirits and keep me optimistic.*

March 28

LISTEN: *"Prophets are not without honor, except in their hometown, and among their own kin, and in their own house."*

MARK 6:4

The rejection Jesus experienced in his hometown exemplified the truth of the saying "Familiarity breeds contempt." Despite his miracles and popularity, his own people scorned him. They had lived closely with him for most of his life and knew him well. They refused to believe that Jesus was superior to them. Maybe some of them were jealous. There is basis for the claim that an expert is someone who lives more than five hundred miles away.

On occasion Jesus's words may apply to you. Although you excel at something, you are overlooked or even snubbed by people who are used to you. They take you for granted. An achievement you are proud of isn't acknowledged, much less celebrated. You are not chosen for a certain role or award.

I could somewhat identify with Jesus's observation after presenting a talk at a conference overseas. Strangers there made me feel like a rock star, but when I returned home, the Sister who picked me up at the airport remarked, "To us you are just Kathleen."

Regardless of how people around you ignore you, criticize you, or dismiss what you say, keep your ego intact. You are the apple of God's eye. He thinks the world of you and knows your value. If you know the hurt of being treated like a nobody, you might consider who in your relationship deserves and needs some attention. Then give it.

RESPOND: *Jesus, make me aware of people I tend to take for granted. Let me honor them by listening to their opinions and ideas and by showing them respect.*

March 29

LISTEN: *"You give them something to eat."*
MARK 6:37

When Jesus told the apostles to feed the thousands of people who were gathered to hear him speak, they faced what seemed an impossible task. They probably wondered if the sun had affected his mind. But then Jesus worked a miracle, and the apostles distributed a meal of bread and fish to the throng.

According to the organization Action for Hunger, in 2023 as many as 783 million people worldwide faced food insecurity and hunger. Globally, that's nearly one in ten people. Like many women, you might derive joy and satisfaction from preparing a homecooked meal for family or friends. Hear Jesus say to you, "Give the starving something to eat too."

You can do a little bit toward solving the world's hunger problem. Cook and serve meals in a food kitchen. Organize or assist with a collection of food items for the needy. Volunteer to make deliveries for Meals on Wheels. Donate to an organization that provides food for the poor, for example, at Thanksgiving.

When you are making a special dinner, invite someone you usually don't dine with to enjoy your feast. People who live alone would especially be glad to receive such an invitation. When friends or neighbors suffer a crisis like a death in the family or are recuperating from an accident or a hospital stay, provide meals for them.

Keep in mind what St. Teresa of Calcutta said: "Not all of us can do great things. But we can do small things with great love."

RESPOND: *Jesus, make my heart sensitive to my brothers and sisters who go to bed hungry. Motivate me to act to alleviate their pain.*

March 30

LISTEN: *"Take heart, it is I; do not be afraid."*
MARK 6:50

As Jesus walked over the water, the apostles, thinking that he was a ghost, were terrified. Jesus may enter your life in such a way that you do not recognize him. Maybe you lose your job, learn that you have a chronic illness, or are deserted by a friend or family member. Your dreams for the future may be shattered or your plans foiled. Your fright will be dispelled if you hear Jesus telling you, "Take heart. It is I."

Jesus allows scary things to happen for a reason. In his wisdom and goodness, he might be planning a better course for your life than the one you intended. Our Blessed Mother's life was turned upside down and riddled with severe trials, but this led to the world's salvation.

Hardships can mold you into a stronger, kinder person, someone who empathizes with others in pain and distress and helps them. For example, a woman who suffered a miscarriage begins a support group in her parish. The mother of a child with a disability meets with other mothers to provide faith classes or social activities for their differently-abled children. A cancer survivor founds a woman-to-woman support group for new patients.

Whatever happens, realize that Jesus is with you, ready to stretch out his hand and sustain you. He only acts for your good. Jesus may assist you through other people such as a good friend or a fellow worker or even an article you read by chance. In whatever guise Jesus comes, you can be sure he is saying, "Do not be afraid."

RESPOND: *Jesus, give me the sight to discern your presence in my life, particularly when strong winds threaten to sink me.*

March 31

LISTEN: *"For saying that, you may go—the demon has left your daughter."*

MARK 7:29

At first Jesus was deaf to the Gentile woman's pleas to cure her daughter; but then he relented and cured the girl due to the mother's persistence and repartee. You might know how a child's constant pestering can wear you down and make you give in. God, your loving father, apparently reacts similarly at times. Remember how Abraham negotiated with God who intended to destroy wicked Sodom (Genesis 18:22–33)? He proposed sparing the city for the sake of fifty good men, then forty-five, forty, thirty, twenty, and finally ten. And God agreed each time.

In a homily Pope Francis taught that we should talk to God as a friend. He said that prayer ought to be "free, insistent, with debate, and should also scold the Lord a little: 'But, you promised me this, and you haven't done it.'"

When you request something from God, ask relentlessly until you receive an answer. Be as determined and tireless as St. Martha, who prayed for decades that her son St. Augustine would be converted from his sinful life. At long last God answered her prayers. So be patient as you ask for healing for a family member, a new job opening, or a buyer for your house. Persevere. But realize, too, that for a good reason God may answer "not yet" or perhaps "no."

RESPOND: *Jesus, give me the hope and the diligence to persist in knocking on heaven's door. I trust that eventually you will respond to prayers for my needs, others' needs, and the world's needs.*

APRIL

April 1

LISTEN: *"Why are you frightened, and why do doubts arise in your hearts? Look at my hands and my feet; see that it is I myself. Touch me and see; for a ghost does not have flesh and bones as you see that I have."*

LUKE 24:38–39

What would you think if a girlfriend who died suddenly appeared before you? Like the apostles upon seeing Jesus, you might assume you were seeing a ghost. Or you might think you were hallucinating. Jesus proved he was really himself by showing his hands and feet wounded by nails, by inviting the astounded apostles to touch him, and by eating a piece of fish.

You are not likely to be visited by the risen Jesus and receive tangible proof that he still lives. Instead, you rely on the word of people who have been told of this phenomenon by eyewitnesses. The Good News of the Resurrection has been passed down for twenty centuries. You probably heard it from your parents. This news is vitally important.

The Resurrection validates everything Jesus did and said, including his promise that you too will rise from the dead. If Jesus hadn't risen, your faith would be useless. Your prayers and good deeds would be in vain. You could not hope to live forever. You could not count on seeing your departed loved ones again.

But Jesus does live again. So dye Easter eggs, buy lilies, send Easter cards, and with all your heart sing "Alleluia" ("Praise God")!

RESPOND: *Jesus, I believe that by dying and rising you won eternal life for me. Give me the grace not to lose that gift.*

April 2

LISTEN: *"Why does this generation ask for a sign? Truly I tell you, no sign will be given to this generation."*

MARK 8:12

To test Jesus, Pharisees asked for a sign from heaven. Oddly, their request came after he had cured hundreds of sick people and multiplied the loaves and fish to feed thousands! Apparently, miracles like this weren't enough to persuade the thick-headed religious leaders that Jesus was God-sent. What more could Jesus do?

Have you ever wished God would assure you of his existence by a sign? Hopefully, you are not as blind as the Pharisees to the signs around you: the mind-boggling marvels of the cosmos that NASA's photos display, the sweet face of a newborn baby, the ingenious variety of flowers and animals, an answered prayer.

God also proves emphatically that he loves you. What greater signs are there than the Cross on Calvary and the Blessed Sacrament in your church? Then there are also the special favors God adds to your days, like meeting up with an old friend, finding a statue or picture you wanted on sale, or your perfect Thanksgiving dinner.

As for a sign that eternal life awaits you, St. Paul wrote that more than five hundred people saw Jesus alive after he was put to death. His disciples spoke with him and ate with him. You can trust Jesus's word that someday you too will see him.

RESPOND: *Jesus, I do believe that you are God and still live. Nevertheless, make me attentive to and grateful for the signs you send me.*

April 3

LISTEN: *"And do you not remember?"*
MARK 8:18

Just after Jesus had miraculously fed four thousand people, incredibly the dense disciples were concerned because they had only one loaf of bread with them in the boat! This merited a rebuke from Jesus. You may identify with the disciples in that although Jesus has worked some marvelous things in your life, you forget about them and become a worrier.

Every now and then God has something occur that takes your breath away. For example, against all odds you take first place in a contest, you find a lost key, you happen to meet someone who gives you advice, or a tornado spares your house. With time, the memory of these serendipities is in danger of fading away.

A few habits will ensure that you preserve the memory of these special favors. First, at the end of each day, mentally scroll through the hours, pinpointing the good things the Lord had done for you that day. Second, record each little miracle in a "blessings book." If you keep a journal, star such events in it. Reread what you wrote from time to time, like a woman reads old love letters.

Recalling the mercies God has shown you in the past will bolster your confidence when you face future ordeals. It will spare you from becoming a nervous and anxious nail biter. When someone loves you, you can depend on them to take care of you. No one loves you more than God.

RESPOND: *Jesus, everyone experiences difficult circumstances and tragedies, and I am no exception. May memories of your goodness sustain and give me courage.*

April 4

LISTEN: *"But who do you say that I am?"*

MARK 8:29

Who are you? Mother, aunt, girlfriend, child, spouse, grandmother, real estate agent, baker? Your identity, signified by your name, is more important and basic than any of these roles. The same holds true for Jesus.

Your answer to the question Jesus posed is crucial for your well-being in this world and the next. Some people say Jesus was a moral teacher, a prophet, a wise man, a miracle worker. Yes, he was all of these, but much more. Jesus is God the Son. When you recognize his identity as such, your whole life changes and is infused with meaning.

As God, Jesus is the Creator, the Alpha and Omega, the utterly Other. He is your origin and your destiny. Your whole life depends on him.

But Jesus is also savior, your savior. His very name means "God saves." He paid a stupendous price to rescue you and guaranteed that you can be with him forever. Jesus deserves to be the center of your life. His great love certainly must evoke love from you.

How you view Jesus dictates your relationship with him. When you truly know him, you commit yourself to him and find times to speak with him. You try to do as he wishes and you are inspired to introduce others to him. Someday you might ask Jesus, "Who do you say I am?" What might he answer?

RESPOND: *Jesus, I adore you as my Lord and God. But I also love you as my Savior who ardently loves me.*

April 5

LISTEN: *"For you are setting your mind not on divine things but on human things."*

MARK 8:33

Jesus chided Peter for refusing to accept God's plan for our salvation that entailed suffering and death. You deserve the same rebuke if you ignore what is good for your salvation.

For most of the day you are focused on things of this world. Of necessity you ponder matters like what to eat at the next meal, where to plan your vacation, what to wear tomorrow, and who to hire to take pictures at a wedding. Followers of Jesus learn to periodically shift their attention to the spiritual realm. Instead of being totally absorbed in the news, they make time to pray. Along with being entertained by movies, television, novels, or games, they occasionally enrich their minds and souls with a spiritual book. Rather than devoting long hours to social media, they visit people in person. Besides working hard in their garden, they cultivate virtues. Yes, they enjoy dining out, but their most important meal is the Eucharist.

Possessions, prestige, or power is the chief goal for many people. Far weightier goals are deepening your relationship with God, living the gospel values, and ultimately attaining heaven. At the end of each day, you might calculate what percentage of it was spent on human things and what percentage was devoted to divine things.

RESPOND: *Jesus, keep me mindful of the things of God and what will benefit me for everlasting life. May my eyes not always be fastened on the ground but raised heavenward from time to time.*

April 6

"The whole world" encompasses everything that people strive for: money, fame, power, success, possessions. Jesus warns that these things mean nothing if the owners lose their soul and eternal life.

The legendary Faust failed to heed the warning of Jesus. He traded his soul to gain knowledge and indulge in worldly pleasures and ended up in hell. The mythic King Midas asked for everything he touched to turn into gold; Aristotle said he died of starvation. Alexander the Great thirsted for power and conquered one country after another. He died at age 32, and his empire disintegrated.

The danger is imitating these deluded men on a small scale. How? Perhaps you can never have enough jewelry, or your closet may be bursting with outfits in every color in the rainbow. Maybe you desire to be elected president of a local organization. Or you like to win contests, see your name or photo in publications, or love to gamble and can't resist buying lottery tickets. It could be that you thrive on demonstrating that you know all the answers, as though you were a *Jeopardy* contestant.

All these traits pursue unworthy goals and empty successes. No achievement on earth is comparable to reaching heaven. That gain has prime value. This life passes quickly. During it, be careful not to commit the ultimate tragedy: trading a happy life that lasts forever for something transitory on earth.

RESPOND: *Jesus, let me never lose sight of what really counts: protecting my soul from sin and doing good so that I am worthy of heaven.*

April 7

LISTEN: *"All things can be done for the one who believes."*
MARK 9:23

After someone says they believe in you, don't you do your utmost to live up to their faith? The person could be a spouse, parent, child, or friend. Their confidence gives you the boost to follow through on a task, be it running a marathon, writing a book, or applying for a new job. I imagine that God feels much the same when you believe in him and his deep love for you. And because he is God, he has the omnipotence to answer you with a positive response. As your loving Father, God will gladly respond to your request, perhaps in a way you don't currently understand. God may even surprise you and grant you more that you ever dreamed!

The Gospels are replete with accounts of Jesus curing sick, disabled, and possessed people. Most of these miracles were brought about because the people themselves or their friends or relatives had faith in Jesus. When you ask for his help in remedying a situation, even the direst, he can do the same for you. After all, he cherished you enough to sacrifice his life for you.

After you place your need before God, relax. You can afford to be as calm and peaceful as a child in its mother's arms.

RESPOND: *Jesus, I believe; help my unbelief.*

April 8

LISTEN: *"This kind can come out only through prayer."*

MARK 9:29

Jesus was speaking about an unclean spirit, one that his disciples were unable to cast out. In our culture powerful evil spirits are reduced to a caricature, mocked as fanciful creatures in red pajamas and carrying pitchforks. The devil, however, is still dangerously at work, creating havoc in the world. He fills a person with depression or chronic fatigue so that it is a feat to get out of bed. He creates obsessions with shopping, food, and social media, and infatuations with a man or woman that cannot be explained or controlled. He infuses jealousy, anger, worry, or low self-esteem that seems impossible to shake off.

When you or someone you love is a victim of this unclean spirit, it is futile to fight him alone. The assistance of a good friend, a therapist, or a spiritual director is required. St. Michael the Archangel, who was victorious over Lucifer before time began, is another possible partner. Your best recourse, though, is to turn to the Creator for help. He is your strongest ally as you battle anything that impinges on your well-being. God conquered Satan before time began and again on Calvary; he can also conquer Satan today if this evil spirit has a foothold in you or another person.

So pray with all your might to free yourself or someone else from the clutches of the invisible enemy who desires your downfall. God, your loving Father, will be happy to restore peace and joy.

RESPOND: *Jesus, cleanse me of any habits that make me less than you wish me to be. Establish your holy kingdom in the world.*

April 9

LISTEN: *"Whoever wants to be the first must be last of all and servant of all."*

MARK 9:35

Naturally we are under the illusion that we are the center of the world, the most important. It's our default setting to put our needs and desires above those of others. Aren't you tempted to choose the largest slice of pizza or piece of cake? Don't you like to be at the head of a line in a store or at the movie theater? Doesn't it please you when people admire you, give you the best seat, or acknowledge you as the boss?

Jesus, however, posed a paradox. In the race of life the winners are the last, not the first. Humbly and with love, they allow others the privilege of first choice and first place.

In God's eyes the greatest people, the superstars, are those who serve. In this way they imitate Jesus, who came to serve. You follow him as you assume the role of a servant—as you prepare meals for your family or at a soup kitchen, as you do the laundry, and as you care for the sick although you have a headache. You are a true Christian when you don't expect others to wait on you but instead are eager to be of service to others.

Squelching the innate urge to promote oneself isn't a cinch. It takes practice and sometimes supernatural grace to pick up the towel and wash feet, faces, and dishes.

RESPOND: *Jesus, your saints are modest and not self-centered. May I keep in mind that I am not any more important than my neighbor.*

April 10

LISTEN: *"Whom are you looking for?"*
JOHN 20:15

O n Easter morning Mary Magdalene was looking for the body of Jesus, which was discovered to be missing from the tomb. You know what it is like to lose someone precious for a time. A child disappears in a store or at the fair. You don't connect with a spouse or a friend at the airport. A teenager isn't home by curfew. Worry and panic set in. Mary was distressed at not finding Jesus's body. He knew she was looking for him, yet he prompted her to state it.

Christians don't ever want to lose sight of Jesus. You would like to keep him in reach. Sometimes you may feel Jesus's distance. During prayer it is as though you stand before a black abyss and your words only echo back to you. Don't conclude that Jesus has abandoned you, that he doesn't really love you, or that you are unworthy. Take heart. The risen Lord is always right there with you, so dry your tears. When you seek him, you will find him.

When Mary assumed she was talking to the gardener who had removed the corpse, she proposed carrying the body back herself—an outrageous feat. But such was her love for her Lord. What would you risk to keep Jesus in your life?

RESPOND: *Jesus, I never wish to be parted from you.
I hope that when I feel you are missing, I search for you and in
finding you, rejoice.*

April 11

LISTEN: *"Whoever is not against us is for us."*

MARK 9:40

The apostle John was disturbed because someone who was not a disciple was casting out a demon in the name of Jesus. An exorcism is a good, compassionate deed, and Jesus would not prevent it no matter who was responsible for it. He is all for inclusivity.

Jesus associated with Jews who didn't share his beliefs: the Pharisees, Sadducees, scribes, and Samaritans, who were half Gentile. He reached out to Gentiles, including a Roman soldier and a Syrophoenician woman. You probably count several Protestants among your friends. Perhaps you married one of them. As I was growing up, we Catholics were not to associate with these fellow Christians. The Catholic Church needed to hear and take to heart these words of Jesus.

Today churches and organizations that are not Catholic accomplish wonderful things for humankind. Envy, egotism, and ambition can cause Catholics to resent their good works. Their victory, however, is our victory. We are all God's children, doing our best to live well on our planet.

Likewise, when a rival school, club, neighborhood, country, political party, or an individual does something praiseworthy, that action deserves applause, not jealousy and criticism. After all, we would expect to be commended for our good deeds.

RESPOND: *Jesus, you love all people. May I always be glad and grateful for the good in others regardless of the faith they profess.*

April 12

LISTEN: *"If any of you put a stumbling block before one of these little ones who believe in me, it would be better for you if a great millstone were hung around your neck and you were thrown into the sea."*

MARK 9:42

At times Jesus called his apostles children, so "little ones" here refers to his followers. He warns of the dire consequences of leading another person into sin. The eternal fires of hell will be more disastrous than death by drowning. The word "millstone" means a massive set of circular stones moved by an animal. Jesus resorted to hyperbole for emphasis.

You may have experienced being tempted by another person who says, "Take some. No one will notice," or "Today couples live together before being married, it's okay," or "It makes no difference which religion you belong to." Peer pressure is real and it is powerful. The actions of others exert influence for better or worse. People who create movies, television, books, and songs define our culture and impact the way we live. They can inspire us or they can drag us down by featuring revealing clothing, coarse and profane language, use of drugs and alcohol, and rampant sex that can throw off our moral compass.

While we are influenced, we are also influencers. It is important to set a good example for others, especially children. Sins like skipping Sunday Masses, speaking ill of other people, gossiping, and lying are contagious. But so are virtuous deeds like praying the Rosary, volunteering at a hospital, and donating to the Red Cross. You can play the role of an angel or a devil in other people's lives. The choice is yours.

RESPOND: *Jesus, prevent me from giving scandal. I want to be a force for good in the world.*

April 13

LISTEN: *"If your hand causes you to stumble, cut it off; it is better for you to enter life maimed than to have two hands and to go to hell, to the unquenchable fire."*

MARK 9:43

Most people seldom think of hell or that they may be headed in that direction. For some sinners, their sins become so routine that they forget that they are sinning. They become immune to guilt. Jesus gave a wake-up call by advising drastic measures to control sins. He named the horror of hell as unquenchable fire and immortal worm. Making use of hyperbole, he recommends destroying any body part that causes sin: hand, foot, or eye.

There are more practical and less grisly separations from sources of sin. Sever your relationship with a man, woman, or group who leads you to sin. Avoid casinos and bars if they foster addictions. Fast from foods that damage your good health. Forgo entertainment that would entice you to sin. Cut short your time on social media if it usurps the time you should be devoting to your family or other responsibilities.

Separations like these are painful and difficult. They require great self-control and prayer. But you are not alone. Jesus, who wishes only the best for you, body and soul, is eager to supply the grace to be holy, that is, to be whole. Just ask him.

RESPOND: *Jesus, I am weak. Give me the strength to avoid all occasions of sin so that my final destination is not hell but heaven with you.*

April 14

LISTEN: *"Salt is good; but if salt has lost its saltiness, how can you season it? Have salt in yourselves, and be at peace with one another."*

MARK 9:50

You have my sympathy if you are on a salt-free diet. Salt is a flavoring that enhances food. It has many uses besides making food tasty. Salt purifies water by causing particles to clump together and settle. A great cleanser, it's used to clean rusty pots and coffee-stained mugs and to remove blood stains and sweat stains. For thousands of years salt has been used to preserve food. It also has healing properties. In addition, sodium is vital for the functioning of our bodies. A low level of sodium causes fatigue, nausea, headache, and dizziness.

Salt is a pure substance, meaning it is composed of one chemical element. Pythagoras noted, "Salt is born of the purest parents: the sun and the sea." An old superstition is that knocking over a saltshaker was bad luck. To cancel it, one had to toss a pinch of salt over the left shoulder, supposedly the devil's side.

Speaking figuratively, Jesus exhorts you to have salt inside you. In other words, he wants you to be zesty and purified of evil. Once you are scrubbed clean of jealousy, pride, gluttony, lust, prejudice, selfishness, and other forms of iniquity, you will be free from the dark power and healthy again. You will love God and neighbor, which leads to being at peace with everyone.

RESPOND: *Jesus, purify our world leaders of sin, unbridled ambition, and thirst for power. When that happens, peace will prevail.*

April 15

LISTEN: *"Do not work for the food that perishes, but for the food that endures for eternal life, which the Son of Man will give you."*

JOHN 6:27

Every cook knows how quickly food can spoil. Milk curdles, meat rots, bread gets stale and moldy, and cookies turn hard. Honey though can last forever. Food is essential for life. Without it living things waste away and die. In the desert God sent the Hebrews manna and quail so they wouldn't starve and water from a rock so they wouldn't die of thirst. Today Jesus provides you with imperishable food to nourish your spiritual life: the bread and wine become him in the Eucharist. Partaking of that holy meal, you are one with divinity and your spiritual life is fortified.

Jesus also gave you words to guide your life on earth. The psalmist said about God's law revealed in the Old Testament, "How sweet are your words to my taste, sweeter than honey to my mouth!" (Psalm 119:103). The same can be said about the teachings of Jesus in the New Testament. At every Mass you are fed at the table of the Word and the table of the Eucharist. Receiving Jesus in Communion and pondering his words keep you spiritually healthy and fit.

Both the gift of the Eucharist and the gift of God's words are lasting and lead to the eternal banquet, where you will be completely satisfied.

RESPOND: *Jesus, you provide my spiritual food with as much love and care as I cook meals for my family and friends. I desire to dine at the table you prepared for me both here and in heaven.*

April 16

After something fantastic occurs, a person relating it might remark, "You have to see it to believe it." As a follower of Jesus, you are expected to believe a miracle that you cannot possibly have seen: a dead, crucified person alive again. You can understand why Thomas was incredulous when the other apostles said that the Lord had visited them.

You have been told the story of the Easter Resurrection handed down from generation to generation, from country to country. Millions have believed this phenomenon without actually witnessing it. You probably heard the Good News of Jesus's saving acts from your parents, grandparents, and teachers. Why do you believe this outrageous story? Because you have faith, a theological virtue you acquired at your Baptism.

Faith is a sheer gift from God, but it must be cultivated and protected. Mingling with other believers bolsters faith; so does learning more about it and, above all, practicing it. Faith is practiced by praying, studying the Bible, and celebrating the sacraments. Strengthen it; otherwise, it may wither away. And do your part by passing on the story for future generations.

RESPOND: *Jesus, I want to grow in faith. I believe; help my unbelief.*

April 17

LISTEN: *"Truly I tell you, whoever does not receive the kingdom of God as a little child will never enter it."*

MARK 10:15

Think of young children you know. They are eager to learn things like the alphabet, how to write their name, and how to ride a bike. They are humble and ask for help in tying their shoes or playing a game. Being needy, they are dependent on adults for food, housing, clothing, and transportation. They trust that others are telling the truth. Their joy is contagious when they open presents, and they love giving hugs and sometimes-sloppy kisses. Like clean slates, they are unmarked yet by prejudices and the worship of power, possessions, and prestige.

Jesus implied that if you hope to enter heaven you must display these same characteristics. You enjoy learning new things and honing your God-given talents and skills. You thirst for spiritual knowledge and are open to guidance from Scripture and religious leaders. You are not pompous and self-serving but simple and humble. You radiate joy because you trust in God's love for you and realize you are offered the gift of God's kingdom. Most of all you are loving. Your love embraces everyone and adores only God. Being childlike is a far cry from being childish.

RESPOND: *Jesus, may I take on the traits of a child so that I may spend eternity with you.*

April 18

LISTEN: *"You lack one thing; go, sell what you own, and give the money to the poor, and you will have treasure in heaven; then come, follow me."*

MARK 10:21

When the rich young man asked how to inherit eternal life, Jesus gave the requirement recorded by St. Mark, along with being his disciple. People like St. Francis of Assisi and St. Katherine Drexel took this advice literally and gave up every material thing. In our era of consumerism and materialism, divesting ourselves of possessions is a challenge. For some people hoarding has become an obsession.

Can you identify with this: Your closets bulge with clothes. Some pieces are too small, but you intend to fit in them someday. You haven't worn some articles for years. You like to buy turtlenecks, T-shirts, and slacks of every color. It's hard to resist a sale or to say, "No thank you, I have enough," when someone offers you an article of clothing. Your shoe collection might make one think you were a centipede. Your kitchen cabinets hold cookware and gadgets that you never use.

St. Basil the Great said it well: "The coat unused in your closet belongs to the one who needs it; the shoes rotting in your closet belong to the one who has no shoes; the money which you hoard up belongs to the poor."

When it comes to possessions, less is more. On life's journey, by donating superfluous items to the poor and traveling lightly you will reach something of inestimable value.

RESPOND: *Jesus, you chose to be incarnate as a poor peasant. May my love for others compel me to own only what it necessary. May you be my greatest treasure.*

April 19

LISTEN: *"It is easier for a camel to go through the eye of a needle than for someone who is rich to enter the kingdom of God."*

MARK 10:25

At times you can barely wiggle a thread through a needle. It can take many attempts and loads of patience. A camel passing through a needle would be impossible, especially if it had two humps! By that hyperbole, Jesus stressed how difficult it is for wealthy people to be good. This would especially be the case for those who attain their riches at the expense of other people, those who get rich by immoral means, and those who fail to share their blessings. It appears that some wealthy people thirst for more and more. There is ever enough.

Jesus's hyperbole suggests that people who view anything more important than God risk salvation. The "wealth" that they strive for and cling to could be health, social status, food, travel, fame, a PhD, or even being righteous, like the Pharisees.

Any benefit you enjoy on earth is a gift from God, not just the result of your own efforts. Acknowledge this with praise and thanks and be satisfied with what you own. Then you will be able to slip through heaven's gates easily.

Take as a model the seven-year-old boy who, with his parents' permission, donated all of his First Communion money to the poor.

RESPOND: *Jesus, let me not be so attached to things of this world that they block me from entering your kingdom.*

April 20

LISTEN: *"They will hand him over to the Gentiles; they will mock him, and spit upon him, and flog him, and kill him; and after three days he will rise again."*

MARK 10:33–34

As Jesus and the twelve apostles were on their way to Jerusalem, he revealed to them the gruesome fate awaiting him there. He also foretold his magnificent triumph: the Resurrection. Jesus was willing to undergo pain and humiliation because it was the path to a new and glorious life for himself and for all humanity.

If you have given birth to a baby, you can identify somewhat with the feelings and experiences of Jesus. You knew the discomfort and inconvenience of being pregnant for almost a year and the agony of labor pains. Yet these difficult experiences led to new life. You also brought new joy into your life and the life of your family.

In this world you, like everyone else, have your share of sufferings: sickness, heartache, problems, misunderstandings, disappointments. When you are faithful to your Christian calling and unite your suffering to the sufferings of Jesus, your life's journey too will culminate in a glorious resurrection. As St. Clement of Alexandria observed, "The Lord has turned all our sunsets into sunrise."

RESPOND: *Jesus, thank you for sacrificing your life for me. With your grace I will live in such a way that your death will not be in vain.*

April 21

LISTEN: *"For the Son of Man came not to be served but to serve,
and to give his life a ransom for many."*

MARK 10:45

The Trinitarians and the Mercedarians were religious orders established to ransom Christian captives in the twelfth and thirteenth centuries, respectively. These men were willing to offer themselves in exchange for prisoners. They mirrored Christ, the greatest Redeemer. By the price of his blood Jesus bought the whole human race back from Satan. He did us a supreme service.

In many ways you serve others by enriching their lives. If you are a mother, you laid your life on the line for the sake of a child. Then you guided their growth from the day of their birth, through teenage years, and into adulthood. As a member of a family, you constantly serve as you clean house, wash clothes, prepare meals, lend a listening ear, and dispense hugs. You may be a nurse, a cashier, or a worker on an assembly line. No matter what job you hold, you serve others in some way, devoting many hours of your life to them.

By sacrificing yourself for others, by making their lives easier you imitate Christ. Hopefully you do so with satisfaction and joy . . . and not counting the cost.

RESPOND: *Jesus, I thank you for the gift of your life that won everlasting life for me. I long to distinguish myself in your service.*

April 22

J esus asked Bartimaeus the beggar this question. Bartimaeus was obviously blind, so the question Jesus posed seems rather senseless. When it elicited from Bartimaeus the plea, "Let me see again," the result was a cure and love at first sight. Jesus won a new disciple. This episode teaches that Jesus wants you to tell him your needs.

Of course, God, who knows everything, is aware of and interested in every aspect of your life. He knows that you would like a raise, healing for your mother-in-law, and peace on earth. Still, he invites you to state your requests. No worry or concern of yours is too small to grab his attention and garner a remedy.

So do be a beggar. Avoid thinking deadening thoughts like, "Why should God answer my prayers when I disappoint him so often?" and "God has more important matters to tend to than my little life." Ignore people who scoff at your faith and dependence on prayer. Onlookers failed to silence Bartimaeus and forestall his miracle. Despite the hubbub of the crowd, Jesus heard his voice.

God cherishes you and desires your happiness. Hear him say, "What do *you* want me to do for you?" Trust in his love for you and, like Bartimaeus, run to him for help.

RESPOND: *Jesus, Son of David, have mercy on me! Grant me*
_____ (insert request).

April 23

LISTEN: *"Is it not written, 'My house shall be called a house of prayer for all the nations'? But you have made it a den of robbers."*
MARK 11:17

For you, God's house is not a temple, but your local church or chapel where Jesus is present in the Blessed Sacrament. As such, it is an awesome building, worthy of reverence. That is why you refrain from carrying on conversations there and teach children not to dash down its aisles or play in its sanctuary.

You decorate and dust your own home, polish its furniture, and keep it uncluttered and clean. Why not do the same for your Father's house? Volunteer to help with the floral arrangements and other decorations for the liturgical seasons, the vessels and candles, linens, and vestments. After Mass, prayer services, and gatherings in church, pick up bulletins, sundry papers, and Cheerios left behind. Contribute to fundraisers for the purpose of beautifying your place of worship.

In addition, you can strengthen your church as a house of prayer by participating in liturgies as altar server, reader, eucharistic minister, or choir member.

Unlike those robbers who desecrated God's house in Jerusalem and evoked Jesus's anger, help make your church a place of beauty and peace, and receive God's gratitude and blessing.

RESPOND: *Jesus, bless and protect my church. May I do something to keep your dwelling on earth a place of beauty and prayer.*

April 24

LISTEN: *"So I tell you, whatever you ask for in prayer, believe that you have received it, and it will be yours."*

MARK 11:24

When you ask your spouse or a good friend for a favor, you expect that they will comply if they can. God loves you infinitely more than anyone else in the world and, being all-powerful, God is capable of accomplishing the impossible. When you ask God for something, you can count on him granting it—unless, in his wisdom, he knows it will not be good in the grand scheme of things.

Jesus claims that when we pray with faith, our prayer will be answered. And Jesus doesn't lie. He frequently worked miracles for someone who showed faith in him and his power: the centurion, the people who carried the paralytic, the woman with the never-ending period, the two blind men, the Canaanite woman. In these cases, Jesus attributed the healings to their faith.

The world today is wracked with wars, divisions, and violence. The homeless live on streets. Death by suicide among young people is increasing. Protestant theologian Karl Barth offered a solution: "To clasp the hands in prayer is the beginning of an uprising against the disorder of the world."

So go to God with confidence, believing that your friend will get well, your house will sell, or you will find a job. Receiving an answer to your prayer will be in direct proportion to your faith.

RESPOND: *Jesus, I trust in your promise that my prayers will be answered.*

April 25

LISTEN: *"Whenever you stand praying, forgive, if you have anything against anyone; so that your Father in heaven may also forgive you your trespasses."*

MARK 11:25

The world was stunned when Pope John Paul II forgave the man who shot him and requested the president of Italy to pardon him. Forgiving someone who has harmed us, even slightly, is one of the most difficult and most beautiful things you can do. Usually your first impulse is to retaliate with an equal offense or at least by giving him or her the silent treatment. Right?

You belong to a fractured humanity. No one escapes being wounded by fellow human beings. You may have been criticized by a friend, disobeyed by a child, sassed by a teenager, slandered by a coworker, or disappointed by someone who broke a promise or a vow. You may need to forgive even more than your offender needs to be forgiven. When you can be big enough and Christian enough to sincerely forgive someone and forgo carrying a grudge, your heart will be lighter. Better still, your heavenly Father will be more inclined to forgive the times you offended him by disobeying.

RESPOND: *Jesus, I realize that we human beings are weak and prone to sin. Fill me with such lavish love that I will forgive others who harm me.*

April 26

LISTEN: *"For when they rise from the dead, they neither marry nor are given in marriage, but are like angels in heaven."*

MARK 12:25

Sadducees, who didn't believe in the afterlife, tried to ensnare Jesus on this topic. They asked, "If a woman had seven husbands, whose wife will she be in heaven?" The answer Jesus gave avoided the trap and also gave a clue that life in heaven will be very different from life on earth. What awaits us there is a mystery. St. Paul apparently had a vision of heaven, but he had no words to describe it. Judging from the beauty and wonders of this world—lush gardens, multihued sunrises and sunsets, starry night skies—you can expect that heaven will be spectacular to behold.

There you will have a glorified body like the risen Lord's. (Notice Jesus said we will be "like" angels; we do not become angels.) You will be radiant, beautiful, and free from suffering. You will not be bound by space, time, or any physical thing and you will be able to travel at the speed of thought. Recall how after Easter Jesus passed through locked doors, appearing and then disappearing.

The love we experience on earth will be magnified, for we will be surrounded and inundated by God's powerful love. And we will enjoy the presence of our saintly loved ones as well as other saints for all eternity. What about your pets that are like family? Some say God will allow animals in heaven; others say no. C. S. Lewis wryly remarked, "A heaven for mosquitos and a hell for men could very conveniently be combined."

RESPOND: *Jesus, thank you for throwing open the gates of heaven for us. I look forward to living happily with you for all eternity.*

April 27

LISTEN: *"The first [commandment] is 'Hear, O Israel: the Lord our God, the Lord is one; you shall love the Lord your God with all your heart, and with all your soul, and with all your mind, and with all your strength.'"*

MARK 12:29–30

A woman confided a concern she had when she was pregnant with her first child. She said, "I loved my husband so much that I was afraid I wouldn't have any love left over for another person. But I found that my heart stretched." When you live out this greatest commandment and love God one hundred percent, your heart stretches to encompass everyone and everything God created.

Why do you love God? It is natural to love someone who loves you. The essence of God is love. God loved you first. He loved you enough to call you into existence out of nothingness. Your Creator loves you with a fiery, passionate, unconditional love. True love yearns for closeness, and so God, who cherishes you so much, desires to live with you forever.

How do you show love for God? By pleasing God and putting him first above all others. St. Bernard stated, "This is why the rightful measure of our love to God is to exceed all measure."

How do you grow in love of God? By spending quiet time aware of God's presence and reflecting on our Creator's awesomeness and goodness.

RESPOND: *God, your love for me was proven in the amazing incarnation and sacrifice of the Son who loved us to death. With all my heart I pray, "Most Sacred Heart of Jesus, I implore that I may ever love you more and more."*

April 28

LISTEN: *"The second [commandment] is this, 'You shall love
your neighbor as yourself.'"*

MARK 12:31

A Gentile asked Rabbi Hillel the Elder, "Teach me the whole law as I stand on one leg." Hillel answered, "What is hateful to you, to your neighbor don't do. That's the entirety of the law; everything else is commentary." Jesus expressed the same law in a positive form. Both statements mean you are to regard other people reverently and lovingly.

Cherishing and caring for yourself are innate tendencies. You protect and pamper your body, nourishing it with healthy food, dressing it to look attractive, and slathering it with lotions. You like to be first and, given an option, will probably choose the best things for yourself. You pride yourself on having a good reputation and are quick to come to your own defense. Making excuses and allowing exemptions for yourself are habits. Some of us have an inflated ego.

God expects you to extend the same generous love toward other people, not only your family members but the crabby woman down the street, the man who cuts you off in traffic, the neighbor whose opinion differs from yours, the beggar living under the bridge, and the desperate immigrant. True love is more than a feeling; it is an act of the will promoting another's well-being.

A parable illustrates this humanitarian love. A man dreams of hell. People sit at a table before a feast, but the only way they can eat is by using three-foot-long chopsticks. They all go hungry. Then the man dreams of heaven. The feast is the same, but all are enjoying it because they are feeding one another with the chopsticks.

RESPOND: *Jesus, you love me though I'm unworthy. Fill me to the brim with such selfless love.*

130

April 29

LISTEN: *"Beware of the scribes, who like to walk around in long robes, and to be greeted with respect in the market-places, and to have the best seats in the synagogues and places of honor at banquets!"*

MARK 12:38

As Jesus is cautioning us to beware of scribes with an oversized ego, he is simultaneously warning you not to be like those teachers. What should you avoid so you are not a modern-day scribe? Here is a list:

- Telling stories about yourself in order to impress others.
- Trying to outdo a neighbor's garden, cooking, or Christmas decorations.
- Being hurt when your work on a project isn't acknowledged.
- Feeling slighted when someone else is praised or promoted.
- Desiring to be the center of attention at parties.
- Trying to be the best-dressed woman at an affair.
- Being a name dropper.
- Searching for yourself in group photos.
- Bragging about your accomplishments.

Who doesn't like being respected and honored? But if you crave attention and adulation, watch out! The deadly sin of pride lurks in your heart. You are far from following in the footsteps of the selfless teacher who humbled himself to become a man and who washed the feet of his apostles.

Christians are to focus on nurturing others' egos, not their own.

RESPOND: *Jesus, keep me mindful that your love and esteem are all I really need.*

April 30

LISTEN: *"Do you see these great buildings? Not one stone will be left here upon another; all will be thrown down."*

MARK 13:2

The Jewish temple atop Mount Moriah in Jerusalem was magnificent, gleaming white, with high, gold-plated gates. It was also immense, spread over thirty-six acres. Its "stones" were massive—some, about forty-six feet long and weighing more than eighty tons. Jesus's prediction that this temple would be destroyed shocked Jewish ears. His words proved true in AD 70 when the Roman army utterly devastated this center of Jewish faith.

A temple where God dwelt and where sacrifices were offered was no longer needed. With Jesus came a new order. The Jewish Christians had to leave behind their old ways. Similarly, the Church changes with the times. You may recall when women were expected to wear hats to Mass, altar girls were unheard of, the Communion fast began at midnight, and Fridays were meatless.

Someone remarked that no one likes change except a baby with a wet diaper. God, whose creativity is boundless, apparently likes new, fresh things. He creates new stars, forms new lands, and produces new humans. He guides us to new realizations and advances in science, medicine, and, yes, theology.

You may find your life's path leading to surprising changes, inviting you to change your attitude or even to rebuild your life. As St. John Henry Newman observed, "To live is to change, and to be perfect is to have changed often."

RESPOND: *Jesus, keep me from resisting change. Instead, make my heart open to it.*

MAY

May 1

LISTEN: *"Beware that no one leads you astray. Many will come in my name and say, 'I am he!' and they will lead many astray."*

MARK 13:5–6

E very now and then these words of Jesus come true. Cult leaders arise and attract many followers. One flagrant example is Jim
Jones, who claimed to be a manifestation of Christ. His claim led to
the 1978 massacre of more than 900 people, a third of them under the
age of seventeen.

The Church of Jesus founded on Peter, the rock, has endured for
two thousand years. You might know someone who broke away from
the Church and established a sect. Jesus is unique. No other church
founder died for you. No one else was crucified and came back to
life. No one healed lepers, the blind, and the deaf to the extent that
Jesus did.

How do you resist going astray? By staying close-knit to Jesus.
Read and ponder the Gospels, which are a unique kind of theological
biography, and pay attention to homilies about them. Pray to Jesus
every day and listen to him speaking to you in your heart. Frequently
meet him in the sacraments, especially the Eucharist when he unites
himself to you in an incredible way. Be inspired and strengthened by
the lives of the saints, those in heaven as well as the living ones in your
parish church. A firm relationship with Jesus and his mystical body
the Church keeps you from veering off the safe, right path.

RESPOND: *Jesus, may I always be faithful to you.
Stay near me please.*

May 2

LISTEN: *"As for yourselves, beware; for they will hand you over to councils; and you will be beaten in synagogues; and you will stand before governors and kings because of me, as a testimony to them."*

MARK 13:9

Chances are slim that this prophecy of Jesus will be fulfilled in you. Almost all the disciples he was addressing met this fate, as did a good number of other early Christians. St. Paul, for example, boasted of being whipped, beaten, and stoned for believing in Jesus. But when arrested, he was able to bear witness to Christ before the Jewish council, the governors Felix and Festus, King Agrippa, and Jewish leaders in Rome.

Christians are still persecuted today. In the United States anti-Catholic hate crimes have increased. You may not be tortured and martyred for the sake of Christ as were St. Agnes, St. Cecilia, and St. Lucy, but you can suffer in nonphysical ways. Say at a party another guest mocks you for accepting a certain Catholic belief. That stings, but it also gives you an opportunity to explain that belief to the taunting person as well as to onlookers.

Are you convinced that your relationship with Jesus is as crucial as the air you breathe? If so, you will be bold in openly practicing your faith and sharing it with others. Some people might not like it, but Jesus will be proud of you.

RESPOND: *Jesus, I am proud and grateful for your gift of faith. Just as others have risked everything to preserve it for me, grant that I may protect and spread it as my precious heritage.*

May 3

LISTEN: *"When they bring you to trial and hand you over, do not worry beforehand about what you are to say; but say whatever is given you at that time, for it is not you who speak, but the Holy Spirit."*

MARK 13:11

You probably will not be hauled into court to defend your faith in Jesus. There may be times, however, when you face criticism or scorn for your beliefs. You may be at a PTA meeting, a cocktail party, or a wedding when someone mocks one of the Church's teachings. Maybe a friend or colleague questions what you believe. As a disciple called to evangelize, you can view this is an opportunity to speak up.

You needn't be afraid. The same Spirit who inspired the apostles (mostly fishermen) to preach and defend the faith also dwells in you. He will nudge you to act and put words on your lips. It helps if you have been educated in the faith and have kept informed about Church developments in our modern world. You can also rely on the gifts of wisdom and understanding that the Spirit infused you with at your Baptism.

When you summon the courage to speak about our faith, at times you will be amazed at the impact you make on others. It could be, however, that you will have to wait until heaven to realize this.

RESPOND: *Jesus, strengthen my belief in the Holy Spirit acting in me so that I may be a more effective Christian.*

May 4

LISTEN: *"You will be hated by all because of my name. But the one who endures to the end will be saved."*

MARK 13:13

William Barclay observed, "Jesus promised his disciples three things—that they would be completely fearless, absurdly happy, and in constant trouble." Christians have been persecuted since the first century. In AD 203 two young African women, Perpetua and Felicity, were martyred. Perpetua was a noblewoman, nursing an infant son in prison. Despite her father's pleas, she refused to deny her faith in Jesus to save her life. Felicity gave birth to a daughter in prison. Both mothers were put to death by a sword in the arena in Carthage and are now acclaimed as saints.

Since the founding of the United States, Catholics were maligned and persecuted, especially by the Ku Klux Klan. Today around the world they are still killed for their faith. You may have experienced anti-Catholicism at a board meeting or a dinner in your own home. Friends and family members, even your children, may criticize you for holding onto your Christian beliefs. Being countercultural does not make one popular. Although you probably will not be martyred, you might be snubbed or sneered at. Enduring such unpleasantness and refusing to forsake Jesus will win you a seat with Perpetua and Felicity in heaven. You have his word for it.

RESPOND: *Jesus, when I suffer prejudice because I follow you, may it only strengthen my faith.*

May 5

LISTEN: *"Then they will see 'the Son of Man coming in clouds'*
with great power and glory. Then he will send out the angels,
and gather his elect from the four winds, from the ends of the earth
to the ends of heaven."

MARK 13:26–27

Caught up in a whirlwind of daily activities at home and at work, you probably don't give much thought to the end of the world; but you might have in 2023 when the news reported that the Doomsday Clock is only ninety seconds to midnight, the time of earth's annihilation. Each Advent you focus on the comings of Christ, including the Second Coming. In the Creed you profess that he will come to judge the living and the dead. On that day he will draw the faithful ones to himself. Naturally, you will "want to be in that number," as we sing in "Oh When the Saints Go Marching In."

When your earthly life ends, your eternal destiny is sealed. How you live each day determines whether you will be in heaven. That is why it is a good practice to take a few minutes each evening to look over the day and examine your conscience.

Don't just pinpoint your failures, but be alert to tokens of love God sprinkled in those twenty-four hours. Then look ahead to the next day and plan how you will respond to people and situations with love.

As St. Francis was hoeing a row of beans, a pilgrim asked him, "What would you be doing now if you knew this was the last day of your earthly life?" St. Francis replied, "I would keep on hoeing."

RESPOND: *Jesus, whether my last day comes slowly or unexpectedly*
I know it's in my future. May I always be prepared for the day
I meet you face-to-face.

May 6

LISTEN: *"Heaven and earth will pass away, but my words will not pass away."*

MARK 13:31

You are familiar with the saying, "Nothing lasts forever." One exception is the words of Jesus. He, who called himself the Truth, spoke words that are eternal. They have already echoed down to you over two thousand years. You read them in the Bible and other spiritual books. You hear them proclaimed at Mass and at prayer services. Hopefully some things Jesus said are inscribed in your heart, ready to sustain, encourage, and comfort you when necessary.

After a difficult, draining day, you might hear him say, "Come apart and rest awhile." When suffering from someone who attacked your person or your reputation, you might recall, "Love your enemies." If you wonder whether you will have the patience to deal with a spouse or children, remember, "With God all things are possible."

Sometimes you are too worried, sick, or tired to pray even one Hail Mary. Repeating a statement of Jesus's over and over is an easy and soothing way to pray. You might compile a go-to list of statements such as "I am with you always" (Matthew 28:20) and "Abide in my love" (John 15:9).

RESPOND: *Jesus, I believe that all your words are true and everlasting. I cherish them. Help me commit some to memory.*

May 7

Listen: *"Therefore, keep awake—for you do not know when the master of the house will come . . ."*
Mark 13:35

When you expect a visitor, you want to make a good impression and show respect. So you dust, vacuum, put away stray items, clean crumbs off the counter, and make sure all the beds are neatly made. It is wise to live by the motto of the United States Coast Guard, *Semper Paratus* ("Always Prepared"). That way you will be ready for any surprise company at your door.

We do not know when the world will end or when death will come calling. This means you had better keep your spiritual house in order. How? If you are caught in an endless round of activities, you need to pause for prayer in order to maintain your friendship with God. If you are tangled in a web of some sin, be freed and strengthened by the Sacrament of Reconciliation. If you need to forgive someone or if you need someone's forgiveness, act now. If you have a bad habit like shopping too much, indulging in too many baked goods, or losing your temper too often, take steps to overcome it.

Strive to be ready at all times to meet your maker without embarrassment and regret.

Respond: *Jesus, help me to be zealous, not lazy, when it comes to caring for my soul.*

May 8

LISTEN: *"She has performed a good service for me. . . . She has done what she could; she has anointed my body beforehand for its burial."*
MARK 14:6, 8

A woman poured over Jesus's head an entire jar of perfume valued at a year's wages. He praised her for the extravagant act of love, while others rebuked her for the waste. This story reminds me of how my girlfriend's father responded when he heard that I was entering the convent. He said, "What a foolish thing to do!" Later when asked why I wanted to become a Sister, I explained that since God had done so much for me, I wanted to give him all that I could.

God's tremendous love for us is obvious. He became one of us and died for us. This lavish love compels us to give him the best gift we can in return.

You don't have to be a consecrated woman to live for God. You offer God your whole self when you pray the Morning Offering. You perform good services for him by donating a generous part of your income to his Church, by being kind to a difficult person, and by spending time with the sick and dying. You express your love by washing a child's face and hands, by preparing a delicious meal even though you are bone-tired, and by going above and beyond what is required at work.

When have you done something outrageous for the love of God?

RESPOND: *Jesus, your love for me is sweeter than honey. I love you too with my whole heart.*

May 9

LISTEN: *"Truly I tell you, this day, this very night, before the cock crows twice, you will deny me three times."*

MARK 14:30

Jesus knew that Peter would betray him that night when he would need his friendship most. The all-merciful Jesus forgave this apostle his flagrant sin and even entrusted his Church to him.

Jesus is aware of the times you failed him as well as your future lapses. Maybe you cowered before people who were critical of the Catholic Church. You might have been silent instead of speaking up for what she teaches. Or perhaps you divorced yourself from Jesus by living contrary to one or more of his values. Here is something to ponder: If you were accused of being a Christian, would there be enough evidence to convict you?

The rest of your life lies before you like a blank book. It's a mystery. Jesus, though, knows that you, a weak human being, will not always be true to him. You will be sorry for disappointing him. A legend holds that Peter was so remorseful that his tears carved grooves in his cheeks. No matter what sin you are ashamed of, Jesus offers loving forgiveness—even more readily than you offer it to a wayward child or a beloved friend. He tells you in Scripture that you are the apple of his eye.

RESPOND: *Jesus, may your grace keep me from sin. But if I do fail you, may I never doubt that you will forgive me.*

May 10

LISTEN: *"I am deeply grieved, even to death; remain here, and keep awake."*

MARK 14:34

As Jesus suffers mental anguish in the face of his coming ordeal, he longs for companionship. You can understand this human need for company in times of stress or distress by reflecting on your personal experiences. Maybe as you gave birth, a family member supported you, or when you were summoned to court a friend accompanied you, or as you performed in a play or recital or gave a presentation, a relative sat in the audience rooting for you.

Hopefully you are aware of the comfort another person's presence can give during frightening times. So why not visit a sick friend or acquaintance, be with someone who is dying, hold the hand of a child or adult who is in trouble, and be there for someone who is attempting a daunting thing? Doing so will impose on your time and might make you uncomfortable, but the person you supported will appreciate your care and you will be glad that you went the extra mile.

By the way, Jesus still yearns to have people with him. When can you remain with him as he is willingly imprisoned in tabernacles? How can you carve time in your day at home to be present to him?

RESPOND: *Jesus, keep me alert to opportunities to express my love for others and you by my presence.*

May 11

LISTEN: *"Abba, Father, for you all things are possible; remove this cup from me; yet, not what I want, but what you want."*

MARK 14:36

Like any sane human being, Jesus preferred not to suffer and die a cruel death. Yet, trusting his Father, he submitted to the inscrutable divine plan. He prayed, "Your will be done." As a result, all creation was saved from perdition.

Jesus was the true son of his mother Mary who said, *Fiat*, ("Let it be") to God's proposal. She was not a prophet who could foresee the many sorrows that her *yes* would entail, culminating in witnessing the Passion and Death of her beloved son. Surrendering herself to God, Mary cooperated with his will for her and set the world on a revised course.

At times you don't know why God lets bad things happen to you any more than Mary did. Maybe your car is totaled, you are let go from your job, or your child has a rare disease. Whatever your plight, you can unite your suffering with the suffering of Jesus and so join in the world's redemption.

When you pray "your will be done" in the Our Father, interpret it to apply to your life. If tragedy strikes, don't pray to change God's will but to understand it—something that may not occur until heaven's hindsight. Possibly, as a coworker remarked to me whenever there was a crisis at work: "It's for your spiritual growth."

RESPOND: *Jesus, may my will always be God's will. Make me more like you and your holy Mother.*

May 12

LISTEN: *"Keep awake and pray that you may not come into the time of trial; the spirit indeed is willing, but the flesh is weak."*

MARK 14:38

Except for John, the apostles forfeited their lives for their faith in Jesus. They stood strong against the temptation to apostatize. Though your trials may not be life-threatening, you certainly are subjected to them: temptations to steal, lie, flirt with someone who is not your spouse, skip Sunday Mass. Jesus recommends prayer as an antidote. Another tip is to build up moral muscles by exercising self-control in small matters.

You can probably identify with the statement that the spirit is willing, but the flesh is weak. How long before you renege on your New Year's or Lenten resolutions? You may intend to eat healthy and forgo sweets, but you hear them calling you and succumb. You may desire to lose weight by exercising, but days go by without going to a gym or doing squats or pushups at home. You want to be humble, but you can't resist mentioning your accomplishments.

The more you overcome yourself in little things, the more successful you will be in repelling temptations. Call on the Holy Spirit to be your ally.

RESPOND: *Jesus, shield me from temptations, or at least make me strong enough to resist them.*

May 13

LISTEN: *"I am; and 'you will see the son of Man seated at the right hand of the Power,' and 'coming with the clouds of heaven.'"*

MARK 14:62

President Thomas Jefferson did not believe that Jesus was God. He compiled his own Bible, excluding verses that indicated the divinity of Jesus, such as his miracles and the Resurrection. Muslims and Jehovah's Witnesses deny that Jesus is God. Yet, Jesus boldly declared to the high priest that he is the Messiah, the Son of God. Ultimately this admission earned him the sentence of death by crucifixion.

The divinity of Jesus was debated in early Christianity. In AD 325 the First Council of Nicea sought to settle the issue and taught that Jesus was God. You profess this doctrine in the Nicene Creed today and teach it to your children. Still, after the Council not everyone was convinced that Jesus is God.

Atheists, agnostics, and those who cease to believe in Jesus exist today, perhaps in your own family. You show that you adore Jesus by worshiping him at Mass, praying prayers of adoration to him, and introducing him to others as God.

At Christmas you sing, "O come, let us adore him." For all eternity those in heaven will praise and glorify Jesus, the Son of God. May you be among them.

RESPOND: *Jesus, I adore you with all my being. I believe you are true God and true man.*

May 14

Dying on the cross, Jesus cried out this pitiful prayer. It is proposed that because he had taken on the sins of all humankind, this condition did indeed separate him from God. Another explanation is that Jesus was truly human, and so his terrible agony made him feel as though the Father had deserted him.

You might identify with Jesus's distress at times. For example, you are devastated by a tragedy such as the loss of a child, a divorce, or an excruciating illness. You wonder where God is. Or you might experience the dark night of the soul in which you no longer feel God's presence when you pray—something St. Teresa of Calcutta suffered for fifty years. Maybe a serious sin creates a chasm between you and God.

One interpretation of Jesus's lament is that he was quoting Psalm 22:1. This messianic psalm prophetically describes in detail the Passion of Jesus, but it ends on a note of hope. Its message is that though life has shadows, it will end in sunlight. In Jesus's case, his life culminated with the glory of the Resurrection. God did not abandon him, and God does not ever abandon you.

RESPOND: *Jesus, I look to you to give me hope during the trials of my life.*

May 15

LISTEN: *"Go into all the world and proclaim the good news to the whole creation."*

MARK 16:15

Modern media and technology make it possible to be bombarded by bad news from all over the world. Reports of wars, crime, and natural disasters can be overwhelming and depressing. As a Christian, you inherited the story of hope and life to the full, the fact that we are redeemed. Jesus commissioned you, his follower, to broadcast this Good News to everyone you can.

You may be able to produce a podcast, website, book, or radio or television program to transmit the Good News of God's love and our salvation. More likely your sphere of influence will be limited to your home, book club, neighborhood, and parish. Teach children and grandchildren the Good News. Don't be shy about introducing the faith in conversations with adults. Pray to Our Lady of Evangelization for the wisdom to take and make opportunities to spread the good word. By evangelizing you will lift people's spirits and make the world a better, happier place.

You can attract people to Jesus by the holy, joyful way you live. As St. Francis sent his friars into a village, it is said that he told them, "Preach the Gospel, and if necessary use words." Whether or not he did, the message is good advice.

RESPOND: *Jesus, help me carry out my responsibility to make you more known and loved.*

May 16

LISTEN: *"Why are you searching for me? Did you not know that I must be in my Father's house?"*

LUKE 2:49

At the age of twelve, Jesus sorely distressed his mother Mary and Joseph by disappearing. The family had traveled to Jerusalem for the Passover, and on the way home, they realized that Jesus was not in the caravan. The couple returned to the city to search for him there.

If you have ever lost a child or sibling in a store or a park for a short while, you can imagine the terror Mary endured—and for three long days. Not only had she lost her son, she lost the Messiah! No doubt she spent sleepless nights.

Like other preteens, the boy Jesus, who was fully human, did not consider how his action would affect his mother and foster father. He assumed that they would look for him in the temple, the dwelling of God on earth. This excuse did not make sense to Mary. Jesus deserved her rebuke.

You too probably can't understand why Jesus caused his parents such anxiety. Afterward, however, Jesus obeyed his parents and grew wiser. Scripture says that Mary kept this mystery in her heart. In this month of May dedicated to Mary, you might imitate her and ponder the mystery of Jesus.

RESPOND: *Jesus, you were a puzzle to your mother on more than one occasion. Give me patience when I don't understand strange things you let happen in my life.*

May 17

LISTEN: *"The Spirit of the Lord is upon me,*
because he has anointed me
to bring good news to the poor.
He has sent me to proclaim release to the captives
and recovery of sight to the blind,
to let the oppressed go free,
to proclaim the year of the Lord's favor."

LUKE 4:18–19

Jesus deliberately read this passage from Isaiah in the synagogue in Nazareth. In it the prophet describes the Messiah. Clearly, Jesus was identifying himself as this Jewish deliverer. God anointed him just as Israelite prophets, kings, and priests were anointed. His mission was to rescue humanity from evil's clutches. He would bring the Good News of salvation to poor sinners. He would bring light to those who were blinded by the darkness of sin.

Jesus is your Messiah. His life, death, and resurrection freed you from sin and restored the possibility of eternal life. Whenever you slip and fall into sin, you can be sure of God's forgiveness once you repent. No need to mull over past failings, the dumb things you did, the ways you hurt others and yourself. Don't let regret wash over you and spoil your joy. Jesus is your Savior. You are free! Alleluia!

RESPOND: *Jesus, I praise you for carrying out your vocation so*
well. Thank you for your great mercy.

May 18

Multiple times Jesus demonstrated his power over evil by expelling demons. In one case, a demon who possessed a man identified Jesus as the Holy One of God. At Jesus's command this demon withdrew from the man without harming him.

Satan still runs rampant in our world, causing confusion and conflict and turning people against one another and against God. You too are his victim whenever sin finds a home in your life. You may have a bad habit, succumb to an addiction, or cultivate a dangerous attraction to something or someone. Little faults like a tendency to gossip or brag, having a quick temper, or going a long time without praying can lead to serious sin. The sly devil uses various ruses to ensnare God's friends and turn them against him.

But never fear. The same Jesus who cast out devils in Israel is ready and eager to come to your aid. Pray to this master exorcist to rid you of any taint of sin. With his all-powerful assistance, you can make your soul as innocent as on the day of your Baptism. His sinless mother, whose "yes" led to the conquering of Satan, will also help you, her daughter whom she loves. In time of temptation, tug at her mantle.

RESPOND: *Jesus, you vanquished Satan when you died and rose.*
Now I trust you to give me the grace to not fall victim to his snares.

May 19

LISTEN: *"I must proclaim the good news of the kingdom of God to the other cities also; for I was sent for this purpose."*

LUKE 4:43

Kingdoms of this world come and go. The kingdom of God is universal and everlasting. It is a kingdom where peace and justice prevail. God the Father sent Jesus to deliver the Good News that this perfect kingdom is intended for us. The saving acts of Jesus restored this inheritance to us.

You have been fortunate enough to hear and believe this Good News. But most people in the world have not. Some have rejected it as fake news. As a Christian, you share in the mission of Jesus. You too are to proclaim the Good News that a peaceful and just world awaits us. You can do this verbally by teaching a religion class, introducing religion in conversation, and consoling bereaved persons by assuring them that this kingdom exists. In addition, you can attest to God's kingdom by advancing it already on earth. You can contact government representative about justice issues and join protests that aim to promote peace and justice.

You can also serve as an example of kingdom living. You can exist peacefully with others, whether with an irritating in-law or an obnoxious neighbor. You can act justly by not cutting corners at work, donating a fair share to your church, and giving seldom worn clothes to the poor.

Moreover, you can pray with all your heart, "Thy kingdom come."

RESPOND: *Jesus, I long for the peace and justice of your kingdom. Help me to actively advance the kingdom of God.*

May 20

LISTEN: *"Put out into the deep water and let down your nets for a catch."*

LUKE 5:4

How disappointed and exhausted Simon must have been after fishing all night in vain! Simon was an experienced fisherman, yet when Jesus the carpenter sent him out to fish again, he obeyed. This time he caught enough fish to feed a village.

You may be discouraged when a project at work looks headed for failure, when you can't seem to keep up with housework, or when you feel like a poor mom or wife. You try so hard to achieve something, but it appears hopeless. Remember that with Jesus nothing is impossible and, besides, he is always eager to help you because he loves you to death. So whenever you are dejected and frustrated by the lack of results, it's time to cry out, as in the country song, "Jesus, take the wheel!" With him by your side to whisper advice and infuse you with renewed energy and determination, you are likely to succeed.

St. Julie Billiart knew this. At the age of fifty-two and after almost thirty years of illness when at times she was paralyzed and mute, she was told to found a religious community. How could this be? Yet she obeyed and miraculously could walk again. However, she met with sundry crosses. A priest took over her community, a bishop ordered her out of the country, after which Napoleon's war soldiers invaded her convents, and then some of her own Sisters turned against her. But today St. Julie's Sisters of Notre Dame minister all over the world. Her favorite expression was "How good is the good God!"

RESPOND: *Jesus, with you I can accomplish even monumental tasks. Help me reach my goals no matter how fantastic they seem to be.*

May 21

LISTEN: *"Do not be afraid; from now on you
will be catching people."*

LUKE 5:10

Jesus made a joke. The fishermen will catch people instead of fish. Because of these original followers of Jesus, the Good News of salvation spread from Jews to Gentiles and throughout the world. Catching people for God is also your divine calling. It's been said that Church obligations are pay, pray, and obey, but Christians must also relay.

You can lure people simply by your example of goodness. Or you might cast your net in more overt and creative ways.

One couple decided to do intentional evangelization by setting a patio table and chairs on their front lawn. Neighbors passing by would join them for conversation, which often included thoughts on spirituality. A Maronite couple designated a day for Bible study in their popular restaurant. Eventually they had to provide more chairs to accommodate the burgeoning group.

An invitation to Mass or prayer service or a parish activity is potential bait in bringing someone into a relationship with Jesus and his Church. One woman became interested in the faith after witnessing a Catholic funeral. Join your parish evangelization committee or if there is none, start one.

Plan ways for you and your family or friends to catch "fish."

RESPOND: *Jesus, inspire me with methods for introducing people to
you. Then give me the gumption to carry them out.*

May 22

You know the satisfaction of making things clean so that they function as they should. You remove dust and smears from windows and mirrors, empty dirt from vacuum cleaners, and dispose of lint in your dryer. When Jesus encountered a leper, a man so contaminated by disease that he was ostracized from society, of course he wanted to heal him. At Jesus's word, the leper's skin became spotless and smooth as a baby's. This cure enabled the man to return to his family and resume his work.

Sin is a sickness. It infects you so that you no longer are the pristine person God created you to be, someone full of grace, reflecting God's goodness and love. Depending on the severity of the sin, to some degree you become separated from your Creator and from the community of believers.

You can "come clean" if you admit your failings, sincerely regret them, and ask God's pardon. Most obviously this occurs during the Sacrament of Reconciliation, but the Eucharist is also effective. In fact, whenever you sin, you can approach Jesus outside of the sacraments and ask forgiveness, the sooner, the better. In his tender mercy for you, he will say, "Be made clean." Then you will regain health for your soul. Once again you will model a statement made by St. Irenaeus: "A human being fully alive is the glory of God."

RESPOND: *Jesus, divine physician, you made lepers whole and well. Please cure me of any imperfections.*

May 23

LISTEN: *"Go and show yourself to the priest, and, as Moses commanded, make an offering for your cleansing, for a testimony to them."*

LUKE 5:14

A man took his wife to a dinner theater for her birthday. After he realized that it was a Friday in Lent, which requires abstaining from meat, both ate fish instead of steak. They chose to follow Church law.

Jesus, the divine lawgiver, is not above following his culture's laws. By doing so, he set an example. Whereas Jesus obeyed Jewish religious laws most of the time, you keep informed about the Church's prescriptions and follow them. This means performing an act of penance on Fridays, burying a loved one's remains, and receiving Communion during the Easter season.

Christians are also expected to be good citizens. So you obey traffic laws. Even though you're on a wide open road with no police car in view, you keep to the speed limit. You refrain from using your cell phone as you drive. As long as you are as healthy as Wonder Woman, you don't park in a space reserved for the disabled. You stop at stop signs, not to mention red lights.

In addition, you prepare your income tax return form honestly and abide by other government regulations even if you don't agree with them, such as wearing a mask during a pandemic.

It's taken for granted that you obey God's rules expressed by the Ten Commandments. Fortunately, Jesus is a merciful judge.

RESPOND: *Jesus, your laws are a gift to me, and I want to obey them. Please help me to stay on the straight and narrow path that leads to you.*

May 24

Listen: *"Friend, your sins are forgiven."*

Luke 5:20

St. Augustine broke his mother's heart by rejecting Christianity and living a life of debauchery. But she never gave up on him. As mothers do, she forgave him everything. Perhaps you can understand because you have forgiven a wayward child, either a young one or a grown one. Jesus, our God-Mother, is always ready to forgive.

When friends carried a paralytic to Jesus to be healed, the man didn't realize that this preacher was God. He didn't think of asking for forgiveness. Jesus gave it anyway, freely and unsolicited.

No one knows you better than God. He is aware of your good deeds and good intentions. But he knows your secret sins as well: your mean thoughts, jealousies, pettiness, selfishness, and ego-centeredness. He also knows the times you fibbed, cheated, or stole. But take heart. No matter what fault you are ashamed of, no matter what sin cripples you, God is more than willing to let his loving kindness wash over you and forgive you.

After you experience God's mercy, like the paralytic, you will stand and walk tall again.

Respond: *Jesus, you have abundant mercy. Forgive me all my sins, those I am aware of and those I have forgotten.*

May 25

LISTEN: *"But so that you may know that the Son of Man has authority on earth to forgive sins . . . I say to you, stand up and take your bed and go to your home."*

LUKE 5:24

After Jesus worked an amazing cure, the healed paralytic returned to a normal life. Doubtless as the man walked to work, went to visit friends, and strolled through town in the evenings, he often thought back on his miracle with gratitude.

If you want peace, be more aware of your blessings than your problems. Occasionally God even brings about miracles for you, some minor and maybe some major. Perhaps a tumor mysteriously disappeared, a family member returned to the Church, or you won a lottery. At first you were blown away by the exceptional event, but as time went on and your daily life resumed, it could be that you gradually forgot God's favor to you. There are ways to keep the memory of it alive.

You make shopping lists, Christmas card lists, and password lists. Keep a gratitude list, a list of miracles. Use this list in prayer to renew your awe at God's love for you and your thankfulness. Ponder God's actions in your heart as our Blessed Mother did.

In addition, share your special experiences with other people. These miracles are your personal Good News. They may draw your listeners closer to God.

RESPOND: *Jesus, sometimes I'm overwhelmed by your kindness. Thank you for the marvels you have done for me.*

May 26

LISTEN: *"Those who are well have no need of a physician, but those who are sick; I have come to call not the righteous but sinners to repentance."*

LUKE 5:31–32

Pharisees criticizing Jesus for eating with sinners elicited this statement of his mission. He came to heal sinners, who endangered their immortal lives by separating themselves from God. The medicine that Jesus, the most powerful physician, prescribed was repentance.

When a child hurts another one or disobeys, you might order, "Now say you're sorry." But repeating these words doesn't necessarily mean the culprit is sorry. Tears may be crocodile tears. Sincere sorrow is shown by a change in behavior. Jesus exhorts everyone diseased by sin to turn their lives around.

Confessing the same sins time after time is a sign that your medicine was a placebo. Your repentance was not real. It requires gumption and grace to eradicate an entrenched sin. The call of Jesus to repent still resounds today. He speaks to all of us. Listening to him will bring about well-being. The One who ultimately died on the Cross to atone for our sins and rose from the dead will not ignore your pleas for help in being cured of them. You can depend on his outrageous love for you.

RESPOND: *Jesus, Savior, protect me from sin. If I do sin, grant me the grace of sincere repentance.*

May 27

LISTEN: *"The days will come when the bridegroom will be taken away from them, and then they will fast in those days."*

LUKE 5:35

The proliferation of dieting ads indicates that there is a need for fasting today. Fasting promotes good physical and mental health, improves one's appearance, and develops self-control. The Church regards it as a spiritual discipline. Jesus fasted for forty days in preparation for his public ministry. After he ascended to heaven, it would also play a role in his followers' lives. St. Catherine of Siena practiced long periods of fasting; however, it would be wrong and unhealthy to fast to the point of anorexia.

Fasting is one of the three primary Lenten practices along with prayer and almsgiving. It is mandatory for most Catholics on Ash Wednesday and Good Friday. An hour fast is observed before receiving Holy Communion.

If you are addicted to chocolate, donuts, Danish pastries, or other sweets or snacks, fasting is a challenge. It requires much willpower and makes a good penance. Saying no to food that you crave strengthens you to say no to sin. So does fasting from games, television, or the Internet once in a while. Someday you may be ready to be received into the bridegroom's wedding feast where your appetite will be forever sated.

RESPOND: *Jesus, implant in me the desire and the power to fast occasionally.*

May 28

LISTEN: *"And no one puts new wine into old wineskins; otherwise the new wine will burst the skins and will be spilled, and the skins will be destroyed. But new wine must be put into fresh wineskins."*

LUKE 5:37–38

The leather of old wineskins is no longer supple. If new wine were poured into them, as it fermented and expanded, the skins would burst. Similarly, the Pharisees' countless exterior practices were unsuitable and outmoded now that Jesus ushered in a new order of grace. He infused religion with a fresh, new vision where love, not washing hands, was the chief concern.

Your practice of faith might need some updating. Here are three ways to do that:

- If you are accustomed to praying the rote prayers your mother taught you, recharge your prayer life by experimenting with new methods.
- Go outside your home and become more involved in current social justice issues.
- Find out about new movements in the Church and join new outreach programs in your parish.

Your life might feel like an old wineskin. The routines of daily life are becoming boring and deadening. If so, it is time for a new hobby, a new friend, or a new job.

Perhaps most challenging, be willing to change old-fashioned attitudes if they are out of step with the new insights of the modern world.

RESPOND: *Jesus, keep me open to thinking and acting in new ways that are compatible with your New Law.*

May 29

LISTEN: *"No one tears a piece from a new garment and sews it on an old garment; otherwise the new will be torn, and the piece from the new will not match the old."*

LUKE 5:36

Cutting up a new dress to patch an old one is ridiculous. Both dresses would be ruined. The new dress should be valued. Jesus introduced a whole new religion, upsetting religious leaders who were attached to the old ways. They couldn't accept his radical change.

This reminds me of my little brother's obsession with his blue blanket. My mother persuaded him to give it to the Easter Bunny, which he regretted, loudly! Mom retrieved the blanket. But after each wash, she cut off a bit, helping to turn my baby brother into a big boy.

The Holy Spirit is at work ushering our Church into the future. Not everyone is happy with the changes. The old ways were more comfortable, like a worn pair of shoes. Rather than clinging to the past, we are called to forge ahead, depending on the Spirit, the Spirit of Jesus, to guide us. St. Turibius of Mogrovejo noted, "Jesus said, 'I am the Truth,' not 'I am the custom.'"

The Church acts to meet the needs of the modern world. In doing so, she develops her teachings, all the while staying faithful to the spirit of the Gospel. You needn't fear this evolution. Trust in Holy Mother Church's wisdom. After all, she has survived for over two thousand years.

RESPOND: *Jesus, preserve me from fearing or resenting changes in the Church. I believe that you are with us all days.*

May 30

LISTEN: *"And no one after drinking old wine desires new wine,*
but says, 'The old is good.'"

LUKE 5:39

Jesus acknowledged that the Jewish religious leaders would have a difficult time accepting his innovations. Indeed, in their eyes, he was unfaithful, possessed, a heretic.

Staying with what is familiar and customary is more comfortable than adapting to new things. My mother was against owning a microwave until we bought her one. Then she loved it! You might know people who resist learning how to use a computer or a cell phone.

Creation still goes on. In a sense, you have to disagree with the saying, "There is nothing new under the sun" (Ecclesiastes 1:9). If that were true, life would be boring and monotonous. Humanity, however, has progressed from horse-drawn carriages, to cars, to planes, to rocket ships. We have moved from #2 pencils and paper, to typewriters, to word processors. It should be no surprise that evolution also occurs in religion. The Holy Spirit constantly breathes new life into the world and the Church, perfecting them. Be open to his movement in your heart so that you may live with peace, joy, and, yes, excitement.

RESPOND: *Jesus, keep all of us attuned to the whisperings*
of your Spirit.

May 31

LISTEN: *"I ask you, is it lawful to do good or to do harm on the sabbath, to save life or to destroy it?"*

LUKE 6:9

By curing a man's hand on the Sabbath, Jesus incurred the Jewish leaders' wrath. From your perspective, their reaction was inane. Jesus did the right thing. History offers other examples of people who dared to balk at authority in order to protect life. When St. Lucy refused to offer sacrifice to an emperor's image, she was martyred. To save lives Dietrich Bonhoeffer, a Lutheran pastor, opposed the Nazi regime and was hanged for it in 1945. St. Óscar Romero criticized the violence of El Salvador's government and was shot to death in 1980.

You never or seldom need to choose to be life-giving or death-dealing. At times, however, you are confronted with a difficult decision that tests your priorities. Which political candidates do you support? Do you go to a business conference or stay home with your children? Do you attend a retirement party or go to a movie with a friend? Your choices will not make the difference between your life or death, but they may bring you closer to eternal life.

RESPOND: *Jesus, give me the wisdom and moral strength to make choices that give God the greater glory. In particular, I want to choose life like you did.*

JUNE

June 1

LISTEN: *"Stretch out your hand."*

LUKE 6:10

Jesus told a man whose right hand was withered to hold it out. When the man obeyed, his hand became normal. Because the man cooperated with what Jesus proposed, the impossible became possible. This often happens. Remember Jonah? When he finally obeyed God and preached to Nineveh—his enemy country—all the people repented. Then there was Moses who, as fugitive in Egypt, was ordered to tell the Pharoah to free the Hebrews, his workforce. And God assisted Moses by sending ten plagues.

Sometimes Sisters were appointed to what looked like impossible jobs. For example, a Sister who did not know Spanish was assigned to teach it to junior high students. As another Sister remarked, "When we accept hard ministries, God's grace will see us through."

You might face a daunting task such as raising a disabled child, leading an organization, or moving to a new home. Take heart. You are never alone. Jesus, who can work miracles, will be right there with you. Rely on him to supply what you need to complete your job successfully and with joy.

RESPOND: *Jesus, sometimes you ask something challenging of me. Let me depend on you to accomplish it.*

June 2

LISTEN: *"But I say to you that listen, Love your enemies, do good to those who hate you . . ."*

LUKE 6:27

Forgiving enemies is hard enough. But loving them? This is a far more difficult teaching of Jesus, one that requires the holiness of a saint. It's more natural to hate enemies, to avoid toxic people. But God's love encompasses all his children. On the Cross Jesus still loved Judas, the Jewish religious leaders, and the Roman soldiers. He redeemed them all. Consider what Abraham Lincoln is credited with having said: "Do I not destroy my enemies when I make them my friends?"

You may not have real enemies, but some people may anger you: the neighbor who complains about your tree, your children, your noise; the woman who criticizes your clothes, your voice, your food; the teenagers who vandalize your home or car; the person who cons you. You feel like retaliating. But Jesus calls you to love your foes and even to go out of your way to do them a favor.

Also, you may plain dislike people because of their personality, mannerisms, faults, or a reason you can't identify. When St. Thérèse of Lisieux had an aversion to a fellow Sister, she treated her with kindness—so much so that one day the Sister said, "Sister Thérèse, will you please tell me what attracts you so much to me? You give me such a charming smile whenever we meet."

The Second Great Commandment is "Love your neighbor as yourself." No exceptions.

RESPOND: *Jesus, help me turn my enemies into friends.*

June 3

LISTEN: *"Bless those who curse you, pray for those who abuse you."*

LUKE 6:28

People who despise you and harm you naturally turn you against them. You may hope that they get what they deserve and are glad when you hear of their misfortune. But Jesus places before you a higher course of action, a super-natural one. You are to wish good things and happiness for your persecutors.

Instead of cursing your tormentors, Jesus asks you to help them by praying for them. In this way you imitate him who, nailed to the Cross, prayed to his Father to forgive his persecutors. When you pray for those who have attacked you somehow—spread lies about you, mocked you, cheated you—your prayers may effect a positive change in them. In addition, your prayers may result in a change in you and the way you perceive your detractors. To soften your heart toward people who have been mean to you, it helps to recall that they have a mother who probably loves them. More importantly, God loves them unconditionally.

When you muster the spiritual strength to treat with kindness those who mistreat you, God will bless you.

RESPOND: *Jesus, your love encompasses all. Make me more like you every day.*

June 4

LISTEN: *"If anyone strikes you on the cheek, offer the other also; and from anyone who takes away your coat do not withhold even your shirt."*

LUKE 6:29

Jesus offers the two proverbs here as ideal goals for his followers. First, when you suffer insults or physical harm, control your temper. Swallow hot words and unclench your fists. Exercise patience and refrain from escalating a situation of hate or violence. Christians are to be peacemakers. Peace is a hallmark of God's kingdom.

Second, share your belongings with those who need them. Be willing to part with your surplus things as well as items you hold on to for sentimental reasons. If someone steals from you, assume that they needed your possession more than you did. Victor Hugo's novel *Les Misérables* powerfully illustrates Jesus's command. In it Jean Valjean, an ex-convict, steals silverware from a bishop. When police capture Jean Valjean, the bishop pretends that he gave the silverware to him and adds two silver candlesticks. This generous act leads to Jean Valjean's conversion. He is able to sell the goods and become an honest man.

You never know how your virtuous actions will be life-changing for witnesses . . . or help form youngsters who look to you as a model.

RESPOND: *Jesus, you endured beatings and whippings without saying a word. Give me the stamina to respond to offenses the right way, the Christian way.*

June 5

LISTEN: *"Do to others as you would have them do to you."*

LUKE 6:31

For some time the expression "What would Jesus do?," abbreviated WWJD, was popular as a compass to right moral action. Jesus himself gave us the Golden Rule that serves as another guide. Some form of his ethical principle can be found in all religions. It is a practical and wise touchstone for determining loving, Christlike acts. Naturally, you like others to treat you with kindness, to smile at you, to let you go ahead in the supermarket line, to notice and compliment your new hairdo, to ask your opinion, to give you small gifts, and to visit or call you. Jesus tells you to turn the tables and do to others what you like done to you.

The inverse of this maxim is the Silver Rule: "Don't do to others what you wouldn't like done to you." Under the umbrella of this precept are commandments that pertain to dealings with other people. A litmus test for choosing an action is to ask, "How would I like it if someone did that to me?" You wouldn't want others to talk about your faults behind your back, help themselves to your roses, or break their promise to meet you for lunch. Thinking about how angry and hurt you would be if you were being mistreated and disrespected would prevent you from harming others.

Ultimately, by following these two rules, you will be reflecting God's loving kindness.

RESPOND: *Jesus, help me to live by the Golden and Silver Rules. That way you will shine through me.*

June 6

LISTEN: *"If you lend to those from whom you hope to receive, what credit is that to you?"*

LUKE 6:34

There is nothing noble about lending or giving something to a person if you expect something in return—invisible invoicing. You may take your neighbor a dozen chocolate chip cookies with the ulterior motive that she will reciprocate by giving you a loaf of potica at Christmas. Or you may let a friend borrow your car because you intend to ask him to help solve computer problems gratis. Maybe you take people out to lunch and then wait for them to invite you. Good deeds like these are spoiled by being self-centered.

It's far better to do something for those who are unable to repay you. Deliver baked goods to a homeless shelter, drop off a box of diapers to a home for pregnant women, volunteer at a hospital.

As a member of a family, you constantly provide for others, wishing for nothing more than "thank you's." For all of your generous deeds without strings attached, at the end of time you will be fully repaid. Jesus promised a great reward for them.

RESPOND: *Jesus, grant me the grace to be unselfish. Free me from greed.*

June 7

LISTEN: *"Be merciful, just as your Father is merciful."*

LUKE 6:36

Eleven-year-old St. Maria Goretti was stabbed to death fending off a twenty-year-old man who was attempting to sexually assault her. On her deathbed she forgave him and said she wanted him to be with her in paradise. After thirty years in prison, the man became a Third Order Franciscan.

Mercy is God's outstanding attribute. As Pope Francis said, "The name of God is mercy." Throughout the Bible our Creator shows compassion and loving kindness, most poignantly by forgiving us. Instead of meting out to us the punishment sin deserves, he transferred it to his Son. Our heavenly Father embraces us sinners with love over and over.

Jesus exhorted his followers to imitate God's mercy. This means that when someone injures you by slamming a door in your face, insulting you, or stealing your idea, you respond with kindness. Granted, this can be as difficult as walking barefoot on hot coals.

Mercy has another meaning besides offering forgiveness. It is having a heart for unfortunate people: the sick in your family, the bereaved widow across the street, the unhoused who live under the bridge, the immigrants at the border, the prisoners in your city jail, and the people in or out of rehab centers. You might be creative in extending mercy to these poor brothers and sisters. At the very least you can remember to include them in your prayers.

Saints like Mother Teresa of Calcutta and Vincent de Paul were known for their remarkable mercy. Let performing acts of mercy bring you peace and joy.

RESPOND: *Jesus, you had mercy on me. Let me pay it forward and extend it to others.*

June 8

LISTEN: *"Do not judge, and you will not be judged; do not condemn, and you will not be condemned."*

LUKE 6:37

Pope Francis caused an uproar: when asked about homosexuality, he responded, "Who am I to judge?" Jesus forbids judging. Judgments can be false due to a lack of information. For example, a few children were running up and down the aisle of a bus screaming while their father sat without saying a word. Disturbed by the racket, one man suggested to the father that he control his children. The father replied that they were returning from the hospital where their mother had just died.

Have you ever thought someone was doing wrong and then to your embarrassment you learned the true or the whole story? You might think ill of someone for being sad and grouchy until you find out they have constant back pain. On the other hand, you may have been the victim of incorrect rash judgment. People might think that you don't volunteer for things because you are selfish when it's because an invalid at home requires most of your free time or you suffer from an auto-immune disorder that requires you to avoid crowds.

Although it's natural to make assumptions about people and judge them, the wiser thing to do is to assume the best about them, give them the benefit of the doubt, or make exceptions for them. After all, only God is all-knowing and the best judge.

RESPOND: *Jesus, give me the grace to think well of others even when they appear to be in the wrong.*

June 9

LISTEN: *"Give, and it will be given to you. A good measure, pressed down, shaken together, running over, will be put into your lap; for the measure you give will be the measure you get back."*

LUKE 6:38

Certain people have the reputation of being magnanimous, that is, large-hearted. You know that when you approach them for a cup of flour, a donation, or help with a sewing project, they will say yes and with a smile. They are like the tree in Shel Silverstein's book *The Giving Tree* that gives itself, bit by bit, to a boy: leaves, apples, branches, and finally its stump. Generous people are admired and loved. Don't you feel good when someone who wins the lottery, earns a load of money on a quiz show or the stock market, or inherits a bundle dedicates a chunk of their windfall to a worthy cause?

Stingy people who, like Ebenezer Scrooge, do not share their wealth are scorned and probably lonely. In the end misers are losers.

Jesus foretold that goodness will be repaid with goodness. In this world generous people are happy and have a bevy of friends. When they are in need, others flock to their rescue. Better still, in the next world untold treasures await them, for God will not be outdone in generosity.

RESPOND: *Jesus, make me a giving person. Show me how I can bless someone today.*

June 10

LISTEN: *"Can a blind person guide a blind person?*
Will not both fall into a pit?"

LUKE 6:39

Everyone wants to know the truth, especially how to find the true path to happiness. Jesus warned that the religious leaders of his day were ignorant and therefore taking people to perdition. David Koresh, a cult leader, perished with seventy-five followers. Jesus, who is the light of the world and who healed the blind, is a safe guide.

Be wise in following people in a position to influence you. This includes religious persons who criticize the Church, politicians whose policies contradict God's laws and the teachings of Jesus, and friends who try to persuade you to accept their ill-conceived advice.

It's better to turn a deaf ear to the blind who say things like "Climate change is a hoax," "A fetus is not human," "Cheat a little; no one will know." At the same time, you can keep your eyes open to truth and prevent cataracts by educating yourself on issues and Church teachings. Just as you depend on a GPS navigator or your phone to lead you to a vacation spot or a friend's house, you can trust the Bible and the Church to direct you on a safe path to your final destination: heaven.

RESPOND: *Jesus, this world is so complex and rife with*
contradictory opinions. Give me 20/20 vision when it comes to
discerning the truth.

June 11

LISTEN: *"Why do you see the speck in your neighbor's eye, but do not notice the log in your own eye?"*

LUKE 6:41

A quirk of human nature is that we are quick to spot defects in other people. A woman driver remarks to a passenger, "That person didn't have the decency to use the turn signal." A few minutes later the driver who criticized sped through a red light and was t-boned. A friend comments to you, "Did you ever notice how she always talks about her children?" You must bite your tongue to refrain from saying, "It's better than always talking about herself and her accomplishments like you do."

How easy it is to find fault with others and be blind to our own failings that may be more serious. It's said that whatever we find most irritating in another person is probably the fault that resides in us. What annoys you most about someone? Is it the tendency to gossip? To exaggerate? To insist they are right? To complain? Beware! Possibly that is your chief fault.

Supposedly Cicero noted, "You can't clear your own fields while you're counting the rocks on your neighbor's farm." It's kinder to give others the benefit of the doubt. Remember that when you point your finger at someone, even more fingers are pointing back to you.

It's better to look on another person's failings with a blind eye, for as St. Jane Frances de Chantal pointed out, we are all capable of each other's faults.

RESPOND: *Jesus, help me to respond to others' flaws gently. That is what I would like others to do for me.*

June 12

LISTEN: *"You hypocrite, first take the log out of your own eye, and then you will see clearly to take the speck out of your neighbor's eye."*

LUKE 6:42

Some saints like St. John Vianney and St. Padre Pio of Pietrelcina had the gift of reading people's souls. In the Sacrament of Reconciliation they knew penitents' sins before they confessed them. Ordinary people lack this power and can be poor judges of others. To be a saint calls for the removal of one's serious sin in order to boost others toward holiness. For example, imagine a mother scolds her underage daughter for drinking at a party and the girl can retort, "Why shouldn't I? You get drunk every weekend." The mother would be in a better position to correct her daughter if she were a good model.

You might already know the log that impairs your vision. If not, you might be humble and courageous enough to ask a trusted friend to identify your fault and suggest ways you can improve. You could also pay attention to clues others give you about a defect in your character. Sometimes during an argument people speak frankly about each other's faults. Learning that you are not perfect may be uncomfortable and embarrassing, but it will be worth it. Because once you are aware of your "log," you can begin surgery to remove it. How? By daily examination of conscience, through receiving the graces of the Sacrament of Reconciliation, and with determination and self-control.

RESPOND: *Jesus, reveal what keeps me from being the person you want me to be.*

June 13

LISTEN: *"No good tree bears bad fruit, nor again does a bad tree bear good fruit; for each tree is known by its own fruit."*

LUKE 6:43

The apple trees in our orchard are no longer sprayed ever since their caretaker died. Because these neglected trees are unhealthy, the apples they yield are small with marred skin and wormholes. They testify to the truth of Jesus's words. The application is also true: good people produce good words and deeds, and bad people produce bad ones.

A corollary is the idiom, "A rotten apple spoils the barrel." Bad persons tend to corrupt others who associate with them. On the other hand, good persons are a good influence. To grow as a virtuous person, choose your friends with care. Stay clear of wicked people who bear bad fruit and show no remorse: the greedy, the rude, the lewd, the selfish, and the irreligious. Build relationships with those who pray, admit when they are wrong, share, apologize, keep secrets, and offer to help others.

One tip is to become friends with the saints, who were extraordinarily good people. Read their biographies, watch movies about them, and be inspired to imitate them. Pray to them. If you do not have a patron saint, adopt one.

RESPOND: *Jesus, inspire me to choose my friends wisely. And please make me a good friend to others.*

June 14

LISTEN: *"The good person out of the good treasure of the heart produces good, and the evil person out of evil treasure produces evil; for it is out of the abundance of the heart that the mouth speaks."*

LUKE 6:45

Imagine two women at a party comment on another guest's outfit. One woman says, "What a lovely dress! It's the perfect style for her. I'm going to tell her." The other woman responds, "That dress is the wrong color on her, and it makes her look fat. I'm glad I have good fashion sense." The women's words reveal what they are harboring in their hearts. The first woman's heart is full of kindness, while the other one apparently has a heart in which jealousy and pride are stored.

Your words reveal who you are at the core of your heart: a heroine or a villain. If you are a virtuous woman, your words are comforting, helpful, complimentary, and kind. If you are basically sinful, your words are mean, spiteful, boastful, and irreverent. It all depends on what you treasure.

Some people value money, fame, and power, while others treasure God, good friends, and Christlike living. To identify what you value, ask, "Where do I spend my time? What do I read, watch, listen to? What do I often think about?"

Mary, the most perfect woman on earth, treasured God and his will in her heart, which is why she was able to utter, "Fiat." If necessary, ask her to help you tame your tongue.

RESPOND: *Jesus, I want to value what you value so my words uplift people.*

June 15

LISTEN: *"Why do you call me 'Lord, Lord,' and do not do what I tell you?"*

LUKE 6:46

The news is full of reports about people who profess to be Christian and yet do not follow Jesus's directions in serious matters. These hypocrites fail to walk the talk.

In prayer you address Jesus as Lord, Master, or King. By calling Jesus by these titles, you acknowledge that he is the chief authority over your life. As your ruler, he deserves to be obeyed. He desires works more than words.

At times obeying God will be difficult for you. It is more comfortable to turn a blind eye to the beggar on the street, to skip a dentist or doctor appointment, to forego attending a funeral, to avoid asking someone's forgiveness. It is more satisfying to take revenge on someone, to overindulge a craving for sweets, to stroke your ego by making others aware of your talents and accomplishments. It might be more pleasurable for you to ignore God's laws regarding drink, drugs, and sex.

While it is tempting to detour from the path Jesus has mapped out, staying on it is safer and brings a great reward. Fortunately, you have a conscience nudging you and grace supporting you. These divine helps can keep you faithful to your calling to be a disciple of Christ.

RESPOND: *Jesus, prevent me from being a Christian in name only. I want to be a shaft of light for others.*

June 16

LISTEN: *"But the one who hears and does not act is like a man who built a house on the ground without a foundation. When the river burst against it, immediately it fell, and great was the ruin of that house."*

LUKE 6:49

The Leaning Tower of Pisa is an example of this parable that Jesus told. In the twelfth century it was built on soft ground, causing it to tilt more and more as time passed. The famous bell tower was finally stabilized in 2008.

The point of the parable is that it is vitally important to found your life on Jesus the Rock and his ethics. Nothing or no one else is as safe or secure. Your life is bound to fail if your chief focus is amassing possessions, climbing the corporate ladder, becoming famous, winning awards at the county fair, or garnering a Pulitzer Prize.

Founding your life on Jesus requires knowing about him. You increase your knowledge about your Savior by reading the Gospels and books about him, viewing movies like *The Chosen*, and taking a Christology course. You make decisions based on his teachings, as challenging as they are.

More important, you build on a rock foundation by knowing Jesus personally. You carve out time in your busy life to converse with him, and you think of him during the day. You sometimes just sit quietly and wordlessly to sense Jesus's love for you and to allow him to speak in your heart. You receive him in the Eucharist, where he unites himself with you by becoming food.

When your life is founded on Jesus, it will not collapse like a sandcastle swept away by the sea.

RESPOND: *Jesus, may you always be the center of my life.*

June 17

LISTEN: *"I tell you, not even in Israel have I found such faith."*

LUKE 7:9

Certain people have faith in you. Friends are confident that you will keep their secrets. Coworkers believe that you will carry out your tasks well. Children trust that you will keep your promises. Of course, you try to live up to their faith in you.

One day Jesus was amazed by a Roman centurion's strong faith in him. When the centurion's servant was very ill, he trusted that Jesus could heal merely by speaking without going to his house and touching the man. And Jesus complied.

Like the centurion, as a Christian you acknowledge the authority and power of Jesus. That is why when you or someone you know is ill or facing surgery, you turn to him in prayer. Your faith in Jesus also prompts you to accept his fantastic words as true. He claimed that God was his Father, and so you believe it. He said that the bread and wine of the Eucharist is his Body and Blood, and so you believe it. He promised that we will rise from the day, and so you believe it.

It is challenging to cling to your faith when many people do not share your beliefs. How wonderful it would be if someday Jesus could say about you, "Never have I found such faith."

RESPOND: *Jesus, I believe in you and I believe you. I accept what you taught as the truth.*

June 18

LISTEN: *"Do not weep."*

LUKE 7:13

Jesus could not bear to see the weeping widow at her son's funeral procession. His compassion moved him to act. He brought the son back to life and changed the woman's tears of grief to tears of joy.

No one's life is free from pain. From the Cross, Jesus had pity on another widow, his anguished mother, and placed her in the care of the young apostle John. This offered Mary some solace.

Whenever your heart is aching, Jesus looks on you with the same tender eyes as he regarded the widow of Nain and his mother. He longs to help you bear the burden of your sorrows. Are you mourning the death of a family member or friend? Have you failed to achieve a goal? Has a partner or spouse disappointed you? Was your home damaged by a natural disaster? Whatever the cause of your sadness, turn to Jesus. He can provide the grace and strength you need to endure any adversity. His greatest hope for you is your happiness.

Graciously accept the comfort Jesus offers, perhaps through the loving support of others. Remember that no storm lasts forever. Eventually dark clouds will give way to sunshine. If you're lucky, the skies may glisten with a rainbow. At the end of time a future awaits you where there are no more tears.

RESPOND: *Jesus, I praise you for your boundless compassion. Remind me to flee to you when I need comfort.*

June 19

LISTEN: *"Young man, I say to you, rise!"*

LUKE 7:14

At Jesus's words, the deceased man in a funeral procession came alive. His heart beat again, his brain functioned, and he opened his eyes to behold his mother's face.

Have you ever felt dead inside, that is, sad and listless? Nothing held your interest, you went about tasks lethargically, life seemed to have no meaning. This desolate feeling could be the result of a calamity or a physical condition. Maybe there was no discernable cause.

You might try coaxing yourself out of this state by taking up a new hobby or talking to a therapist. One sure remedy is to consult Jesus, the ruler of life and death. With him, the black cloud hanging over you can be dispelled. You can be refreshed and have new life.

Just as a downpour can transform a lawn scorched brown by a hot sun and make it lush and green again, a shower of grace can awaken you. Jesus, who called forth the young man from the dead, can enliven you once more. He can restore your enthusiasm and your joy. Entrust yourself to Jesus, whose Sacred Heart was pierced for love of you.

RESPOND: *Jesus, when I'm sunk in doldrums, let me remember to turn to you for help.*

June 20

LISTEN: *"The blind receive their sight, the lame walk, the lepers are cleansed, the deaf hear, the dead are raised, the poor have good news brought to them."*

LUKE 7:22

Jesus cited his many miracles to verify that he was the expected Messiah. As a baptized Christian, you are to be another Christ in the world. Your miracles won't be exactly like the feats Jesus accomplished. Still, you give sight to the blind by sharing the truths of the faith with children and acquaintances. You help the lame walk by doing therapy or offering an arm to an aged parent. You minister to outcasts by befriending a shunned woman and by supporting in person or vicariously organizations that work for prisoners, the homeless, and LGBTQIA+ persons. You learn sign language to communicate with the deaf. You accompany people in deep depression as they return to living life with vitality.

Jesus also fulfilled Isaiah's messianic prophecy by sharing the Good News with the poor. He preached to the twelve apostles who mostly were blue collar workers. His audiences comprised poor Jewish villagers. You bring the Good News of salvation to the poor when you teach religion to children at home or in classes, when you write or speak about the faith, and when you participate in Bible studies.

When you do these Christlike things, you prove not that you are the Messiah but a dear friend of his.

RESPOND: *Jesus, inspire me with ways to follow in your footsteps. Use me to enrich the lives of others.*

June 21

LISTEN: *"And blessed is anyone who takes no offense at me."*

LUKE 7:23

Believing in Jesus demanded a great deal of trust during his public ministry. Some people were offended that he was not the warrior who would deliver them from Rome's oppression. When Jesus taught that those who ate his flesh and drank his blood would have eternal life, many disciples were horrified by what sounded like cannibalism. Besides, Jews were prohibited from eating blood. Religious leaders were scandalized when Jesus flouted their rules.

Today you may be tempted to give up Jesus when his teachings seem incredible. Is there really an afterlife? Must you follow the Church's laws when some leaders have abused children? Is Jesus actually present in the sacred bread and wine? Did his sacrifice mean all my sins were forgiven? Was he really the Son of God? Where is God's kingdom when this world is rife with wars and murders?

Maybe you are disappointed when your countless, ardent prayers for a cure for yourself or a loved one seem to fall on deaf, divine ears. Your faith may be shaken when someone who has done much good endures terrible suffering before dying.

When Jesus doesn't seem to live up to your expectations, cling to him for dear life. Only then will you be blessed, in other words, fortunate and happy.

RESPOND: *Jesus, may this beatitude always be true of me.*

June 22

LISTEN: *"I tell you, among those born of women no one is greater than John; yet the least in the kingdom of God is greater than he."*

LUKE 7:28

You won't find John the Baptist in the book of Guinness World Records, but Jesus lauded him as the greatest human being. He is the only saint besides Mary whose birth and death we celebrate during the church year. An ascetic and a prophet, he prepared the way for the Messiah. After condemning King Herod for adultery with his brother's wife, he was martyred by beheading.

Despite giving John high praise, Jesus acknowledged that all those in God's kingdom surpass him. You, then, are greater than the greatest prophet! This is in the sense that unlike John, who lived prior to the saving acts of Jesus, you benefit from them.

Because of the Cross and empty tomb of Jesus, God adopted you as a beloved daughter at Baptism and filled you with grace. You have the privilege of sharing in the holy banquet Jesus instituted the night before he died. And because the Holy Spirit descended on Pentecost, you host this Person of the Trinity within your very being and enjoy his gifts. You also are blessed in belonging to the community that is the Church. In addition, you know more about Jesus and the kingdom of God than John did.

RESPOND: *Jesus, I give you thanks that I was born after you ascended into heaven. Bless all those who told me about you.*

June 23

LISTEN: *"For John the Baptist has come eating no bread and drinking no wine, and you say, 'He has a demon'; the Son of Man has come eating and drinking, and you say, 'Look, a glutton and a drunkard, a friend of tax collectors and sinners!'"*

LUKE 7:33–34

Sometimes you can't please people. When I was a freshman homeroom teacher, the department head rebuked me for being too strict with the students, but at the same time the principal blamed me for being too lenient with them. The religious leaders condemned both the asceticism of John and the normal life of Jesus. In their eyes Jesus could do nothing right.

How do you handle criticism? It's uncomfortable and annoying when your mother-in-law disagrees with how you raise your children or keep your house. You are insulted when people remark that your skirt is too short, your outfit is too young for you, or your tattoo is ugly. You are deflated (or mad) when your boss deems your work less than satisfactory.

If criticism is constructive, you can be grateful, accept it graciously, and take it to heart. However, realize that critics may speak out of jealousy or because they just don't like you, as was the case with Jesus and the Pharisees. Let such negative comments slide off you like a fried egg slides off a nonstick pan. Always consider the source and protect your ego.

RESPOND: *Jesus, let me discern whether criticism is valuable or mean-spirited. Help me to respond appropriately.*

June 24

LISTEN: *"Nevertheless, wisdom is vindicated by all her children."*

LUKE 7:35

Wise acts yield good children; in other words, good results. A familiar fable is about a wise ant who works hard planting crops while a grasshopper spends the summer singing and dancing. When winter comes, the ant has plenty to eat, but the foolish grasshopper is starving.

Jesus's parables of the wise and foolish virgins and the man who built his house on rock also illustrate the benefits of acting wisely. So does your own experience. When you eat the right foods and in reasonable amounts, you are likely to stay healthy. Overly indulging in desserts and candy leads to trips to the doctor and dentist, not to mention stores to purchase larger clothes. Obeying traffic laws is also a smart thing to do. It keeps you free from causing accidents, paying fines, and perhaps serving jail time. Wisdom teeth appear when people are older and supposedly wise. Judging from our hospitals and prisons, they do not guarantee wisdom.

The wisest thing is to live according to the pattern Jesus outlined. The Ten Commandments, the Two Greatest Commandments (love God and neighbor), the Beatitudes, and Jesus's example are moral standards that guarantee a good life. Following them will result in a clear conscience, peace, and joy in this world and unending happiness in the next world.

The German mystic Meister Eckhart explained wisdom this way: "Wisdom consists in doing the next thing you have to do, doing it with your whole heart, and finding delight in it."

RESPOND: *Jesus, grant me the grace first to recognize a wise course of action. Then help me to choose it.*

June 25

LISTEN: *"A certain creditor had two debtors; one owed five hundred denarii, and the other fifty. When they could not pay, he canceled the debts for both of them. Now which of them will love him more?"*

LUKE 7:41–42

Archbishop Fulton J. Sheen said, "Hearing nuns' confessions is like being stoned to death with popcorn." Sins have different weights. God forgives all sinners, those who commit heinous crimes and those who are only guilty of peccadillos.

Jesus posed the parable here when a Pharisee thought less of him for allowing a prostitute to touch him. The repentant woman's tears trickling down her cheeks fell on Jesus's feet, and she dried them with her hair. The Pharisee wasn't innocent either. He failed to extend to Jesus the customary Jewish acts of hospitality: foot washing, a kiss, and head anointing. No doubt the man was also proud and righteous.

You love God for forgiving your minor offenses like swearing, cheating at cards, telling a fib. But suppose that you are carrying the burden of a serious sin like being unfaithful to a spouse, having an abortion, or stealing a large sum of money. When you are truly sorry and hear God's words of forgiveness conveyed by a priest, you are free from that the heavy weight of sin. You needn't dwell on it anymore and can sleep peacefully. How great then will be your gratitude to God and how your love for him will deepen!

RESPOND: *Jesus, I love you for your great mercy. May I never doubt that I will find it for any sin I commit.*

June 26

LISTEN: *"And he said to the woman, 'Your faith has saved you; go in peace.'"*

LUKE 7:50

A remorseful prostitute believed that Jesus would save her, and so he did. Because he was God, he could forgive her for her immoral life. Jesus sent the woman forth, relieved of her sins and walking into a new life marked by peace and happiness.

This story is repeated whenever a conversion from a godless life occurs. A prisoner studies religions, decides that the Catholic Church is the one, true Church, and becomes Catholic. He leads Bible study and sees that the prison library is stocked with Catholic literature. A woman addicted to drugs turns her life around and establishes a home for women released from prison. Augustine gives up his sinful life and becomes a bishop and a saint.

Your faith in Jesus makes life worth living. You know he loves you to the nth degree and is always ready to take you back when you stupidly stray from him. The relationship you have with Jesus sees you safely through times of self-doubt and adversity. It blesses you with great peace and calm. Over and over Jesus is your Savior.

RESPOND: *Jesus, thank you for being my lifesaver. I am confident that you will never forsake me in spite of my sins.*

June 27

LISTEN: *"Let anyone with ears to hear listen!"*

LUKE 8:8

You are annoyed when children don't listen to you, when others disregard your advice, and when your companion is absorbed in their cell phone or scanning the room for a more intriguing conversationalist. You would like others to listen to you; so too Jesus desires your full attention and compliance with his words. The adage "God gave you two ears and one mouth for a reason" applies to your talks with God.

Allow Jesus space in your day to communicate with you. During prayer time, try to be alone and silent so you can hear the messages Jesus conveys to you. One woman drives to a quiet place and parks in order to escape the noise in her house. Coincidently, the word "silent" is an anagram of "listen." Through prayer Jesus can build a personal relationship with you that will infuse your life with joy and purpose. He can also give directions for your life; for example, paths to pursue and solutions to problems. Read Scripture, the Word of God in the form of human words, and Scripture commentaries. When you hear it proclaimed at Mass, listen with both ears and your brain. Ask what verses Jesus intends for you to take to heart.

You may not like what Jesus says. It may be so challenging that you want to put his voice on mute. On the other hand, you might be able to hear him say, "I love you."

RESPOND: *Jesus, keep my ears open and my heart receptive to your words.*

June 28

LISTEN: *"But as for that [seed] in the good soil, these are the ones who, when they hear the word, hold it fast in an honest and good heart, and bear fruit with patient endurance."*

LUKE 8:15

Chances are that your mother or grandmother gave you some words to live by. Benjamin Franklin's *Poor Richard's Almanack* comprises a slew of maxims. Nothing though compares to Jesus's teaching that brims over with guidance for a good life. Thomas Jefferson cut out these ethical verses from a Bible and pasted them together to make the book *The Philosophy of Jesus of Nazareth.* He described them as "the most sublime and benevolent code of morals which has ever been offered to man."

St. Benedict advised his monks to listen to Scripture with the ear of the heart. When you plant the words of Jesus in the soil of your heart, cultivate them and hold fast to them during storms of trials and temptations, you will reap a good harvest. You will enjoy the precious fruit of the Holy Spirit: love, joy, peace, patience, kindness, generosity, faithfulness, gentleness, and self-control (Galatians 5:22–23). All of these fruits are good for you and nourish the people around you.

Some plants take a long time to achieve full growth from seeds, especially if you are not gifted with a green thumb. When you don't see results immediately from harboring God's word, don't give up. It could be that others notice a change in you.

RESPOND: *Jesus, thank you for the gift of your life-giving words. Make my heart fertile ground for them.*

June 29

LISTEN: *"No one after lighting a lamp hides it under a jar,
or puts it under a bed, but puts it on a lampstand, so that those who
enter may see the light."*

LUKE 8:16

On walking into a dark room, the first thing you do is turn on the light. Without light you can't see and are liable to stumble or crash into things. Light dispels darkness and danger. It reveals objects and keeps you safe. Children intuitively know this and may ask to keep a light on while they sleep. To them, light keeps monsters at bay.

Jesus, the Light of the World, opens your eyes to the truths about God, the universe, and life. He sheds light on mysteries, the ultimate questions humans ponder. This knowledge makes the world a cozier place.

Just as a car's headlights keep you from veering off the road on a dark night, Jesus safely guides you in traveling your life's path. In his parable about the lamp, he exhorts you not to keep him and his teachings hidden. You are to diffuse his light, enabling others to understand eternal truths and live safely. You spread his light by words, freely speaking about him, and by daily actions that align with his teachings. St. Catherine of Siena said, "Be who God meant you to be and you will set the world on fire."

Children sing, "This little light of mine, I'm gonna let it shine." You might sing—and live—it as well.

RESPOND: *Jesus, may I show my gratitude for the gift of your light
by sharing it with others.*

June 30

LISTEN: *"My mother and my brothers are those who hear the word of God and do it."*

LUKE 8:21

If you are a mother, you know how aggravating it is when children are absorbed in a video game, a toy, or their cell phone and don't pay attention to what you are saying. And how frustrating when you tell them to do something but they don't obey! (Especially if it ends with them hurting themselves, others, or something in your house.) God the Father sometimes has the same experience with us.

Jesus regards as his family those who obey his Father. He, your big brother, set an example by doing difficult things that God wished. The Father sent him to come to earth as a man, quite a step down for someone who created the universe and humans. Then Jesus obeyed by undergoing a painful, humiliating Passion and Death.

Scripture is like manufacturer's instructions from our Creator. God spells out how to live happily in this world and in the next. You hear God's will for you in the Ten Commandments and in the teachings of Jesus. At times complying with it is comparable to carrying out the twelve labors of Hercules! In an argument you think of a comeback that would cut your sparring partner like a knife. By mistake you were not charged the whole amount for something and could use the extra money. You'd rather read novels in your easy chair instead of going to a gym.

When you welcome God's Word and take it to heart, Jesus claims you as a family member. Obedience makes you as close to him as a cherished sister. It deepens your personal relationship with Jesus.

RESPOND: *Jesus, thank you for the directions for living my one precious life well. May my ears always be open to your Word and my heart quick to follow it.*

JULY

July 1

LISTEN: *"For this is my blood of the covenant, which is poured out for many for the forgiveness of sins."*
MATTHEW 26:28

You may have donated your blood to prolong or save the lives of others in danger. No doubt Jesus's blood type was O negative, the universal donor! He shed copious blood to save all humankind from eternal death. Fierce Roman whipping drew his blood; so did thorns pressed into his head, and the nails driven into his hands and feet. Finally, a lance piercing his side brought forth blood and water, symbolizing the Eucharist and Baptism as well as the birth of the Church. Coincidentally a woman gives birth with blood and water.

Jesus's sacrifice on the Cross was foreshadowed by the perfect lambs slaughtered and eaten on the first Passover in Egypt. The lambs' blood, smeared on the doorways of Israelite houses, signaled the Angel of Death to pass over them during the tenth plague.

At the Eucharist when the sacrifice of Jesus is re-enacted, his precious blood is present in the chalice and offered to the Father. Your sins are atoned.

St. Catherine of Siena had deep devotion to the precious blood. She began letters with the address, "I, Catherine, servant of the servants of Jesus, write to you in His Precious Blood." This devotion may be new to you. July is the month dedicated to the precious blood. Why not do something special in honor of it this month (or right now), perhaps praying the Litany of the Most Precious Blood?

RESPOND: *Jesus, I can never thank you enough for the gift of your life. Your sacred blood outpoured washed all of us clean of sin.*

July 2

Before exorcizing the possessed man, Jesus asked the evil spirit his name. Historically, knowing someone's name meant having power over them. Originally, when a woman took on her husband's name, it indicated that she was under his authority.

The name you received at your christening identifies you. In the Bible names were changed to indicate their roles: Abram became Abraham (father of many nations), and Simon became Peter (rock). Do you know the meaning of your name?

Your name is precious. Hearing it pronounced is said to be the sweetest sound. You are pleased when someone refers to you by name and when a person remembers it. God says to you, "I have called you by name, you are mine" (Isaiah 43:1). This reflects the intimate relationship you have with your Creator.

You are privileged to know the powerful name Jesus. The apostles worked miracles in this name. You can petition the Father for things in the name of Jesus, and he will grant it. According to the *Catechism of the Catholic Church*, the name *Jesus* contains the presence it signifies. St. Bernard of Clairvaux said, "The name of Jesus is honey for the mouth, music for the ear, and gladness for the heart." The Jesus Prayer, which originated in the fifth century, brings one close to God. It is a prayer repeated over and over. Prayed throughout the day, this mantra is a way to "pray always."

RESPOND: *Jesus, help me foster the habit of praying the Jesus Prayer, which is: "Lord Jesus Christ, Son of God, have mercy on me, a sinner."*

July 3

LISTEN: *"Return to your home, and declare how much
God has done for you."*

LUKE 8:39

Jesus turned the possessed man into an evangelizer. The former out-cast gladly followed this order because he was filled with joy and gratitude. Jesus gives you the same command. At your Baptism, he broke the hold that Satan had over you. Through the other sacraments, he showers graces on you that empower you to repel Satan's temptations. He depends on you to spread the Good News of Salvation.

God constantly does wonderful things for you, his beloved child. Do you live in a pleasant home? Do you have a good job? Are there people who love you? Thanks be to God!

Beyond these essential basics, God favors you with special blessings. You lose your keys and suddenly you discover them. Out of the blue a friend you lost track of calls. You get a promotion. A child in your family narrowly escapes being hit by a car. You need a cup of oatmeal to make cookies, and that is exactly how much you find left in the box.

Each evening you could review your day and pinpoint God's acts on your behalf during that day; don't hesitate to tell others about them. This is not boasting; rather, it is declaring the works of God and perhaps sparking faith in the hearts of others. Your words will also give God glory and praise.

RESPOND: *Jesus, keep me attuned to your actions in my life and
give me the sense to let others know about them.*

July 4

LISTEN: *"Who touched me?"*

LUKE 8:45

Jostled by a crowd, Jesus sensed that someone touched him in a unique way because power left him. A sick woman merely touched the fringe of his robe and was instantly cured. As far as we know, no one else that day was cured. The woman though was healed because of her strong faith. She dared to approach him surreptitiously and she trusted in him.

In Greek mythology Antaeus, the son of Poseidon, god of the sea, and Gaia, the earth goddess, drew strength from touching earth. As long as he was in contact with it, he was invincible. Similarly, you are empowered by staying in touch with Jesus. He is the ground of your being, the source of your strength.

Through prayer and reading Scripture, you encounter the all-powerful God who is the source of life. He fills you with grace to repel Satan and live forever. He heals you from sin and human weakness. You are far more privileged than the woman who touched the clothing of Jesus. In the Eucharist, you come into contact with him physically. You hold him in your hand or on your tongue. You consume him. Be bold enough to receive him in this form and present your needs to him. Let him know if you wish to be healed—body, soul, or both.

RESPOND: *Jesus, let your power work in me and cure me of my sins and faults.*

July 5

Listen: *"Daughter, your faith has made you well; go in peace."*
Luke 8:48

After touching Jesus's garment, the woman was cured, and he subsequently addressed her as "daughter." She alone in the Gospels won this intimate word from his lips. You, too, are a daughter of God. From all eternity God planned to call you into being in your mother's womb. At your Baptism he adopted you into the family of the Trinity. You are God's beloved daughter, destined to live in his kingdom with him forever.

By healing the sick woman and relieving her of her pain and distress, Jesus filled her with peace. He can do the same for you. When you are overwhelmed with problems or misfortunes, go tug on his robe. Believe that he is concerned about you and will dispel whatever erodes your peace if it is for your good. Is your computer refusing to cooperate and driving you crazy? Did you fall and break your right arm? Has a sibling or friend wounded you by words or betrayal? Never fear. The Divine Physician reads your mind and heart and understands your predicament. He has the power and the love for you to make things right again. He can say to you, "Go in peace" and all will be well again, daughter.

Respond: *Jesus, you care about what happens to me. Instill in me such strong faith that whenever I am troubled, I turn to you for help.*

July 6

Listen: *"Do not fear. Only believe, and she will be saved."*

Luke 8:50

Some tenacious person counted how many times "Do not be afraid" appears in the Bible: 365 times, one for every day of the year. Jesus said these comforting words to Jairus, whose little girl had died. Then Jesus proved that Jairus's fear was unfounded. He proceeded to call the child back to life. Jairus needn't have feared with Jesus at his side.

Fear is one of our strongest and most unpleasant emotions. What do you fear? A severe thunderstorm? Your marriage breaking up? Being humiliated? Another pandemic? Most people fear death—the death of a loved one or one's own death.

Jesus calmed Jairus, implying that although the dire situation required a miraculous intervention, all would be well. Likewise, Jesus encourages you to believe that things will work out for the good. You can trust him even when a positive outcome seems impossible. Take to heart St. Padre Pio's advice: "Pray, hope, and don't worry."

As for death, yes, it is inexorable, but because of Jesus's saving acts, everyone will rise again. You can look forward to waking up in the next world. Jesus promised. Believe that his words will come true. In the end it will be as John Donne's sonnet "Death Be Not Proud" predicts: "Death, thou shalt die."

Respond: *Jesus, keep me mindful that you walk with me and are always ready to help me.*

July 7

LISTEN: *"Do not weep; for she is not dead but sleeping."*
LUKE 8:52

When was the last time you cried? Watching a movie? Saying goodbye to someone? Breaking a bone? Sadness, joy, or a touching event moves you to tears. Crying isn't pleasant and ruins your looks. It gives you a swollen face, red eyes, a runny nose, and smeared makeup. But sometimes you feel better after a good cry. Because Jesus was human, he too cried. No doubt he cried as a baby until Mary walked with him, rocked him, or nursed him. As an adult he wept with Mary and Martha, he cried over the future destruction of Jerusalem and its people who refused to accept him, and he shed tears during his agony in the garden.

Jesus encountered several weeping people: the family of Jairus's daughter, the widow of Nain grieving over her son, Mary and Martha when their brother Lazarus died, the forgiven woman whose tears fell on his feet, and Mary Magdalene when Jesus was missing from the tomb. In each case, Jesus acted to stop their crying.

When you cry tears of sorrow or distress, your compassionate Savior longs to comfort you. You might imagine your head on his shoulder and his arms holding you close. Jesus knows that sometimes crying is healing. He also knows that suffering can be a blessing in disguise. As you travel through this "valley of tears" (as the Hail, Holy Queen prayer refers to earth), you can anticipate living in God's home with his saints where "he will wipe every tear from their eyes" (Revelation 21:3).

RESPOND: *Jesus, thank you for the blessing of tears. I offer you all my tears of sadness and joy.*

July 8

To wake up my sister and me, our mother would sing, "Oh, I hate to get up in the morning." Yes, you might find it nicer to stay in bed where it's cozy and safe, particularly if you face a day you dread. Rather than hitting the snooze alarm over and over, you might hear Jesus say, "Child, get up!" Jesus awakened the daughter of Jairus from her "slumber" to new life. He calls you to be alive to a new day full of promise. You never know what unexpected surprises and graces await you. With each sunrise greet Jesus with the words of St. Charles de Foucauld: "Lord, one more day to love you."

On some days lethargy may overtake you so that the smallest task appears to be herculean. Taking your vehicle to the car wash might as well be swimming the rapids. Paralyzed, you just want to sit in your easy chair and, if anything, binge watch Hallmark movies. The sewing and the laundry can wait. You can call your sister tomorrow. You decide to skip that meeting you were planning to attend. Forget about grocery shopping. Your listlessness may be attributed not to illness or much-needed rest but to sloth. If so, in this case too you might hear Jesus say, "Child, get up!"

On the last day of the world, wherever you are, you will hear Jesus command, "Child, get up." Then you will rise from the dead to live a life you never dreamed of. Then Jesus very well might say to an angel, "Give her something to eat."

Respond: *Jesus, my days on earth are limited. Help me to use to the fullest every precious one.*

July 9

LISTEN: *"Take nothing for your journey, no staff, nor bag, nor bread, nor money—not even an extra tunic."*

LUKE 9:3

Some evangelists preach the prosperity gospel, that is, the idea that God rewards virtue and faithfulness by showering wealth and prosperity on a person. That is the antithesis of what Jesus taught. We are not good in order to wheedle money from God. A fat bank account is not the goal of life. Rather, Jesus valued a simple lifestyle and sharing earth's resources. He instructed the apostles to be missionaries with the bare minimum. They were to depend on God and friends to provide for their needs. This is how he lived as he tramped the roads of Israel.

As a Christian, you do not pursue riches or flaunt what you have before others. You are not jealous of those who have more than you. You donate extras to institutions like St. Vincent de Paul or Goodwill stores or give them to needy neighbors. If you win a lottery, you allot part of what's left after taxes to worthy causes. You travel light, not weighed down by superfluous luggage.

Visitors to poor people in countries like El Salvador and Guatemala are amazed at how happy and generous they are. These underprivileged ones, who may live in homes with dirt floors and own only one pair of shoes, preach the Gospel more effectively than millionaires who hoard their money and wear designer clothes.

RESPOND: *Jesus, as your disciple, I want to imitate your simple life. Give me the wisdom and the heart to divest myself of what is unnecessary.*

July 10

People who observed Jesus work miracles or heard him teach viewed him in different ways. Some deemed him to be John the Baptist, a prophet come back to life, or the Messiah. Others viewed him as a possessed person, a rabblerouser, or a lunatic.

Today some people regard Jesus as a great teacher, a hippie, a king, a sage, a revolutionary, a feminist, and even the last pharaoh! To Muslims he was a great prophet; to Hindus, a holy man; and to Buddhists, a fully enlightened being. But Christians identify Jesus as the beloved Son of God who saved the human race from eternal damnation.

What label would people give you? Good Christian woman? Model mother? Good neighbor? Lawyer? Homemaker? Wonder woman? Grouch? Teacher? Saint? Termagant? Some perceptions you may wish to develop, and others you may wish to alter or eliminate. What role in your life is most precious to you?

When you look in the mirror, what do you think of the person you see there? How you see yourself affects your disposition and the way you live. Try to have a true self-image.

Paramount is how Jesus regards you. Who do you think he says you are?

RESPOND: *Jesus, I firmly believe that you are my Lord and my God.*

July 11

LISTEN: *"The Son of Man must undergo great suffering, and be rejected by the elders, chief priests, and scribes, and be killed, and on the third day be raised."*

LUKE 9:22

Stories about underdogs coming out on top are popular. Take, for instance, Cinderella, who was persecuted by her stepmother and stepsisters but then becomes a princess. Real life offers multiple examples. For speaking out for democracy, Victor Havel had his plays banned and was imprisoned several times; later, he became the President of Czechoslovakia and received many awards for promoting democracy and human rights. For anti-apartheid activities, Nelson Mandela was imprisoned for twenty-seven years; after his release, he became the President of South Africa and won the Nobel Peace prize.

No one, though, has a reversal to match that of Jesus. People did not believe his teachings, Jewish leaders resisted him, two of his close disciples turned against him, and he was tortured and killed. But this tsunami of suffering led to the glorious climax of his life: the Resurrection.

When you find yourself at a low point in your life, don't give up. Circumstances and people may work against you. You may feel like a failure as a wife, mother, or wage-earner. Hold fast to hope. As the abandoned Scarlett O'Hara says in *Gone with the Wind*, "Tomorrow is another day."

RESPOND: *Jesus, some days I walk through the dark valleys of life. During these times help me keep my eyes fixed on you and my ultimate goal.*

July 12

LISTEN: *"If any want to become my followers, let them deny themselves and take up their cross daily and follow me."*

LUKE 9:23

Becoming a companion of Jesus has two distasteful requirements: self-denial and acceptance of suffering. Reining in your ego is difficult. Like all humans you desire the best for yourself, whether it's the largest piece of cake, the choicest seat, or the first place in line. You crave praise and attention and enjoy creature comforts like delicious food and drink, sleep, and entertainment. Not satisfying these natural desires takes courage, but it is worthwhile. Self-control builds character and cultivates virtue. More important, it makes you resemble Jesus, who "emptied himself" to become a man and practiced self-denial; for example, when he fasted for forty days, when he prayed all night, and when he preached to a great crowd although he was exhausted.

Like Jesus, you too take up your cross. Yes, every day has its challenges: a disability like hearing loss or diabetes, being a full-time caregiver for a sick parent or child, a fall, an accident, an annoying coworker or boss, disappointments, and worries. Most saints were plagued with problems like ill health and conflict. Legend has it that St. Teresa of Avila once fell off a donkey into mud. When she complained to God, he said, "This is how I treat my friends." The saint retorted, "No wonder you have so few!" Endured with the right spirit and joining your suffering to Jesus's, your hardships contribute to the salvation of the world. It's said that God does his best work through the cross. This was true for Jesus, and it can be true for you.

RESPOND: *Jesus, I want to be the best version of me. Make me strong enough to conquer anything that prevents that.*

July 13

LISTEN: *"For those who want to save their life will lose it, and those who lose their life for my sake will save it."*

LUKE 9:24

Church history is graced with countless martyrs who refused to renounce their faith. St. Lorenzo Ruiz from Manila was captured in Japan during a Christian persecution. For two years he was imprisoned and tortured to force him to recant his faith. Condemned to a cruel death, he declared, "I am a Christian and accept death for God. If I had a thousand lives, I would offer them to him."

You can lose your life for the sake of Jesus this way or by a bloodless alternative called white martyrdom. This is dying to self and being dead to sin, living totally committed to Jesus and offering up suffering. You are a white martyr if: you are a mother or grandmother who heroically takes care of families, doing an immense amount of work with joy and no complaints; you live with a chronic disease or disability without self-pity; you are a wife who stays with her sick and complaining spouse. People like these may not be canonized, but they surely deserve a box seat in heaven.

Some people hoard their life and seek to enrich it with money, possessions, and pleasures. They ignore the fact that sooner or later they will die and be judged on love. Unlike them, you can choose to pour out your precious life glorifying God in prayer and showering other people with love and care. You know that this time-bound world is not the end, but like a dream from which you will awaken. Beyond it lies an eternal kingdom where those who strive to belong to it will enjoy life to the full, a life that never ends.

RESPOND: *Jesus, make me so one with you that I have new life here and in the hereafter.*

July 14

LISTEN: *"Those who are ashamed of me and of my words, of them the Son of Man will be ashamed when he comes in his glory and the glory of the Father and of the holy angels."*

LUKE 9:26

In our secular world, religion and believers are often mocked in the media and at social gatherings. This may make you reluctant to publicly own your faith. You might be embarrassed when a friend prays before a meal in a restaurant. When someone pokes fun at Catholic beliefs and customs, you might keep your lips zipped. You might never introduce Jesus and your faith in conversations. But there is no reason to be ashamed of believing in Jesus and his words. To do so is to betray a best friend.

Jesus taught you the secrets to a successful life. He died for you and commissioned you to spread the word about salvation. Staying mum about him would be shirking your responsibility. If you knew a movie star or popular singer personally, you would be proud of the fact and might indulge in a little bragging. You are privileged to know Jesus Christ, the almighty Son of God. Don't let social pressure make you be quiet about this.

On the last day Jesus will appear in all his splendor and majesty. As he surveys the humans assembled before him, he will be ashamed of his so-called disciples who virtually disowned him. And they will be ashamed of themselves.

RESPOND: *Jesus, make me bold in acknowledging my relationship with you. I pray that Christianity will flourish again, in a small part due to my efforts.*

July 15

LISTEN: *"You faithless and perverse generation, how much longer must I be with you and bear with you?"*

LUKE 9:41

Exasperated by the unbelief of the scribes and Pharisees, the father of the possessed boy, and even his closest friends, the apostles, Jesus lashed out with cutting words. He could hardly wait until his sojourn on earth ended.

You can identify with this human frustration whenever you state a fact and are contradicted or doubted. (Imagine how Galileo felt!) You might warn children or relatives of the risks of smoking, drinking, or drugs and are ignored. Maybe you propose what you consider an ideal plan for a vacation, a project, or new furniture in your house, and it is rejected. Perhaps you set a goal for yourself, like winning a marathon or writing a book, and someone doubts that you will achieve it. You may feel like severing your relationship with people who do not have faith in you. Jesus understands.

Sadly, Jesus might very well utter the angry words he directed to his generation to our generation. Faith is waning, while greed, violence, and sexual misconduct are rampant. Hopefully your faith in Jesus and your blameless lifestyle keep you from being the target of his sharp rebuke.

RESPOND: *Jesus, I hope to never displease you. May I always firmly believe in you and listen to you.*

July 16

LISTEN: *"The least among all of you is the greatest."*
LUKE 9:48

Jesus's paradox proved true for Bernadette Soubirous. As a young girl in France, she did not have a promising future. She had severe asthma, stood only four feet, seven inches tall, lived with her large, impoverished family in a one-room basement, and could barely read and write. Although one of the "least," she was favored with eighteen visions of the Immaculate Conception. But in all humility she said, "The Virgin used me as a broom to remove the dust. When the work is done, the broom is put behind the door again." Now Bernadette is a canonized saint and an incorruptible.

Do not resent being overlooked for a job, ignored in conversations, assigned tasks that no one else wants to do. If you fail to win a chili bake-off, look homely instead of stunning, or have trouble expressing your thoughts, it doesn't matter. It is better to belong to the least category than to have an inflated ego and yearn to be superior to others, or, even worse, to think you are! No one likes an arrogant person.

When you consider yourself one of the least, you are glad to serve others. You don't mind "foot-washing." In this way you are like Jesus, who aligned himself with lowly ones. He was born a peasant, not a king, and he was criticized and hated. He spent endless hours curing the sick, including lepers.

One of the surprises of heaven will be seeing children, beggars, prostitutes, and prisoners, along with all the other people who were considered "nobodies."

RESPOND: *Jesus, it is a blessing just to live. Let me be satisfied with my lot in life and not hunger for power, prestige, and acclaim.*

July 17

LISTEN: *"Do not stop him; for whoever is not against you is for you."*

LUKE 9:50

Has your faith been enriched by reading books by Protestants like Joni Eareckson Tada or Beth Moore, or by listening to a Protestant podcast like that of Joanna Weaver while you folded laundry or knit a scarf?

The apostle John tried to stop a man from casting out demons in Jesus's name because he did not belong to their group of disciples. In other words, he was ready to block good from being done. His words smack of an elitism and exclusivity. Jesus had a different perspective.

This happening reminds me of a joke. An angel was giving a newcomer a tour of heaven. As they passed one door, he said, "That's the room where the Catholics are. They think they are the only ones here." Gone are the days when Catholics shunned anyone who did not share their beliefs. To marry a non-Catholic was taboo.

Today Christians of other faith traditions are acknowledged as brothers and sisters in the Lord. They accomplish a great deal of good in the world. Their efforts to spread the Good News, minister to the needy, and work for justice should not be cause for resentment or envy. We are one in our faith in Jesus. Their success is our success and gives glory to God.

RESPOND: *Jesus, may I cherish my friends of other Christian religions as we journey through life. Let us learn from one another how to serve you well.*

July 18

LISTEN: *"Foxes have holes, and birds of the air have nests; but the Son of Man has nowhere to lay his head."*

LUKE 9:58

After Jesus left Nazareth, as an itinerant preacher who had no fixed residence, he sometimes relied on the hospitality of friends. He still does. Jesus would like to find a home in your heart. Hear him knocking on the door.

When you expect company, you put away stray items, straighten books and magazines, and dust the furniture and knickknacks. You bring out your best dishes and prettiest tablecloth. You might create a pleasant ambience with fresh flowers from your garden and music.

Likewise, you can make Jesus feel welcome by making sure your heart is as pristine as possible. Scrub away the grime of bad habits, straighten out crooked attitudes, hide your ego, and get rid of faults. Beautify your heart with virtues like kindness and humility. Be merciful and do good works. Prepare to give Jesus your undivided attention.

Show your divine guest that you are pleased to welcome him. Tell him that you are honored by his presence and assure him of your love over and over.

RESPOND: *Jesus, you are always welcome in my heart. May you find in me a fitting dwelling place.*

July 19

LISTEN: *"Let the dead bury their own dead; but as for you, go and proclaim the kingdom of God."*

LUKE 9:60

The young man in Luke's Gospel had put off following Jesus until the death of his father. He deemed other things in his life more important than being a disciple. But Jesus wants commitment and action right now. Procrastination won't do.

Your Baptism consecration summons and equips you to be a proclaimer of God's kingdom. You might delay going for a master's degree or applying for a certain job. You might wait until you have more energy to declutter your closets and clean the basement or garage. But you can't postpone responding to those divine nudges to act as a fervent disciple of Jesus.

Maybe now is the time to go to confession, the time to reconcile with your friend, the time to confront a family member addicted to alcohol or drugs, the time to contact your elected government representative about an issue, the time to volunteer at a homeless shelter. Don't wait. The sand in the hourglass of your life keeps flowing downward.

How you spend your time reveals your priorities. Make God your number one priority before you run out of time.

RESPOND: *Jesus, may my daily words and actions proclaim your kingdom.*

July 20

LISTEN: *"No one who puts a hand to the plow and looks back is fit for the kingdom of God."*

LUKE 9:62

When plowing, looking back is a distraction that results in crooked furrows. As you "plow" through your life, Jesus wants you to keep your eyes fixed on the goal ahead: heaven with him. In the past you might have worked to increase your bank account, accumulate possessions, climb the corporate ladder, become popular or famous. Then you decided to live for Jesus and set your sights on spiritual goods. Have no regrets. You are becoming a kingdom person.

The wealthy heiress St. Katherine Drexel sacrificed her inheritance and life of comfort to become a Sister and devote herself to serving the poor and victims of injustice. Dorothy Hart gave up her promising career as a movie star, broke her engagement, and gave away her earthly possessions to become a Benedictine nun. These two women never looked back.

If you have sacrificed some things for the sake of Jesus and his ideals, refuse to dwell on them. You might risk nurturing a longing to reinstate them! Keep on following in the footsteps of poor, humble, self-sacrificing Jesus no matter what the cost. Keep your eyes on the prize.

RESPOND: *Jesus, may my life trace a path that leads straight to you. Keep me blind to tempting detours.*

July 21

LISTEN: *"The harvest is plentiful, but the laborers are few; therefore ask the Lord of the harvest to send out laborers into his harvest."*

LUKE 10:2

Imagine a field of ripe corn that stretches as far as the eye can see. A small group picks some ears but doesn't return. What happens to the rest of the corn? Rotting away, it goes to waste. This is an analogy for the millions of people on our planet who have never heard the Good News because few deliver it. True, valiant missionaries preach the word in foreign countries and at home, but there is still much work to be done.

A movie I saw decades ago provided another analogy. The scene showed, on an otherwise pleasant day, a multitude of people falling off a precipice into a chasm like the proverbial lemmings; meanwhile, other people are picnicking on the grass, oblivious to and ignoring the terror beyond them. This scene powerfully illustrated the need for more Christians to join in the work of salvation and spread the faith.

Even if you are not a professional missionary, you can do the work of a disciple by sharing faith with those within your circle of influence. You can also be a virtual missionary by supporting those out in the field with your prayer and donations. As Jesus exhorted, remember to entreat God to call more people to be missionary disciples.

RESPOND: *Jesus, my faith sustains me and gives me hope. Set me on fire with a desire to bring others this faith.*

July 22

LISTEN: *"Yet know this: the kingdom of God has come near."*
LUKE 10:11

Have you ever seen a bird trapped in a building, flying back and forth, desperately trying to get out? It doesn't know that fresh air, food, and freedom lie within reach. To escape, the frightened bird has only to notice the bright open door or window and fly through it.

Similarly, when the first disciples preached the Good News of God's kingdom of grace and glory, some listeners chose not to enter it. They remained imprisoned, depriving themselves of the hope and happiness that Jesus offered, just as Jesus had the frustrating experience of encountering people who remained deaf and blind to his identity and saving message.

Arguably, if you are reading this book, you believe in Jesus and have accepted salvation and a Christian way of life. You wish that others would do so. Maybe your children or your friends have rejected the faith and turned their back on the kingdom. This distresses you and maybe breaks your heart. Possibly you could gently guide them to the door of eternal life. If nothing else, you can pray that they follow the light and find the way to their God-ordained destiny. Only then will they have the deep-seated joy that no one can take from them.

RESPOND: *Jesus, lead people into your kingdom, especially those I love. Give me the grace to know how to persuade them to follow you.*

July 23

LISTEN: *"I watched Satan fall from heaven like a flash of lightning."*

LUKE 10:18

The *Catechism of the Catholic Church* affirms that Satan is real. Jesus knew it. This evil creature tempted him in the desert three times. Jesus exorcized people and called Satan the father of lies. Originally Satan was a brilliant, beautiful angel named Lucifer, which means "light bearer." But arrogance led to his downfall—he wanted to be god. The Son of God was present when this mighty angel turned against God and was cast out of heaven. Now Satan hates God and strives to lure humans away from the Creator.

No doubt you are familiar with Satan's psychological techniques to corrupt character. He skews your vision so that a sin appears good for you. For example, a dangerous relationship makes you happy, so why not foster it? He makes you discouraged by having you think you are not pretty enough, smart enough, or good enough. He traps you by making you doubt your faith. He urges you to trust your own will and powers rather than God's. When you are in a high position or achieve something great, he prompts you to get a swollen head.

Take heart! You are not alone in your battle to resist Satan's insidious snares. After St. Catherine of Siena was besieged with impure temptations, she asked Jesus, "My Beloved Lord, where were You when my soul was filled with such terrible bitterness?" And Jesus replied, "I was in your heart." In addition to Jesus, you can also summon Mother Mary and St. Michael the Archangel—the leader of good angels—to assist you. Victory is within reach.

RESPOND: *Jesus, I want to follow you, not Satan. Steel me against his strategies to win me over to his side.*

July 24

LISTEN: *"Nevertheless, do not rejoice at this, that the spirits submit to you, but rejoice that your names are written in heaven."*

LUKE 10:20

The seventy disciples returned from their first mission bursting with joy at their success. Jesus cautioned them against being overly proud of their accomplishments. He pointed out that being a citizen of heaven is a greater cause for rejoicing.

Winning a contest, having a book published, getting a promotion, bringing someone into the Catholic Church, and other wonderful achievements can fill you with intense joy. Far more reason to be elated, however, is what God has done for you: he has written your name in the book of life. You are a citizen of heaven, a daughter of God the Father. In fact, God says, "I have inscribed you on the palms of my hands."

Being loved is intoxicating. You are loved by none other than the almighty Creator of the cosmos. God loved you before you were created. After the Fall, to win you back, God stooped to become clothed in skin; otherwise, you would have been separated from him for all eternity, destined for a life of unending misery with no hope. For good reason St. Clare of Assisi urged, "Love Him totally, who gave Himself totally for your love."

RESPOND: *Jesus, thank you for your boundless love for me. May I always remember that my greatest joy is staying close to you.*

July 25

LISTEN: *"I thank you, Father, Lord of heaven and earth, because you have hidden these things from the wise and the intelligent and have revealed them to infants."*

LUKE 10:21

In prayer Jesus thanked God for revealing truths to rather insignificant, simple people. His apostles were fishermen, not rabbis or princes; and his audiences were composed mainly of poor peasants, the sick, and the disabled. He spoke in fields and from a fishing boat, not in palaces or arenas. The scribes, who were scholars, and the Pharisees, who were the esteemed religious leaders, heard his teachings but remained as deaf as stones.

Jesus would like you to focus on little ones too. Is there a sick person you can visit? At a party or other social gathering, can you reach out to someone who looks lost and uncomfortable? Will you make time to serve meals at a shelter or volunteer at a home for women or children in need? Is there a lonely neighbor or acquaintance you can invite to celebrate Thanksgiving, Christmas, or Easter with you?

Taking "infants" more literally, you might share in Jesus's mission by introducing children to him and revealing the mysteries of the faith. These could be children in your family, in your parish, or in a Catholic school.

Be grateful and happy that the Father has obviously thought of you as an "infant."

RESPOND: *Jesus, thank you for enlightening me with the truths of our faith.*

July 26

LISTEN: *"All things have been handed over to me by my Father;
and no one knows who the Son is except the Father, or who the
Father is except the Son and anyone to whom the Son
chooses to reveal him."*

LUKE 10:22

Jesus, the Son of God, and God the Father are one, intimately bound together by love, which becomes God the Holy Spirit. Jesus revealed the Father to us by his teaching, especially through parables but most clearly by his actions. For to see Jesus is to see the Father. To hear Jesus is to hear the Father.

So who is God? Through Jesus you see that the omnipotent one has a heart for the sick, the marginalized, the hungry, the sorrowing. You learn that God is stronger than Satan and can overcome death. You know that God loves all his sons and daughters and extends infinite mercy to sinners. By the Cross you realize that the love you have for your children and friends is merely a pale reflection of the love God has for you. In fact, God loved you first.

You can discover what God is like by reading the Word of God. In your pile of books, among the romance novels and cozy mysteries, the Bible deserves the preeminent place. And in it, the Gospel pages should be well-worn. You come to know people by being with them—having lunch or coffee, playing pickleball, or working on a Habitat for Humanity house. Reading and pondering the Gospels is spending time with Jesus. As you deepen your knowledge of him, you deepen your knowledge of God; at the same time, your love for your Maker grows and blossoms.

RESPOND: *Jesus, may I come to know you more and more. Then
I will have insight into who God is and who God is for me.*

July 27

LISTEN: *"Blessed are the eyes that see what you see! For I tell you that many prophets and kings desired to see what you see, but did not see it, and to hear what you hear, but did not hear it."*

LUKE 10:23–24

How lucky you are to know Jesus! God called you into being in the centuries after he appeared on earth. The great Old Testament figures were not favored like this. Abraham, Moses, Esther, Jeremiah, Isaiah, Ruth, and King David predated the coming of God as Savior, and because they were unaware of God's greatest act of love and mercy, they did not benefit from the teachings of Jesus. In the common era millions of people are deprived of the Good News of Jesus, but you, through God's grace, are blessed to know God's ultimate goodness as revealed in Jesus Christ.

As you praise and thank God for the blessings of things like a loving family, good friends, a home, and a job, remember to include a thank you for the privilege of knowing that Jesus lived on this earth, and that he exists and lives among us now. Because of this knowledge you are able to develop a deep, personal relationship with God. You are aware of Jesus's teachings. Lofty moral principles like the Beatitudes guide your life. You know that your Blessed Mother in heaven loves and prays for you and your loved ones. You celebrate Eucharists with other members of the Mystical Body of Christ. You have the assurance that there is life after death. To sum it up, thanks to Jesus, your life is like a tapestry shot through with strands of gold.

RESPOND: *Jesus, thank you for the grace of living at a time and place that has made me aware of you and your saving actions.*

July 28

Listen: *"Go and do likewise."*

Luke 10:37

Jesus told the parable about the Samaritan who tended to a Jewish man who was beaten and robbed. Then Jesus ordered us to follow the compassionate man's example. St. John Eudes defined Christians as "missionaries of mercy, sent by the father of mercy, to distribute the treasures of mercy to those in need."

So if your friend or neighbor is in the hospital, pay a visit even though you resist being inside hospitals. When a town is devastated by fire, a tornado, or a hurricane, join a rescue effort or donate to a fund to help the victims. If you come across a car accident, a child who has fallen, or someone who lost an item, don't think twice about offering assistance.

The two men in the story were from enemy territories because of religious differences. Regardless, the Samaritan's big heart prompted him to show mercy. He even paid for the man's room and board. It could be that a woman or man spread hateful gossip about you, gloated when they outperformed you, or made fun of you. When that person is in trouble, can you find it in your heart to overlook your hurt feelings and minister to them? After all, this is what Jesus does for you after you wound him by your sins. Someone said that the penalty of sin is not the anger of Jesus but seeing the heartbreak in his eyes. No matter how you might have made yourself an "enemy" of Jesus, he still acts as the Good Samaritan to you.

Respond: *Jesus, I wish to be a Good Samaritan whenever a situation calls for one. Fill me with the love and courage needed for this.*

July 29

LISTEN: *"Martha, Martha, you are worried and distracted by many things; there is need of only one thing. Mary has chosen the better part, which will not be taken away from her."*

LUKE 10:41–42

You may have attended a party where the hostess was so preoccupied with the meal that you didn't have a chance to speak with her. If so, you know how Jesus felt as a guest at a home in Bethany. While Martha fussed in the kitchen, preparing a stellar meal for her friends, Mary sat at Jesus's feet, soaking in his words.

At times you identify with Martha. Cooking, chauffeuring, doing homework, attending meetings, shopping, and dealing with emergencies leave you in a tizzy. You feel like a gerbil running nonstop in a wheel. Taking time to pray seems like an impossible dream.

Yet spending even a few minutes focusing on Jesus is an antidote to frazzled nerves—more potent than any pill or glass of wine. He will help you put things in perspective and infuse you with the grace to cope with a mile-long to-do list. He may enlighten you to realize that everything doesn't call for immediate attention and that some things do not need to be done perfectly. A friend of mine believes that when you partner with Jesus, time stretches, allowing you to carry out your responsibilities calmly.

Listening to Jesus in the midst of a whirlwind of activities brings you peace as well as his praise.

RESPOND: *Jesus, you never forget about me. May I never be so consumed with busyness that I forget about you.*

July 30

LISTEN: *"So I say to you, Ask, and it will be given you; search, and you will find; knock, and the door will be opened for you."*

LUKE 11:9

God already knows what we need and want. Still, our loving Father likes to hear us ask for things. In this verse Jesus underscores this fact by telling us in three ways to petition God: ask, search, and knock.

When people ask you for something—be it to lend you a cup of sugar or to babysit their children—you might be pleased and flattered that they trust you enough to make that request. I imagine God feels that way too. You probably appeal to God for serious situations, like a sick child, the need for a new job, a dying parent, peace in a war-torn country. But don't be reluctant to turn to God with minor requests like finding your lost cell phone and sunshine for a picnic. Nothing is too insignificant for God to handle when it will make you happy. God is a doting Father.

Of course, God's answer to your prayer might be "No" if it is not for your good or the good of others. God might also reply, "Not yet," or "I have something better in mind," or as President Jimmy Carter suggested, "You've got to be kidding!"

RESPOND: *Jesus, let me turn confidently to God for aid in matters great and small.*

July 31

LISTEN: *"If you then, who are evil, know how to give good gifts to your children, how much more will the heavenly Father give the Holy Spirit to those who ask him."*

LUKE 11:13

If you are baptized, the Holy Spirit is alive and acting in you—even more so if you are confirmed. This is the same Person of the Trinity who brought about the Incarnation in Mary's womb, who was present at Jesus's baptism, who came upon the early Church on Pentecost in wind and fire, and who transforms bread and wine at every Eucharist.

The power of the Holy Spirit is easily tapped. Draw on it at prime times: before making a difficult phone call, when confronting someone, at the beginning of a writing or art project, and reading Scripture. The Holy Spirit can rescue you when you are tempted and sustain you during tough prayer times.

The Holy Spirit presents you with a palette of seven gifts. Pray to apply them to make your life more beautiful for God. For example, wisdom will assist you during a job interview, courage will help you persevere in a daunting task, and counsel will inspire you to offer good advice to children and friends.

The Holy Spirit is the supreme gift God offers you. Show your appreciation by unwrapping and using this divine blessing.

RESPOND: *Jesus, I believe that your Spirit dwells in the cave of my heart. Remind me to call often on him for help, or just to talk.*

AUGUST

August 1

LISTEN: *"But if it is by the finger of God that I cast out the demons, then the kingdom of God has come to you."*

LUKE 11:20

People accused Jesus of performing exorcisms by using Satan's power. He pointed out that this was inane and proposed an alternative explanation: His power was of God, therefore, God's kingdom was present. Yes, God walked the earth in the Person of Jesus and is still here though invisible or under the appearances of bread and wine.

God cast Satan and his minions out of heaven, and Jesus banished demons who possessed people. Divine power can also rid you of any "demons" destroying your peace and happiness. Whether you are addicted to drugs or alcohol or driven to hoard things, whether jealousy consumes you or an inordinate ambition threatens your relationships, God is on your side and ready to cleanse you of any habits and traits incompatible with his kingdom. You have only to desire and ask for it.

Likewise, if a relative or friend is Satan's victim, your fervent prayers to Satan's nemesis—the omnipotent God—can win them salvation. Our Creator, who loves you and every person, wishes only good for us: health and wholeness, in other words, holiness. Notice that reversing the letters in the word "evil" spells "live."

RESPOND: *Jesus, protect me from being under Satan's sway even in small matters. I wish to belong to you one hundred percent.*

August 2

LISTEN: *"Whoever is not with me is against me, and whoever does not gather with me scatters."*

LUKE 11:23

No one can be a little bit pregnant. Similarly, with Jesus it's all or nothing; there's no middle ground. He longs to have you follow him wholeheartedly—with no compromise. You are not to pick and choose the truths, laws, and virtues Jesus taught. No, being with Jesus implies zealously trying to live by all his teachings, imitate his lifestyle of love and mercy, and deepen your relationship with him. Sin aligns you with evil, something a disciple of Christ abhors.

A true disciple gathers others to Jesus. Words and deeds that evince an unswerving loyalty to him attract other people. When St. Bernard entered the monastery of Citeaux, thirty relatives and friends joined him, inspired by his example! St. Catherine of Siena attracted a crowd of men and women who traveled with her, ministering to the poor. You may not be a St. Catherine, but you can be a positive influence. You can also set a good example if, like Jesus, you live simply and serve the needy. When you neglect to act as a disciple, who knows how many people will be scattered and lost?

One foolproof way to win others to Christ is to radiate the joy that comes from knowing you are loved and saved. Others will wonder what your secret is.

RESPOND: *Jesus, keep me near to you and on fire to introduce others to you.*

August 3

LISTEN: *"Blessed rather are those who hear the word of God and obey it!"*

LUKE 11:28

When a woman in the crowd praised the mother of Jesus, he responded with this statement that sounds like a putdown of Mary. Actually it was a compliment in disguise, for who more than his Blessed Mother heeded God's word? At the Annunciation, Mary agreed to cooperate with God's fantastic plan although it meant walking in the dark along an uncharted path.

As a daughter of Mary, you follow in her footsteps. It's unlikely that an angel will deliver God's word to you. However, God does send you personal messages in Scripture. You can be alert to these as you read Scripture yourself and as you hear it proclaimed. God also whispers in your heart when you are quiet and listening.

God's words are sometimes a challenge. God may urge you to devote more time to prayer even though your day is glutted with tasks. Like a bolt of lightning God may ask you to forgive your husband or your coworker. Or God may nudge you to volunteer to teach religion or lead a Bible study at your parish.

When you do your best to comply with God's word, you will be blessed. Someday, Jesus might greet you at heaven's gate with the words, "Come in. You remind me so much of my mother."

RESPOND: *Jesus, open my ears and my heart to your words. May I imitate your Mother and surrender myself to whatever plan you envision for me. Help me to follow the path to holiness that you point to in Scripture.*

August 4

LISTEN: *"For just as Jonah became a sign to the people of Nineveh, so the Son of Man will be to this generation."*

LUKE 11:30

God sent Jonah to proclaim, "Repent," and the Ninevites did. Jesus was also a prophet, but not everyone accepted his messages. That is true today despite the stupendous sign of his rising from the dead, prefigured by Jonah's surviving three days in a whale.

No one is perfect; there are reasons to repent. Fortunately, God is patient and has compassion on us weak humans. Although the root words of compassion in Latin mean *suffer with*, in Hebrew compassion is derived from the word for *womb*. There is a strong bond between a mother and child. Nothing the child does is beyond a mother's forgiveness. God shows this kind of love for you.

If you are sorry for doing things you regret, take heart. With infinite mercy God has erased your bad record. You needn't stew over your past. Just as God accepts you with all your flaws, so should you. This is the point of the story of the man carrying water in pots, one at each end of a stick across his shoulders. One pot had a crack, so every day water leaked from it. Finally, this pot lamented, "Sir, I'm sorry that I lose so much water." The man said, "Look behind." All along the side of the path where the water had leaked, beautiful flowers grew.

RESPOND: *Jesus, thank you for your astounding mercy in redeeming humankind and forgiving me my sins.*

August 5

LISTEN: *"[The queen of Sheba] came from the ends of the earth to listen to the wisdom of Solomon, and see, something greater than Solomon is here!"*

LUKE 11:31

When given a choice, King Solomon asked God for wisdom (a wise decision). Therefore, this ancestor of Jesus possessed prodigious wisdom, but Jesus *is* wisdom! St. Paul called him the wisdom of God. The massive Hagia Sophia (Holy Wisdom) in Turkey originally was a basilica dedicated to Christ. The first Advent O Antiphon addresses the Messiah as wisdom coming forth from the mouth of the Most High. Jesus's wisdom is evident from his teachings and parables, his clever retorts to accusers, and his healings. Mother Mary is known as the Seat of Wisdom because she held wisdom incarnate on her lap.

Wisdom is more than knowledge like that displayed in the game show *Jeopardy*. It's more than comprehension or a high IQ. It is seeing things as God sees them. Wisdom is the power to make good judgments based on experience and knowledge. Interestingly, in the Book of Proverbs, the word "wisdom" is feminine as well as wisdom's personification, Lady Wisdom. (See Proverbs, chapters 1, 8, and 9.)

You may have a woman's intuition, but more reliable is the Holy Spirit's gift of wisdom. This wisdom comes into play when making decisions ranging from the serious, like where to live and whom to marry, to the trifling, like what outfit to wear to a party and what nail polish to buy.

Take time to reflect on some wise choices you made in your life. Thank God for them.

RESPOND: *Jesus, make me a woman who grows wiser and holier with each birthday.*

August 6

LISTEN: *"Nothing is covered up that will not be uncovered, and nothing secret that will not become known."*

LUKE 12:2

If you are a fan of murder mysteries, you know that the killer is usually revealed and apprehended in the end, no matter how forcefully he or she claimed innocence. Jesus railed against hypocrisy and foretold that truth will win out.

You might wear makeup to exaggerate your good traits and cover up blemishes. Likewise, if you are like most people, you present the most favorable side of yourself—your talents, successes, and good deeds—and hide your flaws and mistakes. Admit it: we are all guilty to some degree. In all honesty a priest once said, "I don't practice what I preach, but at least I don't preach what I practice."

Some sins tend to be secret, like jealousy, vanity, and lust, but not forever. "The Last Judgment will reveal . . . the good each person has done or failed to do." (*Catechism of the Catholic Church*, #1039) The medieval dirge "Dies Irae" ("Day of Wrath"), formerly sung at funeral Masses, says that on that day "even saints will comfort need." Today our attitude toward that final judgment has changed. Hope has replaced dread. We know that God is just, but God is also loving. Besides, Jesus has atoned for all sin. Nevertheless, if you are smart, you will avoid sin like you avoid a disease. Also, you will continue to ask Mary to pray for you at the hour of your death.

RESPOND: *Jesus, I want to be free from sin, not to escape hell but to spend eternity with you, whose love for me is immeasurable.*

August 7

LISTEN: *"But even the hairs of your head are all counted. Do not be afraid; you are of more value than many sparrows."*

LUKE 12:7

Typically a blonde woman has 150,000 hairs on her head; a brunette, 110,000; a black-haired woman, 100,000; and a redhead 90,000. It must have been difficult to arrive at those figures. According to Jesus, God knows exactly how many hairs are on your head. What a striking way to underscore God's tender love for you! He knows every minute detail of you and your life.

God the Creator cares for the birds, giving them the instinct to build nests, find food, and migrate (sometimes, depending on the species, a 40,000-mile round trip). You, as God's child, made in his image and likeness, have a far greater claim on his affection. With this assurance, why be afraid? No one and nothing should intimidate you. You do not need to worry about anything: hell or high water, disease, death, failing, or what the neighbors think of you.

God holds you in the palm of his hand and gazes on you with love. Your life will unfold safely, although at times your path zigzags and befuddles you. God the Father has planted a homing instinct in you that will take you back to him if you need it. That's a one-way trip.

RESPOND: *Jesus, imbue me with the confidence that comes from knowing that I am God's beloved.*

August 8

LISTEN: *"And I tell you, everyone who acknowledges me before others, the Son of Man also will acknowledge before the angels of God."*

LUKE 12:8

A story tells of the first day Jesus was in heaven after the Resurrection. He met an angel who was astounded at seeing his terrible wounds. The angel asked, "Do all earthlings know how much you suffered for them?" "Not yet," Jesus answered, "but Peter, James, and John, and my friends will tell others. These others will spread the world." The angel asked, "What if they forget? What if they don't do it? Do you have a plan B?" "No," said Jesus. "I have no other plan. I'm counting on them."

"Them" is you. For some reason, you learned about Jesus and were commissioned to tell others about him. When you believe in him, appreciate what he has done for you, and love him with your whole heart, why keep him a secret? That is depriving others of knowing how much God loves them and that he has a fantastic future in store for them. Don't be shy about letting others know about your relationship with Jesus. Bring him up in conversations and mention him in letters and Internet posts, wear a necklace with a cross, send religious greeting cards, have a statue of Mary in your yard and a crucifix in your home. Let people glimpse you praying or reading the Bible.

Jesus promised that if you show others you know and love him, he will greet you at heaven's gate by name and usher you in. Otherwise, he might say, "And who are you?"

RESPOND: *Jesus, you mean everything to me. Strengthen me with the grace to prove to others that you are my God and friend.*

August 9

LISTEN: *"Take care! Be on your guard against all kinds of greed; for one's life does not consist in the abundance of possessions."*

LUKE 12:15

Former Philippine First Lady Imelda Marcos reportedly owned 3,000 pairs of shoes. Undoubtedly your shoe collection is nowhere near that. Still, greed can infiltrate your life in other ways. You might tend to always want more. This is a common fault. Our desire for money and possessions can be insatiable. A Roman proverb put it this way: "Money is like sea water. The more you drink, the thirstier you become."

Do any of the following descriptions sound like you? You hope to win the lottery or hit the jackpot gambling, inherit a substantial sum, or receive a sizable raise at work. One set of dishes isn't enough. You must have a backup set. Your collection of dolls or bears is never complete. You want to buy the best refrigerator on the market. The highpoint of your week is going to the flea market or a garage sale or two, or three.

Jesus warned against greed, which can lead to arrogance as well as crimes like theft, bribery, and tax evasion. No wonder it is among the seven deadly sins. Hours spent shopping for clothes in person or online can be better spent performing acts of mercy. Rather than amassing things for yourself, it's more virtuous to give them to others. Instead of depleting your resources, leave some for future generations. Greed harms those in need. As a wise person advised, "Live simply so others may simply live."

RESPOND: *Jesus, keep me content with having just what I need. Let me remember that the gifts of earth are meant to be shared.*

August 10

LISTEN: *"Life is more than food, and the body more than clothing."*
LUKE 12:23

A large percent of your days revolves around food. You purchase, cook, and eat it, and then wash the dishes and put them away. Another large percent is spent on clothes. You purchase or sew them, decide what to wear, maybe mend and launder them. Taking care of food and clothing is essential, a way of loving yourself. Providing food and clothing to others in your household is ministering to them.

Jesus, however, pointed out that there is something existing on a higher level, beyond meeting physical needs. You, body and soul, are destined for heaven, where you will enjoy a glorified body. You will only reach that state if on earth you pay attention to your spiritual needs.

You do this by living as a kingdom person, promoting peace, justice, and love. Besides winning you grace (a ticket to heaven), this will afford you a more fulfilling life. In your busy schedule, allot time for feeding your spiritual life by prayer and good deeds. Clothe yourself with virtue. Wash away stains of sin through contrition. Do your part as a Christian by spreading the Good News of Jesus, both within your circle of influence and worldwide by supporting missionaries. Lastly, urge others in your family to keep their eyes on what is most valuable in order to lead a truly good and happy life.

RESPOND: *Jesus, I only have one life. May I dedicate much of my days to real essentials.*

August 11

LISTEN: *"Do not be afraid, little flock, for it is your Father's good pleasure to give you the kingdom."*

LUKE 12:32

You may fear any number of things, such as a threatening storm, a dangerous trip, pregnancy complications, a test, or a person who dislikes you. Jesus encourages you not to fear in the most intimate terms. Applying the metaphor of a shepherd caring for sheep, he addresses you as one of his "little flock," an endearing expression. He reminds you that God is happy to offer you his kingdom.

Your heavenly Father does not begrudge you this astounding gift of everlasting peace and joy. You delight in bestowing special gifts on those you love. You search for just the right one or you create a meaningful homemade present, something that will make them happy. Likewise, God is pleased and even thrilled to give you, his daughter, the gift par excellence, his kingdom. Everything else pales into insignificance—your trials and tribulations on earth, the frightening things that haunt your days and dreams.

Rest assured that no matter what challenges your future holds, God is always with you. You will ultimately triumph. As Moses advised the Israelites when pursued by Pharaoh's army, "The Lord will fight for you, and you have only to keep still" (Exodus 14:14).

RESPOND: *Jesus, I trust that our heavenly Father loves and cares for me as he loves and cares for you. May I rely on him to allay all my fears.*

August 12

LISTEN: *"Consider the ravens: they neither sow nor reap, they have neither storehouse nor barn, and yet God feeds them."*

LUKE 12:24

If you have a pet bird, you make sure to stock its cage with nutritious food and fresh water. Maybe you have a birdfeeder in your yard. God is no different. All creatures are dear to God's heart, and so he provides food for them—even ravens. To Jewish people these large black scavengers were unclean and unpopular. The bird in Edgar Allen Poe's poem "The Raven" is evil. It does not sing but croaks. Nevertheless, Divine Providence takes tender care of ravens as well as more appealing birds like majestic eagles and cute hummingbirds.

Some days you may feel like a raven. You are in a black mood because you think no one likes you, or dwelling on your past failings depresses you, or you feel angry, mean, or useless. Realize that God loves you immensely more than the birds that depend on him to stay alive. Imagine God wrapping you in his loving care like a warm blanket on a cold night. He will satisfy all your hungers, not only for food but for hope, forgiveness, peace, and joy. Moreover, God has a huge feast planned for you in the next world.

You can trust God, for you belong to him and he will not let you starve.

RESPOND: *Jesus, I look to you to sustain me, body and soul.*

August 13

LISTEN: *"And can any of you by worrying add a single hour
to your span of life?"*

LUKE 12:25

Writer Erma Bombeck is credited with saying, "Worry is like
a rocking chair; it gives you something to do, but it gets you
nowhere." Jesus would agree. He points out how useless it is to worry.
Being anxious about the future doesn't affect it in the least. What will
happen will happen. Worry affects us though, negatively, draining
our attention away from the work at hand. It can also produce an
ulcer. So keep a tight rein on your imagination.

Sometimes what you worry about never occurs. You worry that
your guests won't like your meal; instead they rave about it. You worry
that a friend's chemotherapy treatment won't work, but it does, better
than predicted. You worry that you will be fired, but you are not and
even get a raise.

The antidote to worry is trust in God, who cradles you in his
hands. St. Teresa of Avila's bookmark offers valuable advice:

Let nothing disturb you,
Let nothing frighten you,
All things are passing away:
God never changes.
Patience obtains all things
Whoever has God lacks nothing;
God alone suffices.

RESPOND: *Jesus, may a firm belief in you preserve me from
needless worrying.*

August 14

LISTEN: *"Consider the lilies, how they grow: they neither toil nor spin; yet I tell you, even Solomon in all his glory was not clothed like one of these. But if God so clothes the grass of the field, which is alive today and tomorrow is thrown into the oven, how much more will he clothe you—you of little faith!"*

LUKE 12:27–28

If you are like most women, you are concerned about your clothing: What color looks best on me? Does this dress make me look fat? Are these shoes dated? I see swimsuits are on sale. Should I save my size 8s when I wear size 14 now? I hope no one comes to the party wearing the same outfit.

Remy Charlip's *Harlequin and the Gift of Many Colors* is the charming story of a boy who has no costume for the town festival. His friends bring his mother scraps from their own costumes, and she makes a multicolored one. The boy was the happiest of all because he was clothed in the love of his friends.

God is your good friend. Your clothes may have been gifts, hand-me-downs, homemade, or purchased. Although you might sometimes lament, "I have nothing to wear," that is not so. The same God who dresses the lilies and fields so beautifully sees to it that you have a wardrobe.

The Book of Revelation describes John's vision of heaven; there, the saints are wearing white robes. Rather than concentrating on earthly clothing, you might focus on collecting enough material for one of those white robes.

RESPOND: *Jesus, you certainly didn't have many clothes. Give me the wisdom to be satisfied with necessary clothes and the will to pass on my surplus to others.*

August 15

LISTEN: *"Make purses for yourselves that do not wear out, an unfailing treasure in heaven, where no thief comes near and no moth destroys. For where your treasure is, there your heart will be also."*

LUKE 12:33–34

If you have had your car stolen, your home burglarized, or a favorite garment riddled with moth holes, you know what Jesus is talking about. Earthly possessions are precarious. A fire, a tornado, or another Great Depression can destroy them. Your savings and possessions will not be yours forever. As it has been said, you never see a U-Haul behind a hearse.

Some people work long and hard to accumulate money and material goods. In the process they sacrifice family time, fun, and rest. But of far more value are spiritual possessions: virtues like honesty, kindness, and integrity as well as good deeds recorded in heaven's Book of Life. Paradoxically, the more you spend your time and money on earth for others and the more you give away what you own, the greater your bank account in heaven. That is the real treasure. As it grows, the closer you are to the ultimate treasure: life in God's kingdom.

When you focus on piling up spiritual wealth, your heart will not fear death as it reaches towards heaven.

RESPOND: *Jesus, align my values with yours so that my life is enriched with grace. I want to be on fire with love for God and for other people.*

August 16

Listen: *"You also must be ready, for the Son of Man is coming at an unexpected hour."*

Luke 12:40

Company knocking at the door early might send you dashing to throw on clothes, stow clutter, comb your hair, or apply lipstick in record time. Being unprepared can embarrass you and your visitors. How much more serious is being unprepared to meet the Lord Jesus when he comes at the end of the world! Scores of doomsday predictions have been made, none of which have come true. No one has an inkling of when this final event will occur, except, as Jesus said, God the Father.

Before it arrives, you might experience a personal coming of Christ—when your life ends. For most of us, how and when this occurs is a mystery. By then you will want to have your affairs in order and your belongings streamlined. You will do well to say to certain people, "I love you," "I forgive you," and, "I'm sorry." Most importantly, your soul ought to be as close to its baptismal innocence as possible. Then you will not be ashamed when you gaze into the loving eyes of Christ.

If you are ready to step into the next world, you will not fear death. It will be the door to a housewarming where countless people will welcome you. The happiest one to greet you will be your heavenly Father.

Respond: *Jesus, may I be prepared to meet you when my days on earth run out.*

August 17

LISTEN: *"From everyone to whom much has been given, much will be required; and from the one to whom much has been entrusted, even more will be demanded."*

LUKE 12:48

A woman in China who was the sole support of her husband became deathly ill. When someone prayed to Jesus for her, she recovered and became a Christian. She wore out nine pairs of shoes walking from village to village preaching Christianity. For this she was imprisoned with three prostitutes who made fun of her faith. She converted them, and then they too spread the word about Jesus.

You could have been born in a country where you never heard of Jesus. You are familiar with the life of Jesus. You know his teachings about God the Father. You have the higher moral teachings of Jesus as a guide to a happy, fulfilling life. You benefit from the sacraments and the presence of his Holy Spirit within you. In the face of death you can hope for eternal life.

This marvelous gift has strings attached! God expects you to share it. When someone gives you a box of chocolate candy, not sharing it is greedy, but not a big deal. Not sharing the faith with others, however, has serious consequences. Your Baptism obliges you to participate in Jesus's mission. Telling others about the Good News is your job description as a Christian. Be bold in talking about the faith and acting as a believer in Jesus. Help missionaries by your prayers and by financial support. You have been chosen and are called to be an active disciple of Jesus. Don't let him down.

RESPOND: *Jesus, don't let an opportunity to tell others about you pass me by. Keep me alert to when and how I can share your Good News.*

August 18

Fire, like Dr. Jekyll and Mr. Hyde, is two-faced. It is our friend when it cooks our hotdogs, warms our homes, and enables us to see. But fire is a dangerous foe as it burns our fingers and devastates our towns. In Greek mythology the Titan Prometheus gave fire to humankind. It's really Jesus who brought fire to earth. His fire is the beneficial kind. Jesus kindled this fire by his saving acts that released the Holy Spirit, who arrived with tongues of fire.

This Spirit's fire enlightens you to see the truth about the world and yourself. It purifies you like gold purified in fire. It comforts you like a crackling bonfire on a chilly night. The Holy Spirit is love.

Theologian and scientist Pierre Teilhard de Chardin, SJ, said, "Someday, after mastering the winds, the waves, the tides and gravity, we shall harness for God the energies of love, and then, for a second time in the history of the world, man will have discovered fire." A fire spreads quickly, as you know from watching wildfires consume forests and houses. Like a holy arsonist, Jesus wishes to enflame the whole world. How can you contribute to his conflagration of love?

RESPOND: *Jesus, may my burning love for you and my neighbor set others on fire.*

August 19

LISTEN: *"Do you think I have come to bring peace to the earth? No,
I tell you, but rather division! From now on five in one household
will be divided, three against two and two against three."*

LUKE 12:51

Belief in Jesus can be dangerous. Since the first century, Christians have been persecuted. Living the faith can cause upheavals in families. St. Clare, who answered the call to follow St. Francis, is an example. Her father and other family members stormed the convent and tried to take her away by force. After St. Elizabeth Ann Seton became a Catholic in 1805, relatives and friends snubbed her. Supposedly when a man in Pakistan was asked why he murdered his daughter, he replied, "I didn't murder my daughter. When she became a Christian, she was no longer my daughter." Even today, anti-Catholicism in the United States is still an "acceptable" prejudice.

Your heart aches to hear of a Catholic church vandalized and religious statues decapitated. You are uncomfortable when an associate criticizes the countercultural Catholic stance on issues like abortion and euthanasia. Mean satires of Catholics directed at the pope, priests, and sisters anger you. Maybe you have been mocked for your beliefs and practices.

You should not be surprised by the antipathy shown toward the Church, and within it; Jesus predicted it. Brothers and sisters squabble over what is true and right. A rational and grace-full response to this turmoil is to endure attacks peacefully, model the beauty of Christlike living, and pray, pray, pray.

RESPOND: *Jesus, make me bold in clinging to you. Give me
patience in enduring prejudice.*

August 20

LISTEN: *"You know how to interpret the appearance of earth and sky, but why do you not know how to interpret the present time?"*

LUKE 12:56

Jesus chastised his audience for not understanding what was happening. They were blind and deaf to the fact that the Messiah was in their midst. They ignored the preaching of John the Baptist announcing him. Not even the miracles Jesus worked opened their eyes.

The situation is not much different now. Like most people, you know that when cows lie down and leaves turn over, rain is coming, and that when monarch butterflies migrate early, a hard winter is ahead. You understand that a solar eclipse is not a bad omen but a natural occurrence, and you know what causes the aurora borealis. But regarding spiritual knowledge, some people are still in the dark. They doubt God's existence, question the Gospels, explain away the Resurrection of Jesus, and deny his real presence in the Blessed Sacrament. This is no surprise. A segment of humankind rejects the fact that the earth is round, that we landed on the moon, and that we are suffering from climate change.

Hopefully you are wise enough to sift fact from fiction. Ask for the grace to read the signs that point to truth. Accept the realities that the Son of God walked on this world, there is a heaven and a hell, and the kingdom of God is among us now. Do what you can to enlighten others.

RESPOND: *Jesus, you place signs in my life that point me to the truth. Give me the grace to read them correctly.*

August 21

LISTEN: *"Or those eighteen who were killed when the tower of Siloam fell on them—do you think that they were worse offenders than all the others living in Jerusalem? No, I tell you; but unless you repent, you will all perish just as they did."*

LUKE 13:4–5

Job's friends assumed that his sufferings were due to his sins. Pharisees thought a man was blind because he or his parents sinned. Jesus corrected the common Jewish thinking that God punishes people for their sins on earth. Many tragedies, though, are the direct result of sin: your car was totaled because the other driver was intoxicated, you lost a great deal of money due to a scammer's lies, you are distressed after a thief stole your purse.

Sinners will receive the punishment they deserve in the next world. That is why Jesus urged repentance. You might spend money on lotions, mascara, and anti-wrinkle creams to improve the face you see in the mirror. Each day is another opportunity to beautify your soul, a task that costs nothing. This could mean repairing a ruined relationship, breaking a bad habit, or quashing an oversized ego. You show determination to quit sin by taking advantage of the Sacrament of Reconciliation. When you put effort into becoming a better self today, you will not need to fear perishing in eternity.

RESPOND: *Jesus, I want to be more worthy of your great love. Keep me steadfastly turning away from sin.*

August 22

LISTEN: *"Woman, you are set free from your ailment."*

LUKE 13:12

You might long to hear Jesus say these words to you right now. If not, the time will come! Judging from the commercials on television, there are innumerable ailments that could afflict you. You might suffer from arthritis, scoliosis, cancer, or infertility.

Growing older brings physical pains and conditions you didn't expect. Jesus, who had power to straighten the crippled woman's back, can heal you. It's possible that he will cure you not through an instantaneous miracle but through doctors.

In addition to physical ailments there are diseases of the soul. You may be plagued with regret for some failing—causing a family member to be estranged, having an abortion, being unfaithful to a marriage partner. Scrupulosity may make you miserable. Grief for a child who died too young may feel like a gaping wound. A sin like jealousy, pride, bitterness, or greed may weigh heavy on you. Jesus can free you from such spiritual illnesses.

Jesus loves you and wants only your happiness. Be patient. The woman in the Gospel had to wait eighteen years for a cure. Pray to the divine physician to heal you and ask others to pray for you. If your sickness continues, trust that there is a reason for it. One advantage is that you will have more empathy for other sufferers. Plus, you can always put your suffering to good use by offering it up for an intention.

RESPOND: *Jesus, I want to give you glory by the way I respond to suffering. I unite my pain to yours for the redemption of the world.*

August 23

LISTEN: *"[The kingdom of God] is like a mustard seed that someone took and sowed in the garden; it grew and became a tree, and the birds of the air made nests in its branches."*

LUKE 13:19

After you plant seeds, it's like watching a miracle take place to see them push through the soil, grow, sprout leaves, and yield flowers, vegetables, or fruit.

A mustard seed is not even a tenth of an inch, yet it can become a tree. Jesus used it as a metaphor for the growth of God's kingdom. Two thousand years ago, Jesus planted the news of God's kingdom in the hearts of a dozen simple Jews. They passed on the message. Amazingly, today people all over the world heard about it and work to advance God's kingdom of justice, peace, and love. Every time you pray the Our Father, you say, "Thy kingdom come." So do millions of other people.

In God's plan, everyone will find a home in his kingdom. That means people of every race, creed, nationality, social status, and sexual orientation. God looks to you to pass on the baton from the first Christians. You are to issue the invitation to his kingdom and help establish his reign. As zealously as you tend your plants, providing water, fertilizer, and sun, oversee the growth of God's kingdom by speaking about it, praying, and acting like a kingdom person. In 2024, Pope Francis said, "The contribution of women is more necessary than ever. For women know how to bring people together with tenderness."

RESPOND: *Jesus, increase my faith like the stunning growth of a mustard seed.*

August 24

LISTEN: *"[The kingdom of God] is like yeast that a woman took and mixed in with three measures of flour until all of it was leavened."*

LUKE 13:21

Jesus spoke this parable from experience, for he often watched his mother bake bread. Like him, you probably know from seeing your mother bake bread, or making it yourself, that a little bit of yeast added to the dough makes it rise. Spreading the yeast throughout the dough by pounding, stretching, and kneading yields a loaf of tasty bread. The tantalizing aroma of bread baking is one of life's joys.

This parable usually is interpreted as an analogy for the spread of God's kingdom on earth. It can also stand for the growth of this kingdom within you. The Holy Spirit initiated the kingdom of peace, justice, and universal love in you at Baptism when the Trinity came to dwell in you. As you age, the kingdom traits can permeate every facet of your being—thoughts, attitudes, values, and goals—and they will be displayed in your demeanor and actions.

You have power to release the kingdom in the home you create, your career, the clubs you belong to, and your relationships. By doing so, by sharing Jesus, you will be bread for the world. You will satisfy people's hunger and fill the air with a healthy, pleasing odor.

RESPOND: *Dear Jesus, help me to spread Your fragrance everywhere I go. (From St. Cardinal John Henry Newman's "Radiating Christ" prayer.)*

August 25

LISTEN: *"Strive to enter through the narrow door; for many, I tell you, will try to enter and will not be able."*

LUKE 13:24

The key word here is "strive," which means putting your whole heart and soul into attaining some goal. Your ultimate goal is not to win a marathon, be the best dressed woman at a party, or see your name in print. Rather it is to enter heaven. Getting there is no easy feat. It is a lifelong task that requires the determination, perseverance, and work of an athlete. To win games or achieve an award, athletes make sacrifices, perform intense exercises, and practice unrelentingly.

Your striving for eternal life can be curtailed when you are entangled in the busyness of everyday life. Daily chores, doctor appointments, and social commitments can make you forget that there is another world coming.

Then too you might stop striving when you fall into sin and fail to repent. You might think, "What's the use?"

Hardships and tragedies may sap your energy and make you lose interest in aiming for heaven. You might ignore the fact that the alternative to heaven is hell. In Dante's *Inferno*, the gate of hell is inscribed, "Abandon all hope, ye who enter here." Souls in hell will be separated from God forever. No second chances.

Sadly, Jesus predicted that many people will not cross the threshold into heaven. They will be carrying too much baggage. Strive while you still have time.

RESPOND: *Jesus, I want to make it through that narrow door. Please keep me focused on you and reaching heaven.*

August 26

LISTEN: *"How often I desired to gather your children together as a hen gathers her brood under her wings, and you were not willing!"*

LUKE 13:34

St. Gianna Beretta Molla chose her unborn child's life over her own and died a week after giving birth. You may know from personal experience the formidable power of a mother's love, either your mother's love for you or your love for your children.

Mothers instinctively protect their children. This is true for mother birds. When a hen faces a predator, she guards her chicks by sheltering them under her wings. Desperately trying to fend off the enemy with her beak and wings, she might fight to the death for them. During a storm she will cover her little ones to keep them dry. Jesus chose this tender feminine image to express how much he longed to save people in Jerusalem who rejected him.

Jesus's love encompasses all God's children, including you. In him you are guaranteed safety and salvation. He already willingly surrendered his life for you. When the storms of life swirl around you, he will protect you. When you are threatened by Satan's snares, take refuge in him. Run to his embrace. Whenever you do succumb to temptation, take heart. Jesus yearns to take you back. His love for you is as strong and unconditional as a mother's love. Nothing you do, no matter how grievous, will ever destroy his wish to live with you forever.

RESPOND: *Jesus, your motherly tenderness enfolds me like a cozy blanket. I trust in your love for me. Keep me under the shelter of your wings.*

August 27

LISTEN: *"For all who exalt themselves will be humbled, and those who humble themselves will be exalted."*

LUKE 14:11

C.S. Lewis said, "True humility is not thinking less of yourself; it is thinking of yourself less." It means thinking more of others. Jesus is the ideal model of humility. He is almighty God, a pure spirit and the supreme, transcendent, infinite Being. Nevertheless, he took on a human nature for our sake. He clothed himself in flesh and blood, was born in poor surroundings, and became subject to human beings, his creatures. He washed his apostles' feet and died on a cross. But then he was exalted and now reigns as king in heaven.

Women perform humble tasks. They change diapers, clean floors, and serve their families. There are, however, other ways to be humble. A humble woman doesn't dominate conversations or speak mostly about herself. She doesn't boast or seek attention. When her success is acknowledged, she gives credit to others. She admits mistakes instead of denying them or hiding them. After hurting someone, she is quick to ask forgiveness. She is not above accepting others' advice and doesn't insist on doing things her way.

People who are puffed up with pride need to heed the warning, "Pride goes before a fall." Satan, Adam, and Eve learned this.

RESPOND: *Jesus, meek and humble of heart, make my heart like yours.*

August 28

LISTEN: *"But when you give a banquet, invite the poor, the crippled, the lame, and the blind. And you will be blessed, because they cannot repay you, for you will be repaid at the resurrection of the righteous."*

LUKE 14:13–14

My former parish has a big heart for the less fortunate. Parishioners regularly prepare hot meals at several hunger centers and at homes for those fighting addiction. They hold food drives for the poor and the homeless. At the annual summer picnic, adults from a nearby facility who have developmental disabilities are always invited.

You too carry out this much-needed ministry when you participate in such programs at your parish. You also do it by inviting to your family meals others who aren't likely to reciprocate: a friend who has nowhere to go for Thanksgiving, a neighbor who uses a cane or walker, a relative whose mental illness you find annoying or sad. Reaching out to people like these is difficult. It demands extra time, energy, patience, and love. You might have to arrange transportation and accommodate your menu to your guest's needs.

When you welcome those on the margins to join you around your table, whether in your home or at a restaurant, you have the satisfaction of bringing them joy. Moreover, Jesus assures you that you will have a place at his heavenly banquet.

RESPOND: *Jesus, keep me mindful of the poor and disabled. Inspire me with ideas for showing love by sharing a meal with them.*

August 29

LISTEN: *"Whoever comes to me and does not hate father and mother, wife and children, brothers and sisters, yes, and even life itself, cannot be my disciple."*

LUKE 14:26

This statement of Jesus is shocking if taken literally. However, he was only conforming to the Hebrews' custom of speaking in hyperbole to get across an idea. His point was that his followers should not prefer anyone or anything to him. That is still a radical requirement, but it makes sense. After all, Jesus is God, the almighty Creator who commanded that we do not have other gods before him.

Jesus is also your Savior. His love for you is unmatched. Once you are committed to Jesus, your whole heart ought to belong to him. No one should mean more to you than he does, not even your spouse or closest relatives. No other person should be able to sway you from living as he taught. The martyrs proved that Jesus was more to them than life. You may not be called to die for being a Christian as they did. But you can live in such a way that it's obvious to all that you consider Jesus number one.

French priest St. Louis de Montfort's motto was "God alone." It is found more than one hundred fifty times in his writings. It is a good motto for all of us to adopt.

RESPOND: *Jesus, I adore you and pray with St. Francis of Assisi, "My God and my all!"*

August 30

LISTEN: *"Whoever does not carry the cross and follow me cannot be my disciple."*

LUKE 14:27

A woman complains to God about her cross. The Almighty takes her to a room where crosses of all sizes are stored and invites her to choose one for herself. Spotting the smallest one, she says, "That's the one I want." And God replies, "That's the one you already have."

You can be like that woman and resist or resent your cross or crosses. Trials like a chronic disease, a mean boss, and a child who breaks your heart are not easy to bear. They fill you with worry, sadness, and frustration. A true disciple of Jesus knows that accepting the cross is an absolute requirement for a Christian. Never fear. You can trust God to act like Simon and help you carry it.

No one escapes crosses. Author Flannery O'Connor observed that people "think faith is a big electric blanket, when of course it is the cross." Some of the greatest saints were blessed with the cruelest crosses. Mary, the mother of God, is a prime example: she gave birth in a stable; a king sought to kill her infant boy, and when he was grown, people called him crazy and possessed; neighbors tried to hurl him off a cliff; and finally, Mary witnessed his torture and execution.

A cross becomes valuable when you unite it to the sufferings of Jesus, for then you share in the world's salvation. Besides, borne with patience, it can make you a better person and more empathetic to people in pain. Yet, it is all right to pray to God to take away a cross. That is what Jesus did in the Garden of Gethsemane.

RESPOND: *Jesus, thank you for bearing the cross for me. When my faith is tried by a hardship or tragedy, let me remember that you give me the strength to carry any cross.*

August 31

LISTEN: *"There will be more joy in heaven over one sinner who repents than over ninety-nine righteous persons who need no repentance."*

LUKE 15:7

A mother who has several children loves them all. One of them may get involved in drugs, crime, and other sins. The poor woman may spend sleepless nights worrying about the child. If that wayward child changes his or her ways, the mother is thrilled. That doesn't mean she loves her other children less.

God wants all his children to forsake sin and attain heaven. One task of God's ambassadors is leading sinners to repent. From her convent, St. Therese of Lisieux prayed that a killer would be converted. She read in the newspaper that right before he was to be guillotined, he asked for a priest. Like her, you can pray for sinners, not only those in the news but those you know.

In addition, you can do your utmost to persuade a sinner to give up a sin. Pray to the Holy Spirit to inspire you with the right words to touch the person's heart.

If you are guilty of a sin yourself, ask God's forgiveness, go to confession, and make a firm decision to eradicate it from your life. This will make Jesus, Mary, the angels and saints, and your friends and relatives in heaven and on earth happy. Besides, according to a French proverb, there's no pillow as soft as a clear conscience.

RESPOND: *Jesus, may I remember to pray for sinners and for the holy souls in purgatory.*

SEPTEMBER

September 1

LISTEN: *"You cannot serve God and wealth."*

LUKE 16:13

Some people can never have enough money and things. G. K. Chesterton said, "There are two ways to get enough. One is to continue to accumulate more and more. The other is to desire less." Our culture is obsessed with money. Gambling is a problem, an addiction that tears some families apart. Game shows on TV offer huge amounts of money as prizes. Lotteries lure people to waste their hard-earned money on winning millions, although the odds are astronomically against them. Greedy people with poor morals will steal, cheat, lie, and even kill to swell their bank accounts.

But then there are large-hearted souls who leave lucrative jobs to work for a nonprofit, who donate to organizations like Boys Town and St. Jude's Hospital, and who fund scholarships.

We were created to know, love, and serve God. Jesus taught that serving God is obeying the commandments and being poor, at least poor in spirit. You do not really need the latest model of cell phone or television or that diamond encrusted necklace. God set the example by entering this world as a poor peasant born in an animal shelter, not a king with a castle and treasure house. As an itinerant preacher, he admitted he had no place to lay his head.

Riches do not guarantee happiness. Research shows that people who use their wealth to benefit others are happier than those who spend money on themselves. A Christian shares wealth with those who are not as fortunate.

RESPOND: *Jesus, I want to keep in mind that money doesn't buy happiness. Please make me rich in virtues.*

September 2

LISTEN: *"Were not ten made clean? But the other nine,
where are they? Was none of them found to return and give praise
to God except this foreigner?"*

LUKE 17:17–18

Mothers teach their children to say please and thank you and to write thank-you notes. Neglecting to send a deserved thank you is impolite and insulting. The donor could forgo giving gifts in the future.

The word "thank" is derived from the word "think." To express gratitude to someone is to remember the source of a gift or favor. After Jesus cured the ten lepers, all but one were so excited and forgetful that they failed to acknowledge the person who gave their lives back. Clearly Jesus expected to be thanked.

God is your greatest benefactor. Everything you have and enjoy is a gift from your heavenly Father. This includes your very existence, every breath and every heartbeat. Each evening you might comb through the day's happenings and pinpoint God's favors. These may be slight like a hug from a friend, a delicious meal, or the release of a new album by a favorite band. Maybe you found a reliable electrician who was able to fix your loose wiring, or you were able to finish reading a book. Or significant like a safe drive home through fog, a cousin who is free from cancer, and finding your lost credit card.

The word "eucharist" means thanksgiving. The Mass is your most perfect way of giving thanks and praise to God. At the next Mass you participate in, recall the gifts God has bestowed on you. Then, be like the one grateful leper. With a strong voice pray and sing glory to God.

RESPOND: *Jesus, thank you for all the good you have done for me.
May I make every day a Thanksgiving Day.*

September 3

LISTEN: *"The kingdom of God is among you."*

LUKE 17:21

When Pharisees asked Jesus when God's kingdom would come, he stated that it was already here. Jesus, in his reign of righteousness, peace, and love, was walking along with them. But it was as though cataracts blinded them to this truth. They failed to comprehend that Jesus's extraordinary teachings and miraculous healings signaled the presence of the kingdom of God.

The kingdom of God is also with you. Jesus is at work around you in the good people you encounter, the neighbor who smiles despite a debilitating illness, the friend who volunteers at a homeless shelter, the cousin who joins protests for justice. The kingdom of God is within you. It is revealed when you settle a dispute between children or adults, when you teach what is right by your words or example, and when you donate time, talent, or treasure to a charitable organization.

If you recognize that Jesus is the kingdom of God, deepen your knowledge of him by reading Scripture and other spiritual books. Be sensitive to the ways he is working in your life. Have 20/20 spiritual vision.

RESPOND: *Jesus, I acknowledge that you are my Lord and Savior, king of my heart and king of the universe.*

September 4

LISTEN: *"Zacchaeus, hurry and come down; for I must stay at your house today."*

LUKE 19:5

I hope Zacchaeus's wife didn't mind unexpected company like Jesus (and perhaps apostles) after her husband's encounter with him. As a good Jew, she knew that hospitality was a hallmark of their faith. God says in Scripture, "Do not neglect to show hospitality to strangers, for by doing that some have entertained angels without knowing it" (Hebrews 13:2). Zacchaeus and his wife were hosting not just angels but the Son of God.

If you are like most women, you enjoy inviting guests and making them feel at home. For one thing, it motivates you to clear the house of clutter and dust the furniture. You prepare one of your signature meals and dress with care. These pains are worthwhile, for in every visitor Jesus is present.

You can practice hospitality in different ways. When Thanksgiving, Christmas, or Easter rolls around, volunteer to provide a feast for your extended family. Occasionally invite a lonely or disabled neighbor to join you for a homecooked meal or take them out to lunch or dinner. For parish functions that involve food—like funeral dinners, picnics, and fish fries—join the cooking staff.

If possible, share your house with someone in need of a home: a friend who has been evicted, a foster child, or a refugee. Welcome every person, even the most disagreeable, as you would welcome Jesus himself. Let your attitude be *mi casa es su casa* (my house is your house).

RESPOND: *Jesus, help me to be a gracious and loving hostess.*

September 5

LISTEN: *"I tell you, if these were silent, the stones would shout out."*

LUKE 19:40

As Jesus entered Jerusalem, a mob of his disciples accompanied him, rejoicing and acclaiming him as king and praised God. When Pharisees told him to stop them, Jesus made this striking statement. The message here is that Jesus, the Son of God, deserves honor and glory.

Of course, stones don't shout. Jesus spoke figuratively. Yet, everything in creation—stars, mountains, trees, flowers, deer—voicelessly declares God's greatness. At the apex of creation are human beings. We alone have the power to glorify God with words and consciously with actions. St. Paul exhorted, "So, whether you eat or drink, or whatever you do, do everything for the glory of God" (1 Corinthians 10:31).

So sing the "Glory to God" and the "Holy, Holy" at Mass with all your heart and soul. Sing Christian hymns of praise as you fold laundry, drive somewhere, or crochet. In the morning offer everything you will do that day for the glory of God who gave you the gift of life. Take care to do things for God's glory, not your own glory. Look forward to the day when you will join the hosts of blessed ones in heaven who sing, "To the one seated on the throne and to the Lamb be blessing and honor and glory and might forever and ever!" (Revelation 5:13).

RESPOND: *Jesus, may I often pray, "Praised be Jesus Christ now and forever!"*

September 6

LISTEN: *"Give to the emperor the things that are the emperor's, and to God the things that are God's."*

LUKE 20:25

Have you ever had something stolen from you, such as an article of clothing, a wallet, a car? If so, you were probably outraged at the injustice of it. Jesus taught the importance of turning over to the government what it has a right to instead of hoarding it for oneself. He did this by pointing out that Caesar's image was imprinted on a coin. You owe taxes for enjoying the benefits your nation, state, and town provide. Paying them is only just.

Likewise, you are responsible for giving God what belongs to him. What doesn't belong to God? All of creation is his, and God expects you to be a good steward of his property. What's more, you, who are stamped with God's image, belong to him. Surrender yourself to God completely. Give God your entire being, your life: your body and soul, your thoughts and actions. Use your gifts to serve God by serving others.

At each Eucharist, you can imagine you are on the paten with the bread and offer yourself to the Father with Jesus. You might also make the prayer of St. Ignatius your own:

> Take, Lord, and receive all my liberty, my memory, my understanding, and my entire will. All that I have and possess. You have given all to me; to you, Lord, I return it. All is yours. Dispose of it as you will. Give me only your love and your grace. With these I am rich enough and ask for nothing more.

RESPOND: *Jesus, may the thought that I belong to God guide my choices and decisions every day. I want to make you proud of me.*

September 7

LISTEN: *"Now he is God not of the dead, but of the living; for to him all of them are alive."*

LUKE 20:38

At a funeral Mass, a woman read a consoling parable during the eulogy. In it mourners are gathered on the shore of a lake, waving off a ship. They call out, "There she goes!" On the other side of the lake, a throng of people are shouting, "Here she comes!"

Christians do not fear death. To us who have faith, death is not the dreadful end of everything. It does not mean we will never see our loved ones again. Rather, we believe that death is merely the door to another form of living, a fantastic one. Jesus clearly taught that there is life after death. He went on to demonstrate this by walking out of his tomb.

You might find it sad to think of leaving this world with its experiences of being loved by family and friends, witnessing breathtaking skies, hiking through forests, and eating hamburgers and ice cream. But the world that awaits you is exponentially superior to this one. You can't imagine what it will be like, but it promises to make you extremely happy. Like Jesus you will have a glorified body. There will be no illnesses, pain, fear, or tears—unless they are tears of joy. You will be reunited with deceased relatives and friends and meet favorite saints including your patron saint. Best of all, you will behold God face-to-face.

RESPOND: *Jesus, thank you for making it possible for me to hope for eternal life with God.*

September 8

Listen: *"Truly I tell you, this poor widow has put in more than all of them; for all of them have contributed out of their abundance, but she out of her poverty has put in all she had to live on."*

Luke 21:3–4

A widow donated a mere pittance to a temple contribution chest. This was, however, a spectacularly generous act, for the two coins were all she owned. She could have begged for alms herself. Jesus recognized that her gift was more valuable than money wealthy people poured into the chest because of what it cost her. She was left with nothing. Apparently, the widow would rely on God to take care of her.

Jesus does not expect you to give away all your money but certainly some of it. Traditionally, Christians tithe, that is, donate ten percent of their income to their church. In addition, there are ample opportunities to use your money to aid poor and suffering people. Your motive for donating is key. Doing it to make yourself feel good or to impress others is not as virtuous or commendable as doing it for love.

In the ordinary course of a day, you actually may have chances to imitate the magnanimous widow. A neighbor asks for flour, and you give her all you have. You have an hour to read a book, but when a friend asks you to babysit for a short time, you sacrifice that hour. Your mother left you earrings that you treasure, but you give them to your niece for her birthday.

Of course, the quintessential donor is Jesus himself, who gave up his life that we may live.

Respond: *Jesus, help me discern what causes to support financially. May I always keep my intentions pure.*

September 9

LISTEN: *"Do this in remembrance of me."*

LUKE 22:19

As my aunt presented me with several figurines, she commented, "This is so you remember me." Without doubt, you have keepsakes like these to remember your aunt, mother, grandmother, or good friend. Jesus made sure that he would be remembered by giving us the Eucharist. Today, more than two thousand years later, people all over the world recall Jesus and his incomprehensible love for us whenever his saving death is re-presented at Mass.

The Eucharist is far more than a memorial. At Mass the living, glorified Jesus truly becomes present in our day. When you receive the sacred bread and wine in Communion, he unites himself with you. This intimate union is greater than your union with any other person. You can speak to Jesus as his contemporaries spoke to him. You can echo the distressed father who said, "Help my unbelief," the leper who said, "Lord, if you choose, you can make me clean," Peter who said, "You know that I love you," and Thomas who declared, "My Lord and my God."

By consuming what Jesus called "the bread of life," you have the grace to become another Christ in the world. In a sense, the Son of God is incarnated again.

RESPOND: *Jesus, thank you for the miracle of the Eucharist. I believe that enables me to be one with you and all the members of your Church.*

September 10

LISTEN: *"Truly I tell you, today you will be with me in Paradise."*

LUKE 23:43

One of the two men crucified alongside Jesus is the only person in the Gospels to address him by name. Ironically we don't know his name, but traditionally he is known as St. Dismas. This criminal made an act of faith. He acknowledged that Jesus was innocent and moreover that he was king. By doing this, the so-called "good thief" stole paradise, Jesus's kingdom.

Paradise is heaven, where people enjoy the intimate relationship with God that Adam and Eve were blessed with in the Garden of Eden. Consequently, paradise is a place of untold delight and bliss. Occasionally you experience a flash of it on earth.

Whenever peace and happiness overwhelm you, that is a glimmer of heaven. This occurs when you hold a newborn infant, after you successfully complete an arduous task, or when a special person showers you with love. It may happen in quiet moments when you feel safe and content sitting alone by a fire or when joy bubbles up inside you during noisy family gatherings. Those wonderful times are a foretaste of the ecstasy awaiting you in heaven. One day, because of your faith and despite any "crimes" you have committed, you may hear Jesus say to you, "Come, be with me in my kingdom."

RESPOND: *Jesus, I rely on you to make me fit for your kingdom.*

September 11

LISTEN: *"Father, into your hands I commend my spirit."*

LUKE 23:46

In his last hour, Jesus calmly handed himself over to his loving Father. He was a model of how to die with dignity, grace, and peace. His death was a culmination of an entire earthly life that was a gift to the Father. For you, a faithful Christian, your life will end continuing the pattern of your whole life. You will entrust yourself into your Father's hands as you did every day.

Each morning you offered God yourself and all that you would encounter: joys, sorrows, accomplishments, good deeds, headaches, and distress. In the course of the day, you renewed your offering by prayers like "God, this painful back is for you," or "Father, I offer you my patience and kindness in dealing with this aggravating person." When making a risky decision, you confidently turned over the results to God, knowing that he desires only what is best for you. During each Eucharist, you offered your whole being along with Jesus to the Father.

Contrary to Dylan Thomas's poem, like Jesus you can go gently into that good night, knowing that it leads to the everlasting day and your heavenly Father's embrace.

RESPOND: *Jesus, may I not dread the hour I return to the God who made me. Rather, let me regard it as my last opportunity to give myself.*

September 12

LISTEN: *"Be opened."*

MARK 7:34

The account of Jesus opening the ears of the deaf man holds a lesson for us. How aggravating it is when someone isn't listening to you! It may be a spouse, children, or a guest talking with you at a party, whose eyes roam in search of a more interesting conversationalist! God speaks constantly, but we sometimes turn a deaf ear. This must frustrate and sadden God immensely.

God speaks to you in Scripture. It's defined as the Word of God in the words of human beings. Read your Bible at home. Keep it on your pillow and read a verse or two at night. Listen carefully to God's loving words proclaimed at the Eucharist.

God speaks to you during prayer. So quiet your restless body and mind, ignore distractions, and pay attention.

God speaks to you in creation. Listen to what he says in the thunder of storms, the whisper of breezes, and the quiet beauty of spring flowers.

God speaks to you through what happens. Each evening reflect on the day's events to detect God's messages.

God speaks to you through other people. Hear them when they offer good advice. Also have ears and a heart that are open to the cries of the poor, the helpless, and homeless.

Once the ears of the deaf man were open, he could speak clearly. After you understand what God is saying, communicate his words to other people. Speak boldly about God and what he has done for all of us and for you.

RESPOND: *Jesus, keep my ears open to your voice. The more I practice listening to you, the more I will be attuned to you and your wishes for my life.*

September 13

LISTEN: *"And see, I am sending upon you what my Father promised; so stay here in the city until you have been clothed with power from on high."*

LUKE 24:49

At a conference a woman began her talk to the audience by stating that she was wearing her power suit: a vivid red one. This bold suit gave her courage and confidence. Do you have an outfit you wear on special occasions because it fits well and makes you look good? Clothes affect how we feel about ourselves and how others think of us.

Jesus told the apostles who were cowering in the upper room after his death that they would be clothed with power. He was referring to the Holy Spirit descending on them at Pentecost. Imbued with this supernatural power, the apostles had the courage and strength to burst out of the room and proclaim the Good News to multitudes.

At your Baptism, you too were clothed with the Holy Spirit's power. Your white baptismal robe signified that you were full of grace. You can tap into the Holy Spirit's gifts you received that day. With knowledge and courage, you can share your faith with others. Because you wear spiritual armor, you can fight off temptations and endure hardships. When it comes to doing God's work, you will find that nothing is too much and nothing is ever enough. If you persevere, in heaven you will be garbed in a white robe, the attire of angels and saints.

RESPOND: *Jesus, keep me conscious so that I am empowered by your Holy Spirit.*

September 14

LISTEN: *"What are you looking for?"*
JOHN 1:38

While searching for a missing item, did you ever come across other things you had looked for earlier without success? When two disciples of John followed Jesus, curious to know who this Lamb of God was, he asked what they were looking for. They discovered much more than they expected. They found the Son of God, the longed-for Messiah, and stayed with him until four in the afternoon.

Hunts are fun for children. They play hide-and-seek and look for hidden Easter eggs. As adults, we are involved in searches that are more serious—and sometimes exasperating. Right now you might be looking for something: a partner to share your life, a positive evaluation at work, health, a new job, a good friend, a school, or a house. Perhaps you are looking for renewed energy because you are paralyzed by lethargy. Maybe you are searching for meaning for your life, which seems to have imploded. It could be that you are in pursuit of hope because everything seems dark. Maybe you are looking for God. It's been said that while God hides, he sometimes clears his throat to give himself away to those who are seeking him.

In prayer, as you communicate with Jesus, tell him what you're looking for. Confide your desires and feelings toward him. Ask him to lead you to what you seek.

RESPOND: *Jesus, essentially, we all are looking for happiness. You are the fulfillment of my quest, for you are the ultimate joy giver. May I always seek you and someday stay with you—not just until four o'clock like the two disciples that day—but forever.*

September 15

LISTEN: *"Do you believe because I told you that
I saw you under the fig tree?"*

JOHN 1:50

Nathanael is amazed that Jesus knows him and more amazed that Jesus saw him under the fig tree. We don't know what happened under the fig tree, but Jesus was aware of it.

You are mindful of your loved ones when they are apart from you at work, at school, or in a nursing home. You are God's beloved. Beyond being mindful of you, Jesus knows what you are doing every moment of the day and night. As the beautiful Psalm 139 suggests, God knows when you sit and when you stand. He reads your mind and knows what you will say before you utter it. This watchfulness and providence of God is reflected in the symbol of the eye within a triangle that is found on our dollar bills. God loves you so much that he can't take his eyes off you!

That God surrounds you and knows you through and through is comforting. God can come to your aid instantly, and he reads your heart when others might judge you rashly. On the other hand, the realization that God is watching you can be uncomfortable at times. How embarrassing if God witnessed you snapping at your children, spreading gossip, or wearing indecent clothing! No matter what unchristian thing you do, God still considers you the apple of his eye.

RESPOND: *Jesus, I'm glad that I am always in your sight and have no secrets from you. I hope that with the help of your grace, I will act in ways that make you proud of me and happy that you created me.*

September 16

LISTEN: *"Come and see."*

JOHN 1:39

Jesus invited the curious Andrew and his friend to see where he lived. Today Jesus lives in our churches, unbelievably confining himself to tabernacles and in the form of bread no less. What love he shows for us! But Jesus also dwells within us. As Paul says, "Do you not realize that Jesus Christ is in you?" (2 Corinthians 13:5). As the water of Baptism flowed over you, the Trinity came to live within you, making you a living tabernacle.

Sister Mary Terese Donze's book *In My Heart Room* teaches children to pray through guided meditations that lead them to visit Jesus living in their hearts. At any time you can accept Jesus's invitation to "come and see" by sinking down into your inner being and meeting him there. Focus on his presence within you and speak with him.

The two men who visited Jesus were so impressed by him that they became his disciples. As you spend time with Jesus, you too will be irresistibly drawn to him. You will want to live for him and follow his way. You will become Jesus for other people.

Neglecting prayer smothers your spiritual life. Pray and find rest from the multitude of tasks that keep you busy all day long. Find peace and quiet and be renewed. Above all, find yourself loved beyond anything you can imagine.

RESPOND: *Jesus, thank you for being close to me. May I take advantage of your presence by carving time out of my day to consciously be with you. Keep me from doing anything that would evict you from my heart.*

September 17

LISTEN: *"Fill the jars with water."*

JOHN 2:7

When wine was needed at a wedding, it made no sense for the stewards to fill jars with water. Sometimes God has us do things that we don't understand. He says things like, "Take time out from work to have this surgery," "Bring up a child with Down syndrome," or "Care for your mother-in-law although I know you can barely manage caring for your four children." At such times we heartily agree with God's statement, "Nor are your ways my ways" (Isaiah 55:8).

When I was head of a high school English department and lacked college math courses, I was sent to get a master's degree in mathematics. That seemed ridiculous but led to many wonderful experiences (and eventually to a degree in education). Perhaps looking back at mystifying things you were asked to do, you realize that they led to good results. Or maybe not. You may have to trust that God knows what he is doing and that he's true to his words, "For surely I know the plans I have for you, . . . plans for your welfare and not for harm, to give you a future with hope" (Jeremiah 29:11).

Just as the stewards were surprised to draw excellent wine out of water-filled jars, you might be surprised when God draws good out of perplexing events in your life.

RESPOND: *Jesus, you are far wiser than I am and know what is best for me. When I am puzzled by what life asks of me, give me faith to trust you, the hope to expect good things, and tons of patience.*

September 18

LISTEN: *"Stop making my Father's house a marketplace!"*
JOHN 2:16

Jesus was outraged by people making money unscrupulously in the temple. Today our churches are God's houses. They are sacred places. Of course, you aren't likely to desecrate your church by making an unjust profit inside its walls, but how do you act there? The presence of God demands your attention and reverence. A peaceful, quiet atmosphere should prevail so that people can pray. Church is not the place to exchange the latest news (or gossip!) or to study the outfits and hairdos of the people in the Communion procession. The aisles are not meant to be racetracks for children. And it would be more fitting for little ones to be occupied with religious books during Mass instead of secular books.

Speaking from a burning bush, God told Moses to remove his shoes because the ground there was holy. You are no longer obliged to wear hats or veils in church as was the custom for women, but your outfit should be appropriate for an audience with God.

God is truly present in the tabernacle and on the altar. It is easy to get used to the idea and take it for granted. When writer Annie Dillard reflected on the power invoked in church, she wrote, "We should all be wearing crash helmets."

RESPOND: *Jesus, what a gift and a privilege your presence is! Help me recapture or deepen awe at this wondrous miracle. May my reverence be obvious.*

September 19

LISTEN: *"Destroy this temple, and in three days I will raise it up."*
JOHN 2:19

Jesus made this statement when asked for a sign that he had authority to purge the temple. His Jewish listeners, assuming he meant the central building of their faith, were stunned. But Jesus was referring to himself as a temple, and the sign he gave to verify his supreme authority was rising from the dead.

The Jewish temple was the site where God and human beings met. It was the only place where sacrifices were offered. Jesus is a temple because in him divinity and humanity merge, and he himself is the sacrifice.

You are a temple because God dwells in you as much as God is present in church. It doesn't matter if you think you are too short, too tall, too fat, or too thin, too pale, or too dark. God is present in tiny, simple chapels as well as in gorgeous cathedrals.

You honor God by taking care of yourself. How? You don't allow sin to stain your soul. You keep your mind and heart pure. But you also keep your body in good condition by eating healthy foods, exercising, and getting enough rest. You make yourself as beautiful as you can. You get your hair styled, splurge for a manicure and pedicure, use makeup that enhances your face, wear clothing that makes you attractive. You do these things not from vanity but from the conviction that you are a walking tabernacle.

At the end of time, God will raise you up. You can look forward to having a glorified body then.

RESPOND: *Jesus, I believe you rose from the dead and live in me now. Your rising proved that all you said was true.*

287

September 20

LISTEN: *"Very truly, I tell you, no one can see the kingdom of God without being born from above."*

JOHN 3:3

The notion of kingdom is somewhat magical and ideal. In the fairy tales of our childhood, a kingdom is a place where princesses live happily ever after. Jesus used the phrase "kingdom of God" to represent the next world in which we will enjoy eternal life. There, all is peace and unalloyed happiness, a contrast to this present world racked with wars and suffering.

We yearn for God's kingdom, especially at the end of a trying day or in the midst of hardships. And we hope for this kingdom when we contemplate the fact that our time on earth is limited. Just as our natural birth catapulted us into life in this world, we can enter eternal life by being "born from above." In other words, by being baptized. The Sacrament of Baptism is the visa that admits us into heaven, where God reigns.

The day of your Baptism deserves to be celebrated with as much gusto as your birthday. Do you know when it was? You might observe it by participating in Mass that day.

RESPOND: *Jesus, thank you for the privilege of being baptized, a sign of your love. May I never squander this gift but bring it to fulfillment. I pray that when I pass from this earthly life, I enter the kingdom of God.*

September 21

LISTEN: *"The wind blows where it chooses, and you hear the sound of it, but you do not know where it comes from or where it goes. So it is with everyone who is born of the Spirit."*

JOHN 3:8

Some children, like my nephew, are afraid of wind, especially when it howls. That's understandable. Wind is mysterious because it's invisible and its origin and destination are unknown. Moreover, wind can be powerful and destructive. On the other hand, a cool breeze on a hot day is a welcome relief. Wind also does good work. It provides electrical power, propels sailboats, and pollinates plants.

The Hebrew word for wind, *ruah*, appropriately means "God's Spirit." Like the wind, the Spirit of God is invisible and powerful. You sense wind's presence by its effects: tree branches bend, papers take flight. You feel wind as it blows over you. Similarly, you discern the Spirit by the Spirit's actions. The Spirit took up residence in you at Baptism and is constantly at work.

Have you ever done something you thought impossible? Thank the Spirit. Did an inspiration inexplicably float into your mind? That was the Spirit. Were you prompted to perform a good deed? Again, that is the Spirit's doing. Sadly, we don't often give the Spirit credit.

Take advantage of the Spirit when facing challenging tasks—not only when taking a test, but before a difficult phone call, a job interview, or a conflict situation. When you were born again through grace, you became like the Spirit, that is, like wind: a mysterious power in the world.

RESPOND: *Jesus, please make me more aware of the Holy Spirit in my life. Let me turn to your Spirit for help, confident that he has the power and desire to be my hidden partner in my life's journey.*

September 22

In Greek mythology the princess Cassandra could prophesy. However, Apollo cursed her so that no one believed her when she predicted such things as the Trojan War. Imagine her frustration! You can identify with hapless Cassandra if you ever stated truth but were ignored or contradicted.

Jesus called himself the Truth. He came to earth as the most perfect revelation of the Father. He shared with us his personal knowledge of the Father as a loving, merciful God. Sent from heaven, Jesus assured us that it existed and someday we can call it our home. Jesus is God who knows all things, including how his creatures can live successfully. He kindly gave us guidelines for a life that culminates in eternal happiness. Yet, too often, his life-saving words fall on deaf ears.

As you carry on the ministry of Jesus as his disciple and spread the Good News, your words are not always accepted or heeded. You might have been derided for your beliefs. Your children might resist the faith, or give it up altogether. Despite any opposition, clasp the truth firmly to your breast. Refuse to cave in to peer pressure. Don't be swayed by our culture's norms and opinions that are contrary to the teachings of Jesus. Be a loyal disciple. The reward is worth it!

RESPOND: *Jesus, give me the grace to accept all your teachings. Let me hear and heed your words in Scripture, and be attentive to people who deliver your messages, so that I may listen to you speaking in the depths of my heart.*

September 23

LISTEN: *"For God so loved the world that he gave his only Son, so that everyone who believes in him may not perish but may have eternal life."*

JOHN 3:16

This Scripture citation pops up in unlikely places: baseball games, cars, and T-shirts. The verse captures the essence of the Incarnation. Martin Luther called it the Gospel in miniature. No doubt, this Bible verse is the most famous and most loved one. It assures you of the immensity of God's love, for Jesus died for love of your love. The verse also carries the promise that there is life beyond the grave.

Pondering the following definitions will deepen your understanding of the great mystery expressed in John 3:16.

- God . . . The greatest lover
- So loved . . . The greatest degree
- The world . . . The greatest number
- That He gave . . . The greatest act
- His only begotten Son . . . The greatest gift
- That whosoever . . . The greatest invitation
- Believeth . . . The greatest simplicity
- In Him . . . The greatest Person
- Should not perish . . . The greatest deliverance
- But . . . The greatest difference
- Have . . . The greatest certainty
- Everlasting life . . . The greatest possession

—source unknown

RESPOND: *Jesus, why should I ever feel unloved or depressed? Inexplicably and marvelously, I am the object of God's infinite love. Every crucifix reminds me of this.*

September 24

LISTEN: *"Indeed, God did not send the Son into the world to condemn the world, but in order that the world might be saved through him."*

JOHN 3:17

When children lie, steal, or sass, mothers scold and mete out appropriate consequences. We have an innate sense of justice that prompts us to desire that people get what they deserve. We like to see criminals sent to prison. Movies are satisfying when in the end the villains are punished. In the grand scheme of things, we are the villains. Our human race rebelled against our Creator, the good God. As individuals, we too offend God by repeatedly going against his wishes. Grave offenses against the all-holy God demand severe punishment.

But surprise! God, whose mercy outweighs justice, did not annihilate us in Eden. Instead, he took an extreme measure to save us. His Son entered the world as one of us, as a helpless baby no less. Almighty God deigned to come crying, speechless, and needing to be fed by his mother's milk. As an adult, Jesus taught us eternal truths. For example, he revealed that God is merciful through a story about a father who not only welcomes home a foolish, wayward son but who celebrates his return. Jesus's life was cut short when he subjected himself to a horrific death, thereby redeeming us by his blood.

Regarding your personal sins, Jesus extends mercy through the Sacrament of Reconciliation. His Sacred Heart is greater than any sin. Moreover, he never tires of forgiving you, even when you confess the same sin over and over as though you were stuck in a revolving door.

RESPOND: *Jesus, thank you for being our hero. When you had every right to condemn us, you saved us. I look forward to praising and loving you for all eternity.*

September 25

LISTEN: *"And this is the judgment, that the light has come into the world, and people loved darkness rather than light because their deeds were evil."*

JOHN 3:19

Sunlight streaming through your windows lets you see motes of dust floating in the air, streaks on the windowpanes, and a film of dust on the television screen. Light reveals dirt! Jesus is light. In his radiant presence, sins appear as they really are. Evildoers prefer to close their eyes to Jesus and hide their sins under the cloak of darkness. Most of us like to think we're rather perfect, and we find it hard to admit our sins. We resent having our failings broadcast. When someone points out a fault of ours, we flinch, at least inwardly.

The sun motivates you to clean the house. Similarly, when you spend time in the presence of Jesus, the all-holy Son of God, you become aware of your sins. You are spurred on to clean up your act.

Chances are, you are not guilty of serious crimes. But like every woman, you have little specks of sin that mar your life. You aren't comfortable confronting them: jealousy of someone who has more or does better, unkind words that stab a loved one, a hot temper, or uncontrolled eating or drinking. Once you face your faults, you can always take them to Jesus in prayer or in the Sacrament of Reconciliation. Natural light has the power to purify and whiten. So does the Light of the World.

RESPOND: *Jesus, enlighten me as to any sin or fault that detracts from the beauty of my soul. Then purify me so that I radiate pure goodness like you.*

September 26

LISTEN: *"Give me a drink."*

JOHN 4:7

The request Jesus made to the Samaritan woman at the well was extraordinary. In his culture men did not address women in public. The Samaritans and Israelites did not get along, to the extent that Israelites would circumvent Samaritan territory to avoid traveling through it. And drinking from the woman's vessel would make Jesus ceremonially unclean. Besides, she had a reputation in town. No wonder the apostles were stupefied to find Jesus conversing with her.

Jesus, though, has a habit of making unusual requests that take us by surprise. Like the day I received an e-mail inviting me to speak at a conference in Abu Dhabi. Responding positively to such unusual requests can lead to wonderful things. The Samaritan woman spoke with Jesus and received salvation for herself and her whole town. And I discovered that Christianity was alive and well in Arabia.

Be ready for Jesus to turn up in your life, thirsting for something and proposing something unexpected. Maybe you will be asked to teach at the parish school of religion. Someone might call to invite you to serve at a food kitchen. An estranged friend or a relative you haven't heard from in years might invite you to lunch, attempting to reconcile. Events like these are opportunities. All it takes is the courage to say "yes." Then watch what happens!

RESPOND: *Jesus, I believe that you are active in my life and behind the unexpected occurrences that break up my daily routine. Keep me from being too afraid to leave my comfort zone. By daring to plunge into new things, show me how I might enrich my life and grow closer to you.*

September 27

LISTEN: *"If you knew the gift of God, and who it is that is saying to you, 'Give me a drink,' you would have asked him, and he would have given you living water."*

JOHN 4:10

Secret identities are the grist of movies and novels. Recall, for example, in *Star Wars* when Darth Vadar declares to Luke, "I am your father." To the Samaritan woman, Jesus was just an unorthodox Jew until he revealed his identity: the long-awaited Messiah.

Millions of people today do not know or do not accept who Jesus is. Some have never heard of him. You, though, were introduced to him by someone (like a parent) or somehow (perhaps by reading a book). You are one of those privileged to know that Jesus, the Jewish teacher who lived two thousand years ago, is God's best gift, his only Son. He is also the giver of eternal life. Because of Jesus you enjoy the living water, an image for the Holy Spirit.

The challenge is to recognize Jesus in the guise of other people. Has a stranger ever approached you for help? Maybe someone asked you for directions while you were busy. Maybe while you were shopping, another customer asked your advice about a product. Maybe as you were preparing dinner, the doorbell or phone rang and someone asked for a donation for the hungry. When we view such strangers as Jesus in disguise and treat them with respect and kindness, we will be rewarded, if not in this life then in the next.

RESPOND: *Jesus, I thank you for leading me to believe that you are God and my Savior. Now give me the eyes of faith to see you in all people and to treat them as I would treat you.*

September 28

LISTEN: *"The water that I will give will become in them a spring of water gushing up to eternal life."*

JOHN 4:14

Water is integrally related to life. In Genesis, before God created light, the Spirit swept over the face of the waters. This parallels the leading theory of the origin of life, namely, that life began when certain chemicals reacted in the natural environment of water. For this reason scientists search for water on other planets as evidence of life. You began life floating in the water in your mother's womb. Water makes up sixty percent of your body. It is so essential that people lost at sea die of thirst before they die of starvation.

In view of water's vital role in our natural life, it is fitting that Jesus used it as a metaphor for eternal life. It also stands for the Holy Spirit. The water Jesus gives is living water, which means moving water, like a stream, which is superior to water in a well.

Jesus is the source of your eternal life, symbolized by the water that flowed from his pierced side. Jesus offers this life not as a trickle seeping through your life, but as a mighty gushing torrent. But to obtain this free supernatural water, to stay hydrated, you must turn on the tap. Only by keeping close to Jesus during your daily round of cooking, cleaning, driving, and so forth will you receive the precious water for which you thirst.

RESPOND: *Jesus, I long to spend eternity with you. Slake my thirst. I was washed with the waters of Baptism and so your Spirit is alive in me. With your help may I bring forth fruit.*

September 29

LISTEN: *"I am he, the one who is speaking to you."*

JOHN 4:26

The Samaritan woman was the first person to whom Jesus openly declared himself the Messiah. Not only that, but Scripture scholars explain that because Jesus said, "I am," he revealed to her that he was God. "I Am" is God's reply when Moses asked his personal name. The Jews yearned for a Messiah, the Christ, meaning *anointed one*, who would overthrow their oppressors and make them a great nation. They didn't expect God made man.

Today the world could use a Messiah who would put an end to all wars between countries and violence on our streets. At times you may personally need a Messiah to save you and establish peace. You may experience conflict with a mother-in-law or a daughter. You may be troubled by a friend who seems angry with you or by someone whose politics are diametrically opposed to yours. You may be held captive by addictions or trapped in depression. Physical illness or accidents may destroy your sense of well-being.

Jesus is your everlasting and compassionate Messiah. You can turn to him to be rescued, perhaps in ways you least expect. Jesus will always hear your pleas for help and either remove the problem or give you strength to bear it. After all, Jesus is God.

RESPOND: *Jesus, you have power to save me when I am distressed. I look to you to be my Christ, my Messiah. I know you will not disappoint me.*

September 30

LISTEN: *"My food is to do the will of him who sent me and to complete his work."*

JOHN 4:34

Most of us eat three times a day (at least) because food keeps us alive and is our source of energy. When his disciples urged Jesus to eat, he claimed that he had different food. Jesus was energized by carrying out his mission: saving the human race. This was his Father's will for him. Jesus knew it because he was in direct communication with the Father. But how do we discern God's will for us? What work are we supposed to do?

Let's say you are torn between two jobs: you can choose to be an office manager or you can be a stay-at-home mom. What would God want you to do? Talk to people who know you and to people who are in each situation. For each option, set up a paper with two columns. List pros in one column and cons in the other. Then weigh them. Determine logically what would be the better decision. Imagine yourself in the two positions. Consider the consequences of each.

Finally, pray. Ask for God's help and then listen to what he says in your heart. The proof that you have made the right decision is that it brings you peace . . . and energizes you.

RESPOND: *Jesus, I want to follow God's plan for me as you did. In all my weighty undertakings, may I rely on God to enlighten and guide me. Then I will know peace and so will others whose lives I touch.*

OCTOBER

October 1

LISTEN: *"I sent you to reap that for which you did not labor. Others have labored, and you have entered into their labor."*

JOHN 4:38

For two thousand years the news about Jesus Christ has been preserved and handed down. Missionaries ventured into dangerous lands to spread it, martyrs gave up their lives to defend it, Church leaders and theologians developed it, and ordinary people passed it on. Thanks to these witnesses you've inherited the precious gift of faith. Without them, you would not have heard of Jesus. You are standing on the shoulders of giants.

My earliest memory is being at Mass with my grandmother and crying because of the incense. Later my mother sent me to catechism class and taught me prayers. (A Spanish proverb proclaims, "An ounce of mother is worth a pound of clergy.") Who labored so that you could enjoy the fruit of knowing the love of God?

Now it's your turn to take up the baton and relay the Good News to people today. Faith begins at home. You can reflect that your family truly is "the domestic church" by displaying Christian images. You can pray together and celebrate the Eucharist each week.

What other labors can you undertake to ensure that future generations have faith? Teach a religion class? Be a sponsor in the Order of Christian Initiation for Adults (OCIA) program? Invite a neighbor to go to church with you? Speak about your faith? Decide to be a giant for future generations.

RESPOND: *Jesus, I'm grateful that knowledge of you has come down to me through an unbroken chain of believers. Help me to think of ways I can be a strong link, and then give me the courage to act.*

October 2

LISTEN: *"Unless you see signs and wonders you will not believe."*

JOHN 4:48

From time to time there are reports of miracles like an image of Mary weeping, a host marked with blood, or an apparition of the Blessed Virgin. Some saints levitated, bilocated, and had visions of Jesus. If you have not experienced such things, take heart. Our faith does not depend on the extraordinary. The ordinary is fantastic enough to convince us to believe in God.

The universe is brimming with God's handiwork. Perhaps you've seen a double rainbow, trees coated with glistening ice, seeds you planted turning into brilliant flowers. Then, too, there are those amazing photos of space—Milky Way planets, stars, and other galaxies. If you've held your newborn baby or grandbaby in your arms, you know God exists.

What if you pray for a miracle and none occurs? A sick relative or friend does not recover. The hurricane does not spare your house. The absence of miracles should not shake your faith, for faith is grounded in the words and deeds of Jesus. You believe in the greatest miracle of all—that God became a man to restore our friendship with him as well as offer us the possibility of eternal life.

RESPOND: *Jesus, may I never look to miracles as the litmus test for my faith. I want to believe in you all the ordinary days of my life. Keep my faith strong no matter how you respond to my prayers whether it be "yes," "no," or "later."*

October 3

LISTEN: *"Do you want to be made well?"*

JOHN 5:6

The answer to this question of Jesus is "of course." No one likes being sick. Even a toothache can ruin our day. Disease, pain, and physical disabilities prevent us from living fully. We can't work as well or enjoy life as much. This is not how God intended or desires us to be. We believe that suffering entered the world along with death only with the original sin. Our wounds are self-inflicted.

Jesus is called the Divine Physician for good reason. He cured the world of sin and death. As a sign of this ultimate work of healing, he performed miracles of physical healing. He still can today. He also has power to cure diseases of the soul that plague us. Some examples are paralysis in doing what we should, addiction to shopping, blindness to people in need, deafness to good advice given by others, an itch to have more, diarrhea of the mouth, a hot temper, hardheartedness, egotism, stubbornness, oversensitivity, restlessness, and an obsession with someone or something.

Suffering from such conditions can be alleviated. Jesus has already given us the prescription. All we need to do is to seek the grace he offers in the Sacrament of Reconciliation. It's free and it's painless.

RESPOND: *Jesus, when our children are sick or other loved ones are ailing, we want to remedy the situation quickly. I know that I am your loved one and you want the best for me. Help me to diagnose my spiritual illnesses and then turn to you for treatment.*

October 4

LISTEN: *"Stand up, take up your mat and walk."*

JOHN 5:8

On some days do you find it hard to get out of bed? You drag yourself around and find every little task daunting. Just bending to pick up a stray thread from the floor is beyond you. Nothing interests you, not even your favorite hobby. On those days, you are a victim of what spiritual writers call *acedia*, which means *without care*. It's also known as the noonday devil, the lethargy that tempts you to take siestas and retire early.

Jesus activated the man who was paralyzed for thirty-eight years. Jesus commands you to stand, assume your responsibilities, and walk. With his help you can fight the noonday devil. You can take action to shake off sadness and listlessness. One means is exercise. Jogging, dancing, brisk walking, and swimming clear the fog in your head, energize you, and stimulate the "happy" hormones in your body. Another trick to dispel *acedia* is getting started on a project you have resisted doing like weeding the garden or washing the windows. The first step is the hardest. For a writer, sometimes sitting down and composing one sentence primes the pump. A third remedy is to do something special to ignite the fire in you again: buy yourself flowers, listen to a favorite song, or go out to lunch with a friend.

Whenever you feel paralyzed, you might imagine Jesus saying to you, "Stand up and walk. I'm with you."

RESPOND: *Jesus, Whenever the blahs overtake me, send me your Spirit of comfort and joy. Then I will be myself again, energized to carry on with my business and yours.*

October 5

LISTEN: *"See, you have been made well! Do not sin any more, so that nothing worse happens to you."*

JOHN 5:14

Jesus cured the sinful paralytic. God also makes you well by Baptism and repeatedly by the Sacrament of Reconciliation. Although you wish you might never sin again, you probably will. In fact, you often confess the same sins. You might as well make a recording of them and play it each time you go to confession. Breaking a habit is hard work. But you can do it if you set it as a goal and commit to it.

The strategies for stopping a bad habit like nail biting can be applied to conquering a sin. Suppose you tend to speak about others' faults. First, be conscious of each time you do this. Then analyze why you did it. Was it to make yourself look better? To impress the listener? To harm someone you don't like? Second, write down the situation. Third, find a substitute action. For example, when tempted to bad-mouth someone, resolve to replace the snide remark with a positive statement. Fourth, whenever you successfully refrain from the sin, reward yourself. Have a donut!

Sin has harmful effects. It disappoints God, fills us with guilt and hopefully remorse, and usually hurts others, sometimes those who love us. The worst thing that could happen to the cured paralytic would be to lose eternal life. That would also be our worst fate.

RESPOND: *Jesus, you hate sin because it puts a wedge between us. I'm sorry for my weakness in surrendering to temptations. Strengthen my will power so that I can exercise the self-control to avoid future sins.*

October 6

LISTEN: *"My Father is still working, and I also am working."*
JOHN 5:17

Although God the Father is pure spirit and has no body, we some-times envision him as an old man with a beard. (It would be more accurate to think of God as pulsing light or pure energy.) All three divine Persons had a hand in creation, but we attribute this work to God the Father. Genesis describes bringing the universe into existence as a six-day job. However, the Father is still working to bring forth new life.

The Father oversees the cosmos, perfecting creation. Each year new flowers bloom and new animals evolve. If you have children, the Father called forth new human beings with your cooperation. Who knows what other forms of life populate distant planets?

One gigantic accomplishment of God the Father was sending God the Son to restore eternal life to us. We attribute the work of redemption to Jesus. His work did not end when he was nailed to a Roman cross. At every Mass the saving acts of Jesus are reenacted. He touches us and will touch future generations in the seven sacraments. Through the Holy Spirit, who is one with the Father and Son, the work of sanctification goes on.

Furthermore, through us, who are God's children and the Mystical Body of Christ, God continues to work in the world. How have you brought forth life? How will you bring life forth today?

RESPOND: *Jesus, I praise and thank you, the Father, and the Spirit for your labors on my behalf. May they not be in vain, but may I eventually become a work of art, one of your masterpieces.*

October 7

LISTEN: *"The Father judges no one but has given all judgment to the Son."*

JOHN 5:22

Silence is required in the Sistine Chapel while people gaze at Michelangelo's fresco *The Last Judgment.* The crowd stands in awe as they ponder the day Jesus will judge us—a day you probably don't often think about. The artist's portrayal is graphic and frightening. No longer the gentle Jesus, a muscular Christ, seated on a throne with arm upraised, dooms terrified sinners to hell. Even the Blessed Virgin at his side cowers. The depiction aligns with the hymn "Dies Irae" ("Day of Wrath"), which declares that on that day even saints will need comfort.

However, the Gospels reveal that Jesus is not a harsh but a merciful judge. When an adulterous woman was condemned to death by stoning, he freed her and simply warned, "Sin no more." He invited himself to dinner at the house of the conniving tax collector Zacchaeus. He healed a sinful paralytic and likened himself to a shepherd who goes after a lost sheep. On the cross he forgave the convicted criminal crucified next to him. And after he rose, he forgave Peter his betrayal and cowardice. Some people believe that Jesus forgave Judas and spared him hell.

Let your main motive for living a virtuous life not be to escape hell's fires and torments but to express love for God, who has loved you to death. Then, with God's grace, you will have nothing to fear when you stand before Christ on Judgment Day.

RESPOND: *Trusting in your boundless mercy and your love for me, I look forward to Judgment Day. For then I will be with you face-to-face, hopefully forever.*

October 8

LISTEN: *"So that all may honor the Son just as they honor the Father."*

JOHN 5:23

We tend to concentrate on Jesus the sweet infant lying in a manger, or the young man tortured and executed by the Romans. We might regard him as our chum, someone we're as comfortable with as an old sweater we can't bear to throw away. Sometimes we forget that Jesus is God the Son, equal to the Father in everything. The Father and the Son are one and the same God. As God, Jesus always was. He is all-powerful, all-knowing, and all-present. His perfections are infinite.

St. Paul reminds us that "at the name of Jesus every knee should bend, in heaven and on earth and under the earth" (Philippians 2:10). John calls him "King of kings and Lord of lords" (Revelation 19:16). All glory and honor are due to Jesus. St. Ignatius of Loyola said we were created to praise, reverence, and serve God.

You praise God when you take St. Teresa of Calcutta's advice and make your life something beautiful for God. You honor our Lord when you adore him in prayers like the Divine Praises and hymns like the "Gloria." You also honor him by living as he wishes. God took the trouble to come to earth to teach us right living. You show respect when you take his advice, just as children in your family honor you when they do as you say. You serve God by serving others with a maternal attitude, especially the poor and suffering.

RESPOND: *Jesus, I praise and glorify you. May I honor you every day by aiming to be like you: radiating love for others.*

October 9

LISTEN: *"For the hour is coming when all who are in their graves will hear his voice and will come out—those who have done good, to the resurrection of life, and those who have done evil, to the resurrection of condemnation."*

JOHN 5:28–29

As a tot you learned that actions have consequences. Touching a hot stove, you get burned. Sharing a toy makes Mom or Dad smile. Being mean to a sibling results in a time out. Your innate sense of justice demands that heroes be rewarded and criminals punished. A movie is satisfying when "the bad guys" get what they deserve. In this quality of justice you reflect God, the all-just one in whose image you are made.

It's no surprise then that when your time on earth is ended, you will be judged on your deeds. In John's vision of judgment, the names of those destined for heaven are written in a book of life. Those whose names are not recorded there are thrown into a lake of fire (Revelation 20:14–15). Michelangelo included this book of life in his painting of Judgment Day in the Sistine Chapel. It shows the Archangel Michael reading from it as people rise to heaven or tumble into hell.

If your good deeds outweigh your bad ones, you will go on to enjoy eternal life. If not, you will be deprived of God's presence and suffer an eternal "time out." Some people think that just as a mother can always make excuses for her child, God will ultimately forgive everyone and there will be no one in hell. Don't count on it!

RESPOND: *Jesus, you are all-just, but you are also all-merciful. Have mercy on me and all sinners, for we are weak and often we do not know what we are doing.*

October 10

LISTEN: *"As I hear I judge; and my judgment is just, because I seek to do not my own will but the will of him who sent me."*

JOHN 5:30

Every time we pray the Our Father, we pray, "Thy will be done." Because God is all-wise and all-good, his will is obviously for the best. At times our will clashes with his. God wills that we keep the Lord's Day holy, but sometimes we want nothing more than to sleep in on Sunday and then catch up on housework. God wills that we love our enemies, but we would prefer to get even with the person who criticized our appearance us or who stole our parking spot. God wills that we welcome the stranger, but some of us would rather not let immigrants into our country.

Jesus, the Son of God, always did his Father's will, even when it meant becoming one of his creatures, and even when it meant being despised, tortured, and executed on a cross like a criminal. In the Garden of Gethsemane, Jesus prayed, "Not my will but yours be done." He is your exemplar when it comes to choosing the Father's will. And so is the mother of Jesus. When the angel Gabriel revealed to Mary the shocking and disruptive course God planned for her life, she did not shrink from it. Rather, she proclaimed, "Here am I, the servant of the Lord."

In the *Divine Comedy*, Dante wrote, "In his will is our peace." If you wish for peace in your heart, simply follow what God prescribes. Obeying him leads to eternal peace.

RESPOND: *Jesus, I would like to align my will with the will of the Father as you did. Help me to live each day as a faithful handmaid of the Lord.*

October 11

LISTEN: *"The works that the Father has given me to complete, the very works that I am doing, testify on my behalf that the Father has sent me."*

JOHN 5:36

You would think after a single miracle—one healing of leprosy, one multiplication of loaves, one raising of the dead—that everyone in Galilee and Judea would view Jesus as God-sent. But not even the stream of healings and other miracles Jesus performed, nor his sublime teachings, were enough to persuade the populace that he was from God, maybe even divine himself. Skeptics proposed that the extraordinary works of Jesus were the work of the devil. How could eyewitnesses be so blind?

Jesus is at work in your life too. And he still works miracles, what someone once called "lovebursts." Did you ever pray for an impossible outcome—such as a healing when doctors gave you no hope—and the impossible happened? Did you ever need to purchase something quickly and, after shooting a brief prayer to heaven, as soon as you walked into a store, you found exactly what you needed . . . and on sale!

We are quick to rationalize away a miracle or even deny it. We might think, "It would have happened anyway" or "It's just a coincidence." (Really it's a God-incidence!)

Maybe at first we are thrilled with the miracle but we soon forget, or assume we imagined or dreamed it. If so, the works of Jesus are ineffective in bolstering our faith in him. We are as blind as those in Israel who did not believe their eyes and accept the miracles Jesus worked.

RESPOND: *Jesus, make me more aware of your actions in my life. May being open to your miracles convince me not only of your existence and your divinity but of your deep love for me.*

October 12

LISTEN: *"You search the scriptures because you think that in them you have eternal life; and it is they that testify on my behalf."*

JOHN 5:39

Do you read your horoscope? Some people look to the stars as well as palm readers, mediums, tarot cards, and tea leaves to obtain secret knowledge. The Jewish people poured over the writings of the Old Testament, hoping for insight into life. They were right to do so because these books were God-inspired. Nevertheless, they failed to comprehend that many Scripture verses pointed to Jesus. As Jesus told his disciples, his Death and Resurrection were so "that everything written about me in the law of Moses, the prophets, and the psalms must be fulfilled" (Luke 24:44).

You have the advantage of hindsight. You know that when God told Abraham that all nations would be blessed in him, this blessing would be in the form of his descendant, Jesus. In the words of prophets like Isaiah, you see hints of the Messiah. You realize that Psalm 22 describes in detail the crucifixion of Jesus. You recognize that some Old Testament people and events foreshadow Jesus: Isaac carrying wood up the mountain about to be sacrificed, Joseph forgiving his brothers who sold him for pieces of silver, the blood of the paschal lamb on the doorway protecting the Hebrews from death.

Besides the Old Testament, you have the benefit of the New Testament in which you meet Jesus himself at work. Reading and pondering it leads you to the sure Way to eternal life.

RESPOND: *Jesus, I thank you for the privilege of living now, when it is possible to know you. Grant my family members and friends the grace to believe in you so that they may attain the everlasting life you won for us.*

October 13

LISTEN: *"Where are we to buy bread for these people to eat?"*
JOHN 6:5

Do you enjoy preparing meals for your family and visitors, refreshments to serve at your parties, and your specialties for parish potlucks? Imagine: Jesus graciously decided to feed people who came to hear him speak—no fewer than five thousand! Miraculously, he provided a meal to satisfy them all.

It's been proposed that the crowd had enough to eat because people who had provisions shared with others. If that were the case, at least one of the six Gospel accounts of the multiplication of bread and fish would have mentioned it. That theory, though, has a valid message: share. Today millions of people are starving, while many of us suffer from obesity. Hunger occurs not only in developing countries, but perhaps in a house on your street. This problem could be solved if we all shared.

You would rather not think about world hunger and the children who go to bed with empty stomachs. It's overwhelming and depressing. You can, however, do your part to alleviate the crisis. You can donate to an agency that feeds the poor, serve in a food kitchen, support laws that benefit the poor, and take a meal to someone in need. You can also remember the hungry in your prayers, looking to Jesus to multiply food as he did in the past. St. John Chrysostom claimed that feeding the hungry is a greater work than raising the dead!

RESPOND: *Jesus, you acted so that people in your audience would not leave hungry. Please do something to fill the stomachs of those who hunger today. It will probably take a miracle. Still, show me how I can help.*

October 14

LISTEN: *"Gather up the fragments left over, so that nothing may be lost."*

JOHN 6:12

Jesus's order is peculiar. Why would he save the scraps from his picnic for thousands when he could easily provide more food if needed? Were the pieces of bread and fish going to be distributed to the poor? Were these leftovers to be consumed by the twelve apostles, whose baskets were filled with them?

Perhaps this command was intended as a lesson for us. In our throwaway culture, we who live a life of abundance could easily discard leftovers. Thankfully with our new concern for creation, we now reduce, recycle, and reuse things. We save leftover food for another meal, ask for doggie bags in restaurants, and donate outgrown and seldom worn clothes to the St. Vincent de Paul Society.

Knowing Jesus, he might be teaching us that he has concern for the littlest people in society—the fragments, the ones few people care about. He came to save everyone, for in his eyes we all are important: the physically impaired, the destitute, the mentally challenged, the addicted. It's up to you as his follower not to lose sight of these people on the fringes but to gather them up, supply what they need, and incorporate them into your life.

RESPOND: *Jesus, it took time for the apostles to walk around the large crowd, gathering the leftovers. Help me to spare the time to save the fragments, both inanimate and human, no matter how inconvenient.*

314

October 15

LISTEN: *"It is I; do not be afraid."*

JOHN 6:20

A striking photo showed a dark cloud and a bolt of lightning, but next to the lightning, a wide rainbow, a sign of hope, curved over the earth like an embrace. That image symbolizes that Jesus sees us through our darkest hours. Before returning to heaven, he promised to always be with us. That promise instills in us the hope that the storms in our life will eventually end.

The disciples were on the lake at night, rowing against a strong wind and large waves. Then they saw Jesus walking toward them over the water. He told them not to be afraid, and in an instant they were safe on the shore.

Who hasn't been in the dark, buffeted by adversities and fighting to stay afloat? We can take heart. Jesus is with us. He can arrange miracles to save us. Can you recall a time when something or someone unexpectedly rescued you from a frightening situation?

Jesus had a habit of rescuing people through miracles. He fed the hungry by multiplying bread and fish. He cured a man blind from birth. And he brought Lazarus back to life, to the astonishment of the man's two grieving sisters.

Whenever you are coping with a distressing situation—an illness, a colicky baby, the loss of a job, the woes of menopause, a lawsuit—don't be surprised if God steps in and acts in an extraordinary way to help. Cling to your faith and hope.

RESPOND: *Jesus, you often rescued people by a miracle. Nothing is impossible for you. In my darkest hours may I always remember that you, the all-powerful one, are with me and that you love me.*

October 16

LISTEN: *"This is the work of God, that you believe in him whom he has sent."*

JOHN 6:29

When people asked Jesus how to perform the works of God, he had one answer: believe in him. To believe in someone is to accept that person as real. As a child you believed in Santa Claus and the Easter bunny, but soon learned they were imaginary figures. Jesus is real, as the Gospels and Tradition attest. The challenge is to believe that this Jewish man was also God, which is the foundation of your Christian faith. The early Church struggled with this concept, as do many people today. Some outright deny the divinity of Jesus. Being able to profess in our creeds that Jesus is the Son of God is a gift, a grace.

There is another dimension to believing in someone. It means to trust that person. People believe in their marriage partners, that they will always love them. We believe in our doctors and dentists, that they have the knowledge and skill to treat us. And we are to believe in Jesus as our Savior, accepting his words as true and trusting that he will keep his promises.

C. S. Lewis observed, "You must make a choice. Either this man was, and is, the Son of God; or else a madman or something worse." Why do you believe in Jesus?

RESPOND: *Jesus, I believe that you are the Son of God who saved me. I believe in you. I believe that you are with me and that you offer me a life of bliss without end. Dispel any doubts I have.*

October 17

LISTEN: *"I am the bread of life."*

JOHN 6:35

We love bread. We use it for appetizers, sandwiches, and wrappings for hot dogs and hamburgers. We bread fish with it, stuff turkeys with it, and toss it to birds. The bread aisle in stores offers a mindboggling assortment of varieties. Bread has been a staple in the diet of many cultures. Jesus wisely chose bread to miraculously transform into himself.

For many countries, bread is truly the staff of life. Just as bread nourishes and sustains our natural life, the bread of the Eucharist feeds your spiritual life. Through it you gain the strength needed to live a good life. You grow in virtue and become more like the Christ you consume. Dining at the table of the Lord on earth will culminate in sharing in the banquet of heaven. There, hopefully, you will enjoy eternal life. The sacred bread of the Eucharist is just a foretaste of the union possible for you to have with God in the next world.

When the Israelites were starving in the desert, God sent miraculous bread. When the multitudes listening to Jesus hadn't eaten, he provided miraculous bread. Today Jesus offers you bread that satisfies all hungers.

RESPOND: *Jesus, keep alive in me a hunger for you that impels me to share in your Eucharistic feast as often as I can. May I never take this miracle for granted.*

October 18

LISTEN: *"I am the living bread that came down from heaven."*

JOHN 6:51

Mothers form children in their womb with the substance of their own bodies. After birth, they may feed their infants with breast milk. Usually, mothers are the ones who prepare meals for their brood until the nest is empty.

A legend tells of a mother pelican who, during a famine, punctures her chest with her beak; as a result, she must nurse the chicks with her blood. In some versions she even brings the dead chicks to life with her blood, and afterwards dies. You might see artwork of this pelican on altars, tabernacles, and stained-glass windows. Obviously her story is a metaphor for the sacrifice of Jesus, who saved us from death by the blood that flowed from his pierced side.

In the Cenacle, the upper room where the Last Supper took place, the mother pelican feeding her children is carved into a pillar. Jesus feeds you, his child, in the Eucharist. The sacred bread and wine you consume at Mass is Jesus himself. It is a life-giving meal that strengthens you and nurtures your spiritual growth. United with Jesus, the Son of God, you become more like him—less self-centered and more selfless, more loving, more compassionate. You are better prepared, then, to partake of his heavenly banquet in the world to come.

Blessed Carlo Acutis, the modern youth (whose canonization has been approved by the Vatican) known for his outstanding devotion to the Eucharist, said, "When we face the sun, we get a tan, but when we stand before Lord Jesus Christ in the Eucharist, we become saints."

RESPOND: *Jesus, your love for me knows no bounds.*
Thank you for sacrificing your life for my sake and for the gift of
yourself in the Eucharist.

October 19

LISTEN: *"Those who eat my flesh and drink my blood have eternal life, and I will raise them up on the last day."*

JOHN 6:54

Did you ever say to someone, "I love you so much I could eat you up"? Jesus has made it possible for us to eat him, literally. For some followers who heard him speak of eating his flesh and drinking his blood, this was repugnant, too much to swallow! They turned their backs on Jesus and left. This is understandable because his words sounded like cannibalism. Also, Jewish people were prohibited from consuming blood and removed it from meat to be eaten. Yet, Jesus did not call, "Come back. I'm only speaking symbolically."

As a Catholic you believe that when you partake of the sacred bread and wine, you are actually consuming the risen Lord. He becomes part of you as much as your daily food does. In the process, you become more divine. Moreover, you are assured of being raised from the dead at the end of time.

Each time the priest raises the sacred host at Mass and declares, "This is my body," you can declare, "My Lord and my God." And when you come to Communion and hear the words, "the body of Christ" and "the blood of Christ," you can give a wholehearted, "Amen"; in other words, "I agree."

RESPOND: *Jesus, thank you for the incredible gift of yourself in the Eucharist. When I receive you in Holy Communion, you are closer to me than anyone could ever be. May I cherish my time with you, and may I offer you my love.*

October 20

LISTEN: *"The words that I have spoken to you are spirit and life."*
JOHN 6:63

We frequently speak words of advice to protect and promote life. To a child we warn, "Don't play in the street." To a spouse we say, "Using a cell phone while driving is dangerous." To an overweight friend, we might remark, "Did you know there are about ten teaspoons of sugar in a can of soda?"

God, who is concerned about your welfare, teaches and offers advice through several channels. God speaks through the writers of Scripture, in creation, and in the silence of your heart. Then, incredibly, God made himself more understood when he became a human being and spoke in human language. When Jesus went about Israel teaching, God communicated directly, clearly, and personally.

Jesus taught truths that lead to a happy, fulfilled life here and hereafter. Just as not everyone listens to your advice, not everyone accepted what Jesus said. Some of his disciples found his words difficult, and some still do. Whether or not you understand, it is only when you are fully open to the teachings of Jesus, only when you follow his "advice," will you safely arrive at your eternal destination. You will have protected more than your natural life. You will have protected your supernatural life.

RESPOND: *Jesus, you speak the words that lead to everlasting life. Keep my ears and heart open so that I may be receptive to your teachings and live wisely.*

October 21

LISTEN: *"Do not judge by appearances, but judge with right judgment."*

JOHN 7:24

A wise Native American proverb says, "Don't judge your neighbor until you have walked a mile in their moccasins." You never know what burdens another person is carrying. Chances are that you have been guilty of judging a person or situation incorrectly. Did you ever have the impression that a woman was snobbish and unpleasant and then after you got to know her, she became your good friend? You too might have been misunderstood. Perhaps you have done something that appeared wrong but really wasn't and you hoped that no one was judging you!

We jump to conclusions so easily and tend to think the worst. The huge man walking toward you covered with tattoos and scowling might be the kindest man on earth. The teenage girl behind you in line with facial piercings, chewing gum, and talking on the cell phone might be the most reliable babysitter. The obese clerk at the supermarket might not be guilty of overindulging but rather gained weight as a result of a medication's side effect.

From outward appearances, Jesus was a troublemaker who flaunted Jewish laws and customs. He was labeled a glutton, a drunkard, and a possessed man. Only those who took the time to know him and listen to him learned the truth.

RESPOND: *Jesus, give me a gentle, loving heart. When I see people who seem to be doing wrong, make me willing to give them the benefit of the doubt.*

October 22

LISTEN: *"Let anyone among you who is without sin be the first to throw a stone at her."*

JOHN 8:7

If we were in the crowd surrounding the accused adulterous woman, we wouldn't cast a stone. The reason would not be because we felt sorry for her or because we thought it unjust that she was accused and not her male accomplice, but because we all have sinned (except for Jesus and his mother, Mary). Our weak human nature is prone to make wrong choices. Like St. Paul we rue the times we knew what we should do but didn't do it.

Just as a blemish on your face and a brown spot on your hand detract from your physical beauty, sin spoils the splendor of your soul. The grace, the divine life in you by which we mirror God's holiness, is eroded. But because Jesus atoned for all sin, grace can be restored. You can be as relieved as that poor woman was. You are freed by meeting Jesus in the Eucharist and by celebrating the Sacrament of Reconciliation. He will say to you as he said to the woman, "Go, sin no more."

While the religious leaders looked to Jesus to condemn their prey, twice he wrote with his finger on the ground. One theory is that he wrote the sins of the woman's accusers. Jesus knows your sins too, but he also knows the good you do even in secret.

RESPOND: *Jesus, you have a heart for sinners. After all, you died for them. May I never be discouraged by my bad habits and failings. Your mercy is far greater than any sin.*

October 23

LISTEN: *"I am the light of the world. Whoever follows me will never walk in darkness but will have the light of life."*

JOHN 8:12

If while walking in a dark room you stumbled over shoes on the floor or bumped your shin on a table, you know the danger of being without light. Jesus was wise to call himself light. The metaphor fits on several levels. Following Jesus we are safe. He is like a lighthouse guiding storm-tossed ships, a lantern leading people through a dark cave, and the high beam of our car when driving down an unlit road.

Some days the world seems dark and dreary. There is no end to violence and the threat of war. Personal problems overshadow us like dark clouds. Some days you feel lost and confused. You don't know what to do or you can't understand why bad things happen to good people—like yourself! At such times you only need to turn to Jesus and his teachings. He sheds light on any situation.

Just as the sun is the source of all life on earth, Jesus is the Son who bathes you with radiant light to walk safely through this world. Living as he taught, you grow and thrive. Moreover, you will reach your final destination where you will live forever in the radiant glory of God. In this kingdom there is no need for lamps, for the night is as brilliant as day.

RESPOND: *Jesus, keep me safe in your light. Illumine me with your grace and love, and let me be a beacon reflecting your light to others.*

October 24

LISTEN: *"If you knew me, you would know my Father also."*
JOHN 8:19

Sons often take after their fathers. We even have a saying, "Like father, like son." Jesus did not just resemble his Father. The two of them, along with a third Person, the Holy Spirit, constitute one God. This is a mystery you will never understand but must firmly believe.

Because Jesus and the Father are one, what you know about Jesus is true for the Father. Jesus is the perfect revelation (or self-disclosure) of God the Father. You come to know Jesus by reading the Gospels. There you find that he is wise and knows when to follow the law and when to bend it. He is loving and calls human beings his friends, not his servants. And Jesus is merciful, forgiving common sinners as well as his betrayers and executioners.

You are made in the image and likeness of God. Like Jesus you have the opportunity to reflect God's qualities to your family members, friends, and strangers. Mary, the mother of Jesus and your mother too was full of grace. She resembled her Son. May it be said of us, "Like mother, like daughter."

RESPOND: *Jesus, help me to be like you and my heavenly Mother Mary. In this way I will be a true child of my Father in heaven.*

October 25

This was the response Jesus gave when he was asked his identity. It's said that "I am" is a reference to the personal name God revealed to Moses at the burning bush: "I am that I am." This can also be translated, "I am who I am for you." We Christians profess that Jesus is God and our Savior. Not everyone believes this. Some of your relatives and neighbors might not. You yourself might have doubts some nights as you drift off to sleep or when the news reports horrendous events.

Jesus said that his "lifting up" would open our eyes to who he is. This refers to his being lifted up on a cross, the way the bronze serpent was lifted up to save the Israelites bitten by poisonous snakes in the desert. How could God be executed? Enemies charged Jesus to come down off the cross if he were God. But as has been observed, it would have been human to come down but it was divine to stay there. The sacrifice of Jesus culminated with his rising from the dead and being lifted up into heaven. Now we await the return of the Son of Man who will come to lift us up to heaven.

RESPOND: *Jesus, I believe you are true God and true man. When I am plagued with doubts, strengthen my faith.*

October 26

LISTEN: *"If you continue in my word, you are truly my disciples; and you will know the truth, and the truth will make you free."*

JOHN 8:31–32

I responded to an ad that offered "free" compression socks. They weren't free, because my Visa statement showed a monthly $25.00 payment for membership in a health club! If you have fallen victim to false advertising or a scam, you know the value of truth. Jesus offered the truth about God, ourselves, and the way to live. He taught that God is our loving Father, that he himself is our divine Messiah, and that the Holy Spirit is our helper. He preached keeping the Ten Commandments that require us to love God and our fellow men and women and even demanded more. He gave us the Beatitudes, attitudes that lead to blessings. By accepting these truths and living by them, we are free.

Being free means not being enslaved but having the power to make our own decisions. Being free means we are not controlled by addictions to food, alcohol, drugs, sex, or shopping. Being free means we are not swayed to act according to popular but immoral public opinion or peer pressure. Living by the words of Jesus, we are free and happy.

If we forsake his teachings, we become slaves of Satan, otherwise known as the father of lies. This is not fake news.

RESPOND: *Jesus, may I read and ponder your words that have come to me in Scripture. Then may I be faithful in living by them until the day I die.*

October 27

LISTEN: *"Very truly, I tell you, everyone who commits a sin is a slave to sin."*

JOHN 8:34

Being a slave to sin means that sin is your master and you are no longer free. Serious sin will block your way to heaven like a traffic accident halts your journey. One sin can lead to another, and before you know it you have fallen into a habit of sinning in which you lose control of your life.

If you are basically a good person, a sin committed weighs heavily on you, makes you feel guilty and ashamed, fills you with regret, and robs you of sleep. A sin made public can tear your reputation to shreds. It can turn friends and relatives away from you.

But Jesus still has faith in you after you sin. His Death and Resurrection broke the chains of sin and death and made it possible for you to be forgiven your personal sins. He knows your weakness, and that we are a fallen race. Despite your sins he loves you just the same—with an unconditional love. He is like a mother who can always make excuses for her child. Not only will Jesus forgive your sins, but he will strengthen you to avoid them in the future.

RESPOND: *Jesus, you know all about me. You understand my weakness and are aware of the experiences, circumstances, and motives that cause me to sin. I do not want to belong to sin but to you. Bless me with the grace to say no to temptations.*

October 28

If a friend claimed that she was alive before George Washington, you would have three possible explanations: she is joking, she is lying, or she has lost her mind. Jesus claimed to have existed before Abraham, the forefather of the Jews, who lived some eighteen hundred years earlier. Jesus really meant his words, as his introductory expression "very truly" indicates. Jesus is no ordinary man. In fact, his statement "I am" echoes God's name revealed to Moses. By applying this identification to himself, Jesus is equating himself with God. To the religious leaders of that day, this was blasphemy.

Today Christians accept Jesus as God, the second Person of the Trinity who became a human being like us more than two thousand years ago. As God, Jesus always was and always will be. He is everywhere, he knows all things, and he is all-powerful. Whether you are cooking dinner, conducting a meeting, suffering bothersome monthly cramps, or laughing hysterically, whether you are enduring a very bad day or floating on cloud nine—be aware that Jesus is alive this year too. He is with you, looking on you with eyes of love. Speak to him.

RESPOND: *Jesus, I acknowledge that you are God. You were present at the creation of the world and at my birth. With the help of your grace, I will spend all the days of eternity with you.*

October 29

LISTEN: *"I came that they may have life, and have it abundantly."*
JOHN 10:10

Some days it's great to be alive. Outside the skies are blue, the sun is shining, and your garden is in full bloom. Dreaded tasks like going to the dentist and cleaning the garage are behind you. No one in your family is sick or facing a problem. You're looking forward to an evening out. On these days you feel wonderful and are perfectly happy. Life is good, and the thought of it ending someday is unthinkable.

Unless you are in the depths of despair, your survival instinct is always at its most powerful. You want to live more than anything else. Jesus fulfilled your hope for life without end. By coming to earth as a man and dying and rising, he conquered death once and for all. He made it possible for you to live beyond the grave. In fact, in heaven you will live as you've never lived before. There you will experience abundant life characterized by never-ending joy and passionate love. Surrounded by the glory of God and in the company of all his holy ones, including your family members and friends, it will be as though the skies are always blue and the sun never sets.

RESPOND: *Jesus, my heart overflows with gratitude to you. You have won a future life for me that is beyond my wildest dreams.*

October 30

LISTEN: *"I am the good shepherd. The good shepherd lays down his life for the sheep."*

JOHN 10:11

When you think of it, perhaps no shepherd would die in order to protect a flock of sheep that perhaps weren't even his own. Would you die in place of your dog or cat? Yet, Jesus was that extraordinary shepherd who gave his life to save an entire flock, the human race. He fended off not lions and bears but evil spirits who held us captive and threatened us with everlasting death. By sacrificing his life, Jesus vanquished these enemies and secured eternal life for us.

Jesus still shepherds us today. As Psalm 23 says, because of him, you shall not want for anything. He takes you to green pastures and still waters. When you are weary or depressed, he restores your soul. He guides you in making choices that lead to a good life and happiness. When you are in trouble, he protects and comforts you. He provides food for you, the bread on your table and the bread on the altar, and he showers you with blessings.

You can look to Jesus for help in being a good shepherdess for the sheep and lambs who are in your care. Modeling yourself on him, you will show them nothing but goodness and mercy.

RESPOND: *Jesus, what love you and your Father have for me! I hope to be worthy of it, all the days of my life.*

October 31

LISTEN: *"My sheep hear my voice. I know them,
and they follow me."*

JOHN 10:27

We are so attuned to the voice of a loved one that we are able to detect it in a throng of people talking. We recognize it immediately on the phone—no need for caller ID. Christians who deeply love Jesus pay attention to his voice in the midst of the clamoring noise of the world.

Our good shepherd speaks to you in several ways. He guides you through Church leaders. That is why bishops' crosiers are shaped like shepherd crooks and why we call our priests pastors. Jesus communicates with you in Scripture. Following his teachings contained in those Scriptures guarantees a safe journey to heaven. Moreover, as you read or hear Scripture, a particular passage may strike you personally, bearing out the words of the prophet, "Is not my word like fire, . . . and like a hammer that breaks a rock in pieces?" (Jeremiah 23:29).

Jesus speaks to you in ordinary ways, like through the good people he puts in your life, especially those who know you best. He may send messages through experiences you have when you ponder them.

And sometimes Jesus speaks to you in the stillness of your heart. Usually this occurs when you manage to be alone, withdraw from the busyness of your life, and be silent. When you are all ears, you can hear him more clearly.

RESPOND: *Jesus, keep my ears open to hear your words and keep
my heart open to follow your advice.*

NOVEMBER

November 1

LISTEN: *"The Father and I are one."*

JOHN 10:30

Jesus not only resembles his Father; the two are one. This doesn't only mean that they think alike. They actually are one.

The bond of Jesus and God the Father is at the heart of the mystery of the Trinity. What the monotheistic Jews viewed as blasphemy, you see as truth, but a truth beyond your comprehension. Nevertheless, we attempt to grasp the Trinity through metaphors like a three-leaf clover and water, which has three forms: liquid, vapor, and ice. The Trinity presented mathematically is not $1 + 1 + 1 = 3$ but rather $1 \times 1 \times 1 = 1$.

By equating himself with the Father, Jesus clearly reveals that he is divine. And this is another mystery of our faith—that a human being could also be God. In a different but real way, God also shares his divinity with you. At Baptism you became one with Jesus. At Mass through Communion you and he are united closer than your bond with any human, no matter how profound your relationship. This is symbolized when the celebrant adds water to the wine. He prays, "By the mystery of the water and wine, may we come to share in the divinity of Christ who humbled himself to share in our humanity." As St. Athanasius taught, "For the Son of God became man so that we might become God." (He didn't mean we become equal to God but that we should strive to attain God-like traits.) Because God is love, love should be your chief quality.

RESPOND: *Jesus, I firmly believe that you are true God and true man. Your words are God's words, and your acts of love and mercy are God's acts. Thank you for giving me the gift of faith.*

November 2

LISTEN: *"I am the resurrection and the life. Those who believe in me, even though they die, will live."*

JOHN 11:25

The day after I set a lovely potted geranium outside, I found that deer had eaten it. Weeks passed and then one day I noticed that the plant bore five buds. Maybe you've had the experience of seeing a plant that was apparently dead spring into life.

In this world there are hints of our own resurrection. Every winter trees and bushes are black skeletons, but then in spring they burst into lush greenery. Every night we crawl into bed and become "dead to the world" for several hours, but then in the morning we awake to another day. The sun too disappears, but then rises again with its life-giving rays. Caterpillars form "tombs" around their bodies and then emerge as lovely creatures capable of flying.

Of course, after Jesus predicted that we would rise from the dead, the greatest sign that this was true was his own Resurrection. His empty tomb was the first of what will be a multitude of empty tombs and graves someday. Jesus conquered death once and for all. He is our resurrection and our life. We believe in him and we believe him.

RESPOND: *Jesus, I trust in your words. I look forward to the day I will be united forever with you and with all my faithful family members—those who have already died and those still on earth with me.*

November 3

LISTEN: *"Lazarus, come out!"*
JOHN 11:43

Jesus commanded dead Lazarus to come back to life. And so Lazarus, full of breath again, emerged from his tomb to the astonishment of all, and to the joy of his two grieving sisters.

Who hasn't felt lifeless sometimes, as though imprisoned in a dark cave? Grieving for a parent, husband, or a good friend can make you feel this way. So can being diagnosed with a life-threatening disease, failing to achieve something, having your hopes dashed, or being wearied by daily drudgery. Sometimes depression casts a pall for no reason that you can name. When you are sunk in gloom, you would like to hear Jesus firmly call to you, "Come out!"

The name Lazarus is derived from the Hebrew for "God is my help." Jesus would like to help you. He wants you to be fully alive and happy. He is with you and will be glad to see you through bad days. Just ask. But you must do your part. Some remedies to relieve sadness are talking with someone who cares about you, engaging in a favorite activity, exercising, and, if necessary, seeing a therapist. Psychologist Karl Menninger gave good advice to banish the blues: "Lock up your house, go across the railroad tracks, find someone in need, and do something for them."

RESPOND: *Jesus, I look to you on days when I'm downcast and listless. You, the source of all joy, have the power to lift my spirits.*

November 4

LISTEN: *"Leave her alone. She bought it so that she might keep it for the day of my burial."*

JOHN 12:7

The forgiven woman who poured costly perfume on the feet of Jesus was criticized. Her beautiful expression of love and gratitude was viewed as a foolish waste. Jesus, who sees clearly and reads hearts, came to her defense.

How quick we are at times to find fault with others. For example, we make comments like, "Someone her age shouldn't have such long hair," or, "That was a fine dinner, but your spaghetti was too salty." We make rash judgments about others. The girl with the nose ring and tattoos that we think is a juvenile delinquent might be the smartest and kindest girl we know. We misinterpret others' actions and leap to wrong conclusions. The speeding driver who we assume is on drugs might be taking his pregnant wife to the hospital. If you have been a victim of this form of injustice, you know how uncomfortable and hurtful it feels.

When you infer a base ulterior motive behind someone's actions or when you think someone made a mistake, it could be you who is mistaken. The wiser course is to give people the benefit of the doubt. After all, that is what you hope people would do for you. If you are tempted to criticize someone, especially out loud in front of others, imagine Jesus saying, "Leave them alone."

RESPOND: *Jesus, you were repeatedly criticized for things like healing on the Sabbath and eating with sinners. Your accusers were blind. May I always look at things optimistically with eyes of love.*

November 5

LISTEN: *"Unless a grain of wheat falls into the earth and dies, it remains just a single grain; but if it dies, it bears much fruit."*
JOHN 12:24

If you have a green thumb, after you plant seeds they give rise to flowers, vegetables, or fruit. There is no trace of the seeds. By giving you their life, they are transformed into an even greater form of life. Likewise, burying your ego results in new, glorious life in eternity.

You control your ego by patiently preparing meals for others when you don't feel like it, by refraining from informing others of your achievements, by biting your tongue when you want to complain or criticize, and by doing others a favor—even those people you don't like. There are thousands of ways to die to one's self.

St. Thérèse of Lisieux gave good advice: "Miss no single opportunity of making some small sacrifice, here by a smiling look, there by a kindly word; always doing the smallest thing right and doing it all for love." She imagined that her sacrifices and acts of love were changed into a variety of flowers. With a string of beads she kept track of them, pushing one bead down for each act.

In the evening you might review the times you planted a seed that day. The more you can count, the more you will have beautified your life and the lives of others.

RESPOND: *Jesus, you surrendered your earthly life on Calvary so that humankind might live. Help me to offer you little gifts of self-denial.*

November 6

LISTEN: *"Those who love their life lose it, and those who hate their life in this world will keep it for eternal life."*

JOHN 12:25

Now this paradox is puzzling. Hate is such a strong word—and hating life? I love being alive. I bet you also enjoy working, playing, loving, and being loved on this magnificent planet we call home. And after all, creation is God's gift to us. So how could Jesus tell us to hate our life in order to be saved? Didn't St. Catherine of Siena say, "All the way to heaven is heaven"? Obviously, Jesus is employing hyperbole. What is he really saying?

People who focus on this life with no thought of the next one will be sorry. They spend their years busy building their bank accounts and accumulating possessions, forgetting that you can't take it with you. They are self-centered, indulging in all sorts of pleasures they think will make them happy and delighting in wielding power over others. In doing so, they ignore three recommendations Jesus gave for right living: share your belongings with the poor, take up your cross, and be humble.

Those people who deny themselves and those who enrich the lives of others are the ones who are guaranteed a full life in the world to come. It is that eternal life which we ought to value more than this fleeting life on earth.

RESPOND: *Jesus, keep me mindful of my life after death. Let me strive to spend each day on earth in such a way that I will someday be a citizen of heaven.*

November 7

LISTEN: *"Whoever serves me, the Father will honor."*

JOHN 12:26

A podiatrist said that surgery might cure my mysterious foot pain. Needing a second opinion, I consulted another podiatrist. He, too, advised surgery, which meant that two men served me by caring for my foot. It happened to be Holy Thursday, the day Jesus washed the apostles' feet, setting an example of service! You might not be a podiatrist, but through your occupation you serve others in some way.

In addition, how many meals do you serve others during a week? Do you serve an elderly parent by shopping for them, by bathing them? Do you volunteer at a food distribution center? Do you weed a neighbor's garden? Do you comfort a grieving friend? Do you tutor? If so, you serve Jesus.

Besides these acts of mercy, you do something for Jesus directly by participating in Eucharists, leading Bible study or prayer groups, teaching religion class, and sharing the faith in conversations.

Devoting hours to service is often a requirement for the Sacrament of Confirmation. Hopefully it is the beginning of a lifelong habit. The *Baltimore Catechism* states that we were made to know, love, and serve God. If we know and love God, it follows that we will serve God. To serve him is to reign. Your service on earth probably won't merit you a trophy or plaque, but in heaven the Father will reward you with a high place and perhaps a gold crown.

RESPOND: *Jesus, help me meet the needs of those around me. I want to be more like you.*

November 8

In your garden you grow a multihued assortment of flowers, for variety is the spice of life. In the Garden of Eden, God fashioned the first human from soil and planned on creating others who would showcase diversity, not cookie-cutter dull.

Bigotry infects humanity like a plague, and it appears to be on the rise. Some find it difficult to tolerate people who differ from us in their religion, skin color, sexual orientation, or political views. A Christian ought to be immune to this disease because Jesus's love embraces every human being.

After a few Gentiles expressed the desire to see Jesus, this Jewish Messiah declared that his Death on the Cross would encompass all people. He flung heaven's gates wide open not only for his own Jewish people, but for everyone. Scripture confirms this in John's vision of heaven. He says that by his blood Jesus "ransomed for God saints from every tribe and language and people and nation" (Revelation 5:9). This does not mean every person will enter heaven, but that we have an equal opportunity.

Every individual is a unique and wonderful creation of God, in fact, his precious child. Small-minded and hard-hearted bigots who don't accept others as their brothers and sisters on earth may discover that they are their neighbors in heaven; that is, assuming they themselves are admitted.

RESPOND: *Jesus, you created a fantastic variety of men and*
women. Teach me to appreciate our differences and respect and love
all people who share this world.

November 9

LISTEN: *"And whoever sees me sees him who sent me."*
JOHN 12:45

Do you have your grandmother's hair? Your mother's eyes? That is natural because you inherited their genes. Jesus and his Father, though, are more than similar; they are identical. Here's what we can infer about the Father by reflecting on some of the extraordinary acts of Jesus:

- Multiplying bread and fish, changing water into wine, and calming storms reveal that God is all-powerful.
- Curing ten lepers, the woman with the flow of blood, blind and deaf people, the crippled, and the possessed shows God has compassion for those who are sick or disabled.
- Forgiving the adulterous woman, the paralytic, the good thief, and Peter indicate that God is merciful.
- Bringing Jairus's daughter, the widow of Naim's son, and Lazarus back from the dead show that God is for life.
- Suffering a horrific Passion and Death points to the depths of God's love for us.
- Instituting the Eucharist shows how much God longs to be with us now and forever.

You will never comprehend the Trinity, but Jesus gives a window into what God is like. Above all, he proves that God is good, very good.

RESPOND: *Jesus, I don't have words to thank you for the sacrifice you made in coming to earth as one of us. Because of you, I have faith, hope, and love.*

November 10

LISTEN: *"I have come as light into the world, so that everyone who believes in me should not remain in the darkness."*

JOHN 12:46

Light is associated with truth. A sudden realization might evoke the expression, "The light dawned on me." In cartoons a light bulb in a character's word balloon signifies an inspiration. A brilliant thought is referred to as a "bright" idea. A nightlight assures a child that no monsters lurk in the bedroom. In our darkness Jesus is the light because he is the ultimate Truth.

From time immemorial human beings have pondered weighty questions like, "How did the universe come to be?" "Is there a God?" "What is the key to happiness?" By becoming man and teaching for about three years, God shed light on these realities. Jesus revealed that God is our loving Father who cares about us and all of creation. He explained that he would atone for the sins of the world. He gave us the Beatitudes, eight ways to be blessed and happy. To our great relief, he promised that there is life beyond the grave.

Christians, those who believe in Jesus and accept his answers, are truly enlightened. They are not in the dark about God, themselves, and life's origin, meaning, and final destiny.

RESPOND: *Jesus, thank you for bringing us out from the shadows and darkness of ignorance. May I stay close to you and take steps to deepen my understanding of the truths you teach.*

November 11

LISTEN: *"For I came not to judge the world, but to save the world."*
JOHN 12:47

If you ever were tried in court, you know that awaiting judgment is grueling. You wonder if you will be found guilty and be charged a hefty fine or face jail time. Jesus did not become incarnate to accuse people of a crime and level punishment. Instead of stoning an adulterous woman, he defended her and let her go free. He turned an immoral Samaritan woman into a disciple without shaming her. On meeting Zacchaeus, a swindling tax collector, instead of accusing or scolding him, Jesus invited himself to his house. His first words to the apostles who abandoned him during his Passion and Death were, "Peace be with you." He said this three times! His role was to save everyone.

Today Jesus doesn't judge you either but looks on you with kindness and mercy. After you hurt someone's feelings, drink too much, tell a lie, lash out in anger, or commit some other sin, you deserve punishment. But if you regret your lapse, you can immediately ask Jesus for pardon and be forgiven. Venial sins are forgiven when you receive Communion. Then there is the Sacrament of Reconciliation where all sins are forgiven and you are fortified to rebuff temptations. Jesus has been generous in providing ways to correct your detours and reset you on the path to holiness.

Be careful though. The same Jesus who breathed our air and ate our food as man and Savior will appear as a powerful judge at his second coming. But you needn't fear. He is a just and perfect judge who reads hearts.

RESPOND: *Jesus, I praise you for your mercy in atoning for all sin and forgiving my sins. Give me true sorrow for them and the grace to refrain from committing them.*

November 12

LISTEN: *"So if I, your Lord and Teacher, have washed your feet,*
you also ought to wash one another's feet."

JOHN 13:14

Women wash a lot of feet, cute little baby feet and parents' feet that are wrinkled and calloused from a lifetime of loving. The feet Jesus washed at the Last Supper were a different matter. They were the feet of men who wore sandals on unpaved roads—dirty, smelly feet that perhaps hadn't seen soap and water for some days. Ordinarily servants carried out the distasteful task of foot washing. And that is precisely why Jesus decided to do this. By his humble service he, who is Lord of heaven and earth, taught a powerful lesson: we are to serve one another.

Women like you serve in homes by preparing meals, doing laundry, cleaning, and helping with homework. You are the backbone of the Church as you run parish organizations, teach, act as sacristans, and pass on the faith to children. It's often women who guarantee smooth-running workplaces, plan and carry out social affairs, and act as peacemakers. Some women are both homemakers and breadwinners. God blesses these selfless ones for their service.

Mary served Jesus and Joseph in Nazareth, Elizabeth and Zachary in Ain Karem, and, no doubt, the apostles after Pentecost. In the footsteps of Mary and her son, you can consider it an honor and a joy to make life easier and more pleasant for God's sons and daughters. Think of how often you depend on others to wash your feet.

RESPOND: *Jesus, I wish not so much to be waited on but to jump at*
the chance to be of service to others. I know that by serving them,
I am serving you.

November 13

LISTEN: *"I give you a new commandment, that you love one another. Just as I have loved you, you also should love one another. By this everyone will know that you are my disciples, if you have love for one another."*

JOHN 13:34–35

Love is the hallmark of a Christian community. Jesus loved his disciples although they tried his patience. He loved them despite their wrangling for high places in heaven, their slowness in accepting his teachings, their cowardliness in deserting him on Calvary, and even their betrayal. He asks us to love one another the same way: unconditionally.

It is fairly easy to love our family members even when they drive us crazy. It's easy to love people we like: the charming ones, the gifted ones, and those who like us. We overlook their faults and make excuses for them. But Jesus asks more of us. We are to love all fellow Christians including the driver who cuts us off in the church parking lot, the guild board member with the annoying laugh, the neighbor who brags about her children, and the slovenly coworker who spends more time talking than working.

When we master our negative feelings toward certain people and reach out to them with understanding and love, we are treating them as our brothers and sisters in God's family. And we are carrying out the new commandment Jesus gave us.

RESPOND: *Jesus, help me to be identified as a Christian by the love, tolerance, and acceptance I manifest to all my fellow Christians all of the time.*

November 14

LISTEN: *"In my Father's house there are many dwelling places.
If it were not so, would I have told you that I go to
prepare a place for you?"*

JOHN 14:2

When someone is coming to stay at your house—when, for example, you are welcoming a new baby into your family, or your mother-in-law or a foreign exchange student is moving in—you prepare a room. You clean it from top to bottom, see that it has good furniture, supply it with anything the person might need, and perhaps add a bouquet of flowers and a welcome sign.

Jesus is expecting you to stay in his Father's house, the temple of heaven. At the Last Supper he says heartening and touching words. Not only is there is room for you in heaven, but he is readying a place for you. What kind of place will your glorified body dwell in? Heaven is beyond your imagination. Planet Earth is magnificent and awe-inspiring, so heaven must be even more so. One thing you can be sure of is that Jesus will be a gracious host. He will provide everything that will make you happy.

By his Death and Resurrection, Jesus purchased the right to God's house for you. If you are faithful in living as he taught, someday you will be home with him, your Father, and your Blessed Mother forever. Heaven is a family home.

RESPOND: *Jesus, thank you for making it possible for me to live in
the Father's house. May I do nothing on my life's journey that will
prevent me from reaching heaven.*

November 15

LISTEN: *"And if I go and prepare a place with you,
I will come again and will take you to myself, so that where I am
there you may be also."*

JOHN 14:3

The dozens of movies on the apocalypse reflect our fascination with it. As a child I was terrified at the thought of the end of the world. Today I rarely think of it except during Advent when we ponder Jesus coming in history, mystery, and majesty. The positive side of the world's end is that the second coming of Jesus will occur. At that time he will gather all of the faithful people to himself. And don't worry: if you happen to die prior to that time, Jesus will come for you personally.

When you love people, you want to be with them. You want to see them, to hear their voice, and to feel their touch. In their presence, you are filled with joy and time speeds by. When a loved one departs, you feel a little lost and lonely. Incredibly Jesus, the Son of God, loves you! He appeared to St. Margaret Mary Alacoque and asked her to promote devotion to his Sacred Heart. Revealing his heart, he said, "Behold this Heart which has so loved men that it has spared nothing, even to exhausting and consuming itself, in order to testify its love." He desires to have you with him for time and for eternity. If you love Jesus with all your heart, you will be perfectly, deliriously happy with him in heaven.

RESPOND: *Jesus, I know you are with me spiritually and in the
Eucharist in good times and bad times. Still I long for the day
when I will see you face-to-face.*

November 16

LISTEN: *"I am the way, and the truth, and the life."*

JOHN 14:6

Sometimes you are lost in a labyrinth and don't know which way to turn for safety and peace. You may be facing a major decision or plagued by a problem you can't solve. You feel confused and frustrated. Jesus is the way, and you can depend on him to guide you to the right answers. Before his teachings were known as Christianity, they were called the Way.

People hold contradictory opinions. At times you don't know who or what to believe. For example, is it right to believe in evolution, climate change, the Eucharist as the Body and Blood of Jesus, that your cat or dog will be in heaven? Jesus speaks the truth, the whole truth. He communicates it through Scripture, Tradition, and the teaching Church. While Satan is the father of lies, Jesus never lies.

You want to go on living. Seventy or eighty years of life is not long enough. The thought that you will someday cease to be is abhorrent. Losing your loved ones is traumatic. Jesus is the life. He won eternal life for everyone by dying on the Cross. This new life is light-years better than the life you experience now.

Jesus is the fulfillment of three of your most deep-seated desires: you want to know what to do to live right, you want to know what is real, and you want to continue to exist. You also yearn to be loved. Jesus also could have added, "I am love."

RESPOND: *Jesus, you are the source of all good, the key to my happiness. Keep me close to you as I strive to meet the challenges each day brings.*

November 17

LISTEN: *"No one comes to the Father except through me."*
JOHN 14:6

You can't get into certain websites unless you remember your password. We human beings don't have access to the Father without Jesus, the Word. He was essential for the salvation of the world in the Father's plan of action.

The gates of heaven were barred to us after the first couple God created offended him. But then Jesus, our big brother, threw open the gates by atoning for all sin through his Death and Resurrection. He made it possible for everyone to come to the Father. Now any person has the opportunity to be united with God for all eternity.

Don't misinterpret this statement of Jesus to mean that non-Christians will not be allowed into heaven. What it really means is that no one and nothing other than Jesus, God's Son, has the power to free us from sin and death and restore our status as heirs of heaven. In God's providence, Jesus was the only way our salvation could be achieved. That is the basis of the saying "Hail Cross, our only hope." You are responsible for introducing Jesus and his Paschal Mystery to the next generations. That is a privilege. What will you do about it?

RESPOND: *Jesus, may I never forget you and the stupendous thing you did for all of us. I hope I spend all eternity thanking you.*

November 18

LISTEN: *"Very truly, I tell you, the one who believes in me will also do the works that I do and, in fact, will do greater works than these, because I am going to the Father."*

JOHN 14:12

Jesus healed people, multiplied bread, and brought the dead back to life. If, as he said, you will do greater works, you might wonder why you are not working miracles! The miracles were only signs that Jesus was divine. The main tasks on his job description were to call people to repent and to teach about God.

After the Holy Spirit came upon the apostles, the Church accomplished great things for civilization. She spread the Good News to Gentiles, provided unity for Europe after the Roman Empire was destroyed, promoted culture, and initiated all kinds of social works. Jesus worked among a small group of people. Today the Church works throughout the whole world.

You have done works that Jesus didn't do. Although you haven't raised the dead, perhaps you've given birth to a child and taught them about the spiritual life. Jesus never wrote anything, but perhaps you've written articles, a book, or some blogs about the faith. Jesus didn't work in parish organizations or support the missions in developing nations outside Israel, but perhaps you have. In a sense, you work your own miracles every day as you impact the people in your sphere of influence.

RESPOND: *Jesus, use me to carry out your work. Let me be attentive to the chances to teach someone to know you better, to turn around a sinner's life, and to bring your healing love to those in need.*

November 19

At first glance, this promise of Jesus seems to indicate that he will grant anything you ask whenever you add, "I ask this in your name"—like magic results from saying "abracadabra." Think again. "In my name" can't mean asking Jesus for something in his own name, by his own authority. That would make no sense, comparable to saying to your boss, "Mr. Cline, I ask for Friday off in your name." Instead, "in my name" in the Scripture verse here means asking for something that is in accord with the teachings and will of Jesus.

Asking for illness to strike an enemy is an evil prayer that won't be granted. Neither will a prayer to win the lottery so you can quit work and live in a mansion. Praying that your baseball team wins doesn't guarantee a positive answer because a fan on the other side might be praying that her team wins. Prayers for beneficial things prompted by worthy motivations are likely to be heard and answered. Of course, you must approach Jesus with faith. Then if your prayers aren't answered, possibly in heaven you will be thanking God for the times he didn't answer your prayers!

Respond: *Jesus, may all of my petitions come from a pure heart set on doing your will. I hope my prayers never spring from selfishness, bitterness, or other unholy motives.*

November 20

LISTEN: *"If you love me, you will keep my commandments."*
JOHN 14:15

Naturally you try to please people you love. You might go so far as to say, "Your slightest wish is my command." Just as children show love for their mothers and fathers by obeying them, you show love for your heavenly Father by acting according to his will. Jesus expects you to love God and others as spelled out in the Ten Commandments: to pray; to honor God's name and God's day; to obey and honor parents and other authority figures; and to respect life, others' property and reputation, the truth, and marriage.

Jesus took these laws to a higher level by saying forgive, share with others, be humble, watch your thoughts, don't be greedy, don't judge others, follow the Golden Rule, love your enemies, and pray for persecutors. He enumerated the Beatitudes—attitudes that result in blessings and happiness.

Jesus, who is sinless, is the touchstone for living out these moral ideals he set before you. Above all, Jesus showed tremendous love for God the Father by fulfilling his daunting wish, namely, by assuming a human nature and atoning for all sins by suffering and dying. You prove your love for Jesus by living as he wished.

RESPOND: *Jesus, may my main motivation for doing good and avoiding evil always be to show you that I love you, who loves me so much.*

November 21

LISTEN: *"And I will ask the Father, and he will give you another
Advocate, to be with you forever."*

JOHN 14:16

When going for a doctor's visit, you are encouraged to take along a companion. That person will see that you describe your situation accurately and completely, ask questions, and later remind you of things the doctor said that you may not remember. Someone who does those things is acting as an advocate or a helper. Another advocate is a lawyer who guides you and speaks on your behalf.

Jesus is your advocate, who championed your ability to hope for eternal life once more. He saved you and now intercedes for you with the Father. But at the Last Supper, Jesus said he would advocate for you by asking the Father to send "another Advocate." This helper is no less than the Third Person of the Blessed Trinity, the Holy Spirit. This Spirit came upon the apostles and fortified them with the wisdom and courage to guide and grow the early Church.

This same Holy Spirit, the Spirit of Jesus, is with you today, giving you counsel when you are in doubt, strengthening you when you are spiritually weak, and comforting you in times of trouble or distress. The Holy Spirit also intercedes for you before the Father, obtaining blessings that you may not think to ask for yourself.

RESPOND: *Jesus, I'm grateful that you are my advocate and that at
your request the Father sent the Holy Spirit to be my helper too.
I pray that I may be sensitive to the Spirit's nudges during the day.*

November 22

LISTEN: *"You know [the Spirit] because he abides with you, and he will be in you."*

JOHN 14:17

One reason that your Baptism was so important is that through this first sacrament the Holy Spirit took up residence in you. He is a very welcome guest. As hostess gifts, the Holy Spirit brought along the seven gifts of wisdom, knowledge, understanding, counsel, fortitude, piety, and fear of God—which he strengthened in you when you received the Sacrament of Confirmation.

The Holy Spirit abides, or remains, as your constant partner throughout your life. With the help of this advocate, you can deal successfully with all the challenges your days present. And you can stay true to your baptismal vows to live according to the Gospel, a feat that is not for the faint-hearted.

St. Basil said that just as the sun penetrates crystal to make it dazzle, so too does the Spirit makes souls into radiant powerhouses beaming with grace and love.

As with any guest, it is good etiquette to offer the Holy Spirit hospitality. From time to time remember that he is with you, speak to him, and above all listen to him. When you let the Holy Spirit take charge of your life, it's unlikely that you will admit any evil spirit into your heart. The Holy Spirit is one guest you do not want to leave—ever.

RESPOND: *Jesus, what a gift we have in your Holy Spirit! May I take advantage of his presence in me to become all that you want me to be.*

November 23

LISTEN: *"I will not leave you orphaned; I am coming to you."*
JOHN 14:18

Tragedies like wars and natural disasters create orphans, children who lack the support, security, comfort, and love of their biological parents. In Jesus's day, orphans were penniless and homeless. On the night before Jesus died, he assured the apostles, whom he called his children, that he would be back with them. He kept his promise by appearing to them periodically after the Resurrection. He also kept it long-term by sending the Holy Spirit, his Spirit, to be with them.

Jesus is your constant companion too. When you were baptized, you became a dwelling place for the Trinity. At every Eucharist, Jesus—body, blood, soul, and divinity—becomes truly present to you. For easy access he remains in the tabernacle in the form of sacred bread, "a prisoner of love." You also meet Jesus in every person you encounter, not only a sweet baby or your spouse but the beggar on the street and the rude driver who cuts you off in traffic. You especially encounter Jesus, as St. Teresa of Calcutta found, in the distressing disguise of the poorest of the poor.

Your mother or father or both may have already died, to your great sorrow. But you will never be an orphan. You always have a heavenly Father, who counts all the hairs on your head; a divine brother, who surrendered his life for you; and, thanks to Jesus, a heavenly mother, Mary, who watches over you and prays for you.

RESPOND: *Jesus, I believe that you are always with me whether I feel it or not. Thank you for making it possible for me to be God's daughter.*

November 24

LISTEN: *"Those who love me will keep my word, and my
Father will love them, and we will come to them and make
our home with them."*

JOHN 14:23

The family of the Trinity—Father, Son, and Holy Spirit—makes a
home in us. When we love Jesus, God moves into our hearts and
lives there day and night. Our triune God is closer to us than anyone
else can ever be. St. Augustine refers to God as "the One who is in me,
more myself than I am." God's tremendous love for us compels him
to unite us in this intimate relationship. Our communion with God is
like the combining of two flames or two drops of water.

This divine indwelling means that God's dynamic life pulsates
within us. The Father is begetting the Son, and in mutual love they
are breathing forth the Holy Spirit. God keeps pouring into us his
divine life, which we call grace. The whole purpose of Calvary was
this indwelling, both on earth and perfectly in heaven.

St. Teresa of Avila explains that we are like a beautiful castle of
clear crystal with many mansions, and in the center of it God dwells.
This mystery gives us immense dignity and reason to take good care
of ourselves, body and soul.

RESPOND: *Jesus, keep me mindful of the presence of the Trinity
within me. May my every action, thought, and word reflect that
I am a sanctuary of God.*

November 25

LISTEN: *"The Advocate, the holy Spirit that the Father will send in my name—he will teach you everything and remind you of all that I told you."*

JOHN 14:26

When you think about it, your religion strangely has its roots in a group of twelve simple men, mostly fishermen. What is even more amazing is that Jesus sometimes chided those apostles for their lack of understanding! How then did all those teachings that fill the *Catechism of the Catholic Church* come about? Some of our beliefs, like the Assumption of Mary, are not found in Scripture.

The answer is that Jesus's prediction of the Holy Spirit's arrival was fulfilled on Pentecost. This Spirit opened the minds of the apostles, assisting them to remember what Jesus taught while enabling them to acquire new knowledge. He is the author of the Gospels and the one who inspired the work of the Church councils that defined our beliefs. This same Spirit is with the Church today—two thousand years after Jesus lived—guiding her to instruct humankind.

That Holy Spirit is with you personally, helping you to know, understand, and accept the truths of the faith. He is your divine teacher who instructs you and through you instructs others who are entrusted to you.

RESPOND: *Jesus, I want to grow in wisdom and knowledge. Let your Holy Spirit release his power in me and open my eyes to discern what is true and good.*

November 26

LISTEN: *"Peace I leave with you; my peace I give to you."*
JOHN 14:27

halom, or peace, is a Hebrew greeting, a blessing for peace, well-being, and wholeness. On the lips of Jesus, peace has a weightier meaning because it refers to the peace he has established between God and us; in other words, salvation. By his coming to earth, dying and rising, the Son of God restored you, all other people, and all creation to original goodness. You again can hope for eternal life with God. For good reason Jesus is known as the Prince of Peace.

Wars can rage around us in other countries, in your own city or town, and in your home. At times you can be beset by trials and problems: a miscarriage, an argument with a friend, a car accident, the sickness of a loved one. Yet, peace can reign deep in your heart, for you have the assurance that God loved you so much, he saved you at great personal expense. He walks with you, seeing you through all the ups and downs of your life. This conviction can give you courage and stamina. It can also fill you with peace until you reach the end of your days when you will enjoy everlasting serenity.

RESPOND: *Jesus, thank you for the gift of peace. When I am frustrated, rattled, worried, or disappointed, let the thought of you and your love keep me calm and at peace.*

November 27

Listen: *"Do not let your hearts be troubled, and do not let them be afraid."*

John 14:27

What if your best friend told you that he or she was going to leave you, that you would be betrayed and denied by trusted people, and then executed? Certainly your heart would be troubled, and that was the case for the apostles at the Last Supper. Yet, Jesus told them not to worry! Hindsight lets you know that everything worked out for the best.

The word "worry" is from a German word that means "to strangle or choke." That is understandable, for if you worry, your life is compromised. When you fear for the future, you too can hear Jesus say, "Don't worry, I've got your back!" Life is full of frightening things: your teenager just got a driver's license, a tornado is spinning your way, the doctor informs you that you are a prime candidate for a heart attack. No doubt your greatest fear is death, your loved ones' and your own.

At Mass, after the Our Father, the celebrant prays that we may be "safe from all distress" as we await the coming of our Savior, Jesus Christ. You do not have to be anxious or afraid. God holds you in the palm of his hand. He has planned a future for you beyond your wildest dreams.

Trust Jesus to draw out good from any misfortune you encounter. That is what the apostles hiding behind locked doors learned when the risen Lord surprised them. The times that God hasn't protected you from trouble, it could be his scheme to perfect you.

Respond: *Jesus, keep me from being a worrywart. I know that you always plan the best for me. When I'm ambushed by a crisis, deepen my trust in you.*

November 28

LISTEN: *"I am the vine, you are the branches. Those who abide in me and I in them bear much fruit, because apart from me you can do nothing."*

JOHN 15:5

Unwrapping a new azalea bush, to my dismay I found that a large branch had broken off. Lacking a green thumb and unfamiliar with grafting, I discarded the limb. Without the moisture, minerals, and nutrients that the main stem provided, it would die. It would never bear the brilliant red flowers that intact branches yield.

Jesus used this image from nature to symbolize your dependence on him. United to him, you are so bursting with life that you cannot help but bring life and joy and love to others. Apart from him, you would be useless. You need the supernatural life of Jesus to flow through you and give you the energy, strength, and stamina to produce good works. When you are one with Jesus, there is no limit to what you can accomplish. You might even surprise yourself!

Knowing that you are tapped into a powerful source, you can endure trials and sufferings, you can dare to volunteer for challenging jobs, and you can go the extra mile to show love to your family members and friends. By Baptism you were grafted onto Jesus, and only deliberate, foolish, and serious sins will cut you off from him.

RESPOND: *Jesus, keep me mindful that you are always with me, helping me to make my life meaningful and fruitful. Never let me be separated from you.*

November 29

LISTEN: *"As the Father has loved me, so I have loved you;*
abide in my love."

JOHN 15:9

I read that men want to be admired while women want to be liked. I'd edit that to women want to be *loved*. Being loved is the most exhilarating experience. Children offer sweet definitions of love: "Love is when my mommy makes coffee for my daddy, and she takes a sip first to make sure the taste is okay." Or, "Love is when you give somebody most of your French fries without making them give you anything." Or, "When you love somebody, your eyelashes go up and down and little stars come out of you."

The love of Jesus for you is unconditional, constant, and everlasting. For good reason, G. K. Chesterton advised, "Let your religion be less of a theory and more of a love affair." In the "Hound of Heaven," the poet Francis Thompson compared God to a hound pursuing you unwearyingly—you might say doggedly (forgive the pun, but it is apt).

Your divine lover invites you to abide in his love. Let your mind dwell on him during the day. At times give yourself the luxury of being alone and silent with Jesus and just soaking in the love he has for you. No one but Jesus can ever be your perfect soulmate. He will always love you with a warm and tender love and will never break your heart.

RESPOND: *Jesus, I'm overwhelmed and humbled to know you love*
me. May I return your love with all my heart until I see you face-
to-face and live happily ever after.

November 30

LISTEN: *"I have said these things to you so that my joy may be in you, and that your joy may be complete."*

JOHN 15:11

We say, "Happy birthday," "Happy Thanksgiving," "Merry Christmas," and "Happy New Year" because the best thing you can wish for people is that they have happiness. God made us to be happy, we like to be happy, and we like to make other people happy. At the Last Supper, Jesus is glad to reveal God's plan to his friends the apostles because he knows that his news about the Holy Spirit, heaven, and the Eucharist will bring them intense joy.

You live in an era when the promises of Jesus have been realized. You have received the gift of the Holy Spirit and the Lord in the Eucharist; you have also received the assurance that heaven is possible for you because Jesus has risen from the dead. The joy that comes from Jesus is a deep joy that no one can take from you. Your checks may bounce, your children may drive you crazy, your microwave may stop working, and though trials like these and even tragedies like the death of a good friend shake you, a quiet river of joy may still run through your heart. Why? Because of Jesus. What a sad world it would be if we did not have the hope he offers!

Someone noted that joy is the result of putting (O) nothing between (Y)ou and (J)esus: JOY. Cling to him alone and your days will overflow with laughter.

RESPOND: *Jesus, you are the source of all our joy. Keep my eyes fixed on you so that someday I will live with everlasting joy, close to you.*

DECEMBER

December 1

LISTEN: *"I do not call you servants . . . ; but I have
called you friends . . ."*
JOHN 15:15

Friends are precious blessings. Do you keep in touch with friends from your grade school days? Probably some friends played a brief role in your life and then moved on. Now you are making new friends maybe by participating in a book club, a parent association, or senior center activities. You may consider your spouse to be your best friend.

If Jesus regarded you as a servant, it would be understandable. After all, he is the almighty, ineffable God, and you are one of his creatures. Yet he calls you his friend.

Jesus certainly acts like a friend. When you are troubled, worried, or scared, he comes to your rescue. When you have a knotty problem, he untangles it for you. When you are sad, he offers comfort. When you happen to offend him, he quickly forgives. When you face a weighty decision and feel like you're trapped in a maze, he suggests a way out. He accepts you as you are, warts and all, and encourages you to be better.

Friends tell each other secrets. Jesus said he revealed to you all that he heard from the Father. You can frankly confide in Jesus things you don't share with anyone else. Friends like to be with each other. Jesus is always with you, especially in the Blessed Sacrament. You reciprocate by carving out time in your busy life to focus on his loving presence. Friends exchange gifts. What can you give to Jesus who gave his life for you?

RESPOND: *Jesus, I appreciate your unlikely and undeserved
friendship. May we become closer friends each day.*

December 2

Think of a time you were chosen, maybe as class or club president, employee of the year, or fiancée. Remember the thrill and joy you felt then? Nothing compares to being chosen by God.

First, God chose you to exist. Out of uncountable possibilities, he decided to create you with your unique DNA and fingerprints and with your talents and, yes, quirks and flaws. Your strings of genes trace back through many couples over many centuries.

Second, Jesus chose you to be a disciple, an intimate friend. You could have been born before Christ and never heard of him. You could be living in a country where the Good News hasn't penetrated. But no. One day you were baptized, probably as an infant (even a sleeping one) when you had no choice. But Jesus chose you to become a Christian. You were told about him, probably by your mother or grandmother. You learned about him in school and read about him in the Gospels. You are privileged to encounter Jesus in prayer and in the Eucharist. You have the hope of living forever and seeing your deceased loved ones again. Jesus chose you to share in his ministry by introducing him to others and relaying how his Death and Resurrection rescued humanity.

You did nothing spectacular to win God's favor. His choice was based solely on his ardent love for you. Now you have the power and hopefully the love to choose to follow him every day.

RESPOND: *Jesus, I don't deserve all your loving kindness in calling me to be your disciple. Grant me the grace to live up to your expectations for me.*

December 3

LISTEN: *"If the world hates you, be aware that it hated me before it hated you."*

JOHN 15:18

Has anyone ever said to you, "I hate you"? If so, something in you withered. To be hated is devastating, or at least uncomfortable. Why? Because we all love to be loved.

As a Catholic, you espouse some values and opinions that are countercultural, like cherishing life from womb to tomb, believing that sex outside of marriage is wrong, and acknowledging the pope as head of the Church. For that reason, people may despise you and may treat you with scorn and mockery. Jesus predicted that this would be the fate of his faithful followers.

When you go against the grain of what the world thinks and practices, you can expect to lose friends, have disagreements with relatives, and be barred from some social events. As you are subjected to this subtle persecution, you can identify with Jesus. Although he is the Truth, the religious leaders of the day challenged and criticized his ideas and actions. In the end his own people turned against him and had him put to death. Similarly, down through the centuries Christians have been martyred by emperors and fanatics opposed to their faith.

Being the object of derision because of your faith is sharing in the Cross of Christ. If you hold fast to Jesus and his teachings, ultimately you will not be the victim but the victor.

RESPOND: *Jesus, give me the courage and stamina to weather any attacks I may endure because of my faith in you. Keep me steadfast in living according to the kingdom values you taught.*

December 4

LISTEN: *"When the Spirit of truth comes, he will guide you into all the truth."*

JOHN 16:13

Sometimes you don't know what to believe. Ads tell you a certain cream has a magic formula that makes wrinkles disappear. Politicians claim they will make the country or your state prosperous and safe. Some people hold that climate change is a fantasy. Recently a friend tried to convince me that the earth is flat!

Jesus, who knows all things and is supremely trustworthy, taught fundamental truths. At times he was exasperated with the apostles' failure to comprehend his lessons. It wasn't until the Holy Spirit filled them on Pentecost that they understood and confidently communicated the truth to thousands hungry for it. Church leaders and faithful Christians have done this for more than twenty centuries.

This same Holy Spirit came to live in you at Baptism and more fully at Confirmation. He infused into you the gifts of wisdom and understanding. Tap into them when Jehovah's Witnesses appear at your door, when a family member no longer believes Jesus is God, or when a stranger on a plane asks why you are praying a rosary. Rely on this all-wise One to direct you in making decisions in a perplexing situation. When you engage in a difficult conversation, ask the Holy Spirit to place the right words in your mouth. Thanks to the Holy Spirit's enlightenment, you can be a beacon of truth for those around you.

RESPOND: *Jesus, preserve me from swallowing falsehoods and half-truths. Let me delve ever deeper into the realities you reveal, especially the fact that your love for me is profound and unshakeable.*

December 5

LISTEN: *"So you have pain now; but I will see you again, and your hearts will rejoice, and no one will take your joy from you."*

JOHN 16:22

Being separated from a loved one feels as though a heavy stone weighs on your heart. A classic example of faithful waiting is Penelope in Homer's *Odyssey*. For twenty years she waited for her husband Odysseus to return from the Trojan War. To deter suitors, she wove during the day and told them she wouldn't marry until she finished the project. At night she unraveled her work.

Over the course of three or so years, the apostles had become deeply attached to Jesus. He knew that when he disappeared from their lives, they would be lost and in shock. But before Jesus left, he promised to come back to them.

You did not have the privilege of living when Jesus did. You never had the chance to meet him when he walked on our earth. Still, because of his promise of resurrection, you can anticipate seeing him face-to-face someday. In the meantime you wait patiently, weaving the tapestry of your life as best you can, staying true to Jesus. In faith you know that when your last stitch is done, you will encounter him in his glorified flesh. On that day, you will be overcome by an immense joy that will never end. You will be reunited with the God who created you for that very purpose.

RESPOND: *Jesus, I appreciate the ways you are present to me today: in your Word, in the Eucharist, in other people. Still, I long for the day when I will see you in all your glory in heaven. Keep my eyes fixed on the goal of being eternally one with you.*

December 6

LISTEN: *"Do you now believe?"*
JOHN 16:31

The disciples witnessed Jesus's miracles and heard his unparalleled teachings. Finally at the Last Supper they professed that they believed Jesus was from God. Little did they know that they were on the verge of having their faith tested to the nth degree as God's Son was arrested and executed.

You who are privileged to have the gift of faith cannot take it for granted. Future trials may shake it in unimaginable ways. A family member might die unexpectedly, your marriage partner might prove unfaithful, you might wake up some morning in terrible pain. Such tragedies might leave you questioning whether God truly exists . . . and if he does, does he really love you?

You can strengthen your faith through study and meditation. But by far the most effective way to grow in faith is to cultivate an intimate relationship with Jesus through prayer. The disciples' faith was grounded in their experience of the resurrected Jesus to the extent that almost all of them became martyrs. Your faith can be made steadfast in the same way.

RESPOND: *Jesus, I believe in you with my whole heart. Grant me the grace to remain faith-filled and faithful to the end of my days no matter what adversities I may face.*

December 7

The world can be a frightening place. It is rife with sin. Countries stockpile weapons, officials present blatant lies as truths, trusted leaders steal to fatten their bank accounts, violence stalks our streets, singers and actresses vie to flaunt the most revealing outfits. In addition, you are plagued by personal traumas, like illness and accidents, and your own faults and addictions. Somedays you might feel like echoing the title of the musical *Stop the World—I Want to Get Off!*

The Son of God entered our world as man and sacrificed himself for you. By doing so, he overcame the devil, sin, and death. Because of your divine hero, you can take heart: good ultimately will triumph. When swamped by worries and heartaches, you are not alone. As Moses told the Israelites when Pharaoh's forces pursued them, "The Lord will fight for you, and you have only to keep still" (Exodus 14:14).

Knowing that Jesus is on your side will dispel your fears and fill you with deep and lasting peace. You can enjoy life on this earth as God intended.

Respond: *Jesus, when I am beset with trials and feel overwhelmed, may I remember that you walk beside me. The thought that nothing is impossible with God encourages me. So does your love for me.*

December 8

LISTEN: *"I glorified you on earth by finishing the work that you gave me to do."*

JOHN 17:4

Jesus's resume might read as follows:

- Did carpentry and construction work for twenty years
- Spent three years as an itinerant teacher in Israel
- Occasionally practiced medicine as an ophthalmologist, ENT, dermatologist, and chiropractor
- Established the Christian church

Of course, the preeminent task of the God-man, the reason the infinite One became finite, was to bring eternal life to humankind. Everything Jesus achieved, including the sacrifice of his life and his rising from the dead, gave glory to his Father.

A common belief is that each of us was put on earth for a certain purpose. It's as though at birth we were handed a job description. Were you born to care for a disabled child, to foster your spouse's holiness, to be a community leader, or to promote social justice? What task or tasks do your heavenly Father expect you to carry out?

In all that you do, you glorify your Creator, whether it's speaking at a convention, listening to a hurting friend, or picking up after children. Someday you will be compensated generously.

RESPOND: *Jesus, may I be as dedicated to you as you were to me. I want to carry out my purpose with joy and love, giving glory to our Father.*

December 9

LISTEN: *"Holy Father, protect them . . . so that they may be one, as we are one."*

JOHN 17:11

The three persons of the Trinity are one God. That is why Jesus could say, "Whoever has seen me, has seen the Father" (John 14:9). At the Last Supper he prayed that we would enjoy a similar unity. What does that mean? Jesus longs for his followers to have the same beliefs and the same values. Moreover, he wants us to be bound to one another in love.

We humans hold different opinions and like different things. These differences can lead to conflict. Witness the cracks in our republic that is supposed to be one and indivisible. Look at the Christian church in which someone counted 3600 divisions. Then there is the Catholic Church where liberals and conservatives threaten to scuttle Peter's boat. Despite our dissimilarities, love is to be the cement that keeps us together.

You might not agree with your spouse about how to spend your money. You may disagree with your neighbor about whom to elect. Your children might have their own ideas about curfew and mealtimes. Yet, deep love and commitment to one another maintain your unity.

When you are overwhelmed by the lack of unity and peace in our institutions, you might follow St. Teresa of Calcutta's advice: "If you want to change the world, go home and love your family."

RESPOND: *Jesus, we are your one Mystical Body. May we strive to stay united on earth that someday we may be one with you and the Father in heaven.*

December 10

LISTEN: *"As you have sent me into the world,*
so I have sent them into the world."

JOHN 17:18

The Father sent Jesus to earth and to its inhabitants to reclaim its original glory. Jesus has delegated to us the all-important task of restoring the world to God. We Christians are his ambassadors to the people living today, as well as to those who will live in the future. By virtue of your Baptism, you share in the prophetic office of Jesus to further the kingdom of God. A prophet is someone who speaks for God. You are to speak for God, and, remember, actions speak louder than words.

You needn't stand on a podium and preach, write articles, or create podcasts about the kingdom of God. You are swimming in practical opportunities to spread it. Whenever you encourage a child to be kind, whenever you comfort a grieving neighbor, whenever you invite a friend to go to church with you, you participate in the saving work of Jesus. You also do this vicariously by supporting missionaries with money and prayers.

The word "apostle" is from a Greek word meaning "one who is sent out." Jesus sends you out into this world—your world. He commissions you at the conclusion of each Mass, for you are dismissed with the words, "Go forth, the Mass is ended." You are a modern-day apostle. Go be a prophet!

RESPOND: *Jesus, you rely on me to continue your work among the people on earth. May your Spirit inspire and embolden me to carry out your will. I don't want to disappoint you.*

December 11

LISTEN: *"Am I not to drink the cup that the Father has given me?"*

JOHN 18:11

Jesus uttered these words as he stopped Peter from defending him from his captors in the Garden of Olives. Jesus accepted the fact that the Father was not going to remove the cup of suffering destined for him. Demonstrating the submission of an obedient Son, he would drink it to the dregs. By doing so, he would achieve the world's salvation.

As a child of disobedient Adam and Eve, and so subject to the proverbial death penalty, you have inherited your share of sorrow and pain. Why does your loving Father allow you to suffer? This is one of life's ultimate mysteries. You must be content with God's answer to Job: How can you question your mighty God?

The agonizing suffering of Jesus was not in vain but generated new life just as a woman's labor pains bring forth a new life. Your sufferings needn't be useless either. The same Jesus who turned water into wine can transform the bitter wine of your life into life-giving water. Uniting your pain to Jesus's sufferings and offering it to the Father makes you a partner in winning eternal life for humankind. The misery caused by a broken arm, the death of a family member, or a personal failure can be meritorious and redemptive when transformed into a gift to God. More than that, you can welcome suffering for it purifies you, strengthens you, and makes you more compassionate toward others who suffer.

RESPOND: *Jesus, may I always accept sufferings with peace, love, and even joy. I know that this will lead to eternal life for myself and others.*

December 12

LISTEN: *"My kingdom is not from this world."*

JOHN 18:36

The news is replete with reports of conflicts, homicides, and corruptions. No doubt you yearn for a better world, especially if any of these horrors have directly touched your life. An ideal world may not exist here, but it does in a different dimension. The kingdom of God is one of perfect peace and justice where everyone lives in love and harmony. Jesus, whom this world persecuted, reigns there, and his hope is that someday you will join him.

Each time you pray the Our Father, whose words Jesus taught, you declare, "Your kingdom come." Primarily this is a plea for the coming of Christ at the end of time. But it also expresses a wish that this reign of peace and justice will infiltrate the present world. It reminds you that as a follower of Jesus you have a duty to promote this blessed kingdom. United, women are a powerful force in confronting evils. Besides marching and protesting they form organizations, for example, those that aim to end human trafficking, reduce drunken driving, and care for the children of prisoners.

As an individual, you also can be effective. You spread God's kingdom as you raise children who value goodness. You promote it as you contact government officials and press for just laws. You bring about peace and justice whenever you forgive someone or persuade another person to forgive. In these ways you show you belong in God's kingdom.

RESPOND: *Jesus, may I always live as a loyal citizen of your kingdom. Instill in me the wisdom, courage, and stamina to plant peace and justice in the people around me and in the larger world.*

December 13

LISTEN: *"For this I was born, and for this I came into the world, to testify to the truth."*

JOHN 18:37

What a shame some people are not born with a nose like Pinocchio's! With fake news, false claims, exaggerations, and skewed facts, it is difficult to know whom or what to believe. Truth is refreshing. It is one of the three classic values: the good, the true, and the beautiful. Mothers are quick to teach their children the difference between what is true and what is a lie. This is important, for truth leads to wise actions. The smooth functioning of societies and human interactions depends on being truthful.

While appearing before Pilate, Jesus claimed that the main purpose of his Incarnation was to teach the truth. He would undo the damage that Satan, the father of lies, wreaked upon humanity.

You are on a quest for the meaning of life, knowing who God is, and how best to spend your life on earth. Jesus gave you the true answers. Through him you learn the eternal truths. Jesus called himself the way, the truth, and the life. When this ultimate Truth is the foundation of your life, you can't go wrong. He will guide you to happiness in this world and the next.

RESPOND: *Jesus, thank you for teaching us what is true. May I be moved to read and ponder the Gospels, and may I expand my knowledge of you and your teachings.*

December 14

LISTEN: *"Woman, here is your son. . . . Here is your mother."*

JOHN 19:26–27

From the Cross, Jesus bequeathed his mother Mary to us. Like a true mother, Mary guides, protects, and comforts. When you implore her help, with motherly concern she intercedes. Mary is the perfect model for what a woman should be.

You can also draw lessons from her life. Mary shows us how to listen to God with implicit faith. When the angel Gabriel proposed that she become the mother of God, she didn't think twice. With her "yes" she assumed this unique role that would involve heart-piercing events.

Mary teaches compassion. Hearing that her elderly cousin Elizabeth was pregnant, Mary, pregnant herself with the world's Savior, made an arduous journey to assist her. Much later, when wine ran out at a wedding, Mary spared the newlyweds and their parents embarrassment by daring to prod her Son into action.

Mary teaches prayer. The words of the Magnificat fell from her lips. After the shepherds' visit, and after Jesus was discovered in the temple, she was rapt in contemplation. For nine days Mary prayed among the apostles while awaiting the descent of the Holy Spirit.

When you resemble your Blessed Mother in these three ways, you please her Son. You also become a model for other women.

RESPOND: *Jesus, give me a heart like your mother's. May I show gratitude for the gift of Mary by being devoted to her.*

December 15

Perhaps at least once you have heard a child asking for a glass of water after being tucked in bed. Water is essential for your survival, and you would die faster from lack of it than from lack of food. It is estimated that, on average, a woman's body is sixty percent water. When you are dehydrated on a hot day, you need to replenish. You crave water and gladly gulp down a tall glass of it.

While dying on the Cross, Jesus declared that he was thirsty. Given the blood and sweat he lost, he must have been severely dehydrated. As a human being, Jesus knew the agony of extreme thirst. He asked for something to soothe his parched lips and dry mouth. Even the sour wine given to him brought some relief.

The thirst of Jesus has been interpreted beyond the physical level. It is a metaphor for his yearning to be appreciated, understood and, most of all, loved by you. In the words of St. Gregory Nazianzen, "God is thirsting for us to thirst for him." Jesus also longed that through his sacrifice many people would attain eternal life.

In a parable Jesus says to the saved, "I was thirsty and you gave me something to drink" (Matthew 25:35). He views good done to others as done to himself. St. Teresa of Calcutta displayed in her convents the words "I thirst." She knew that by quenching the thirst of God's little ones by ministering to them with love, she was slaking Jesus's thirst.

Respond: *Jesus, may I satisfy your thirst not only by giving you my whole heart but by showering other people with love.*

December 16

LISTEN: *"It is finished."*

JOHN 19:30

After nine months of uncomfortable pregnancy and hours of labor pains, when a baby is born, a woman might very well say with relief, "It is finished." She has successfully brought new life into the world. The mission of Jesus on earth lasted some thirty-three years and culminated in the agony of torture and crucifixion. His final words were, "It is finished." With that he breathed new life into the world. He had conquered sin and death, patched the gap between God and human beings, and thereby enabled us to live eternally.

We can only imagine what our redemption cost the Son of God. He, the omnipotent Creator of the universe, condescended to become like one of his creatures. Having a human body, he endured thirst, fatigue, and hunger. As a revolutionary teacher, he faced the criticism and scorn of his religious leaders. In the end he suffered scourging, thorns pressed into his head, heavy wood laid on his back, and nails driven into his hands and feet.

At each Eucharist, the sacrifice of Jesus is re-presented. We remember his offering on Calvary and unite ourselves with his mission, which is not yet finished; it goes on and on all over the world, until the end of time.

RESPOND: *Jesus, I thank you for the obedience, humility, and incredible love that allowed you to give your life for my sake and the sake of the world.*

December 17

LISTEN: *"Woman, why are you weeping?"*
JOHN 20:15

When Mary Magdalene found Jesus's tomb empty, she cried, thinking that his body had been stolen. Jesus was there all the time, watching her. He knew very well that frustration and grief were behind her flood of tears. Yet, he asked her why she wept. He wished to hear her name the reason.

Likewise, when sadness makes you cry—at the death of a family member or friend, the loss of a home or a job, a physical or mental trial, or the suffering of another person—Jesus is there. He sympathizes with you. Scripture attests that he too cried. He wept at the death of his friend Lazarus, over the destruction of Jerusalem, and during his agony in the garden. Although Jesus reads your heart, still he invites you to turn to him in sorrow and verbalize why you are sad. He longs to comfort you.

Mary Magdalene shed tears of joy when Jesus spoke to her. When you experience life's gifts such as beauty in creation, someone's kindness to us, or the birth of a baby, you probably are overcome with emotion and tears glisten in your eyes. At those times Jesus is there, waiting for you to speak to him about it. He shares your joy.

RESPOND: *Jesus, during the highs and lows of my life, may I always be aware of your loving presence and talk them over with you.*

December 18

LISTEN: *"Whoever welcomes one such child in my name welcomes me, and whoever welcomes me welcomes not me but the one who sent me."*

MARK 9:37

Children are delightful. Their innocence and antics are appealing. At the time Jesus lived, children were dispensable, viewed only as part of the family workforce. Of course it makes sense that he identifies with them because he knows what it is like to be a child. No wonder then that his teachings emphasize that we should cherish our children. By accepting these weak and insignificant ones, you are accepting him and consequently God his Father, who is the Father of all children.

What children should you be welcoming? All of them, but in particular the children waiting in the womb, children in foster homes, children who are disabled mentally or physically, migrant children, children who pester us, stubborn children, crying children, abused children, bratty children. Whenever we show love for these children, we are acting in the name of Jesus, we are acting like him. He welcomed children, took them into his arms, embraced them, and blessed them. He also loved adults who were childlike: the guileless Philip, the foot-in-mouth Peter, the doubting Thomas, and the tree-climbing Zacchaeus.

Think with gratitude of the many people under whose care you grew and flourished: parents and grandparents, aunts and uncles, teachers and coaches, and neighbors. Now you are called to do the same for other children.

RESPOND: *Jesus, you were once a child who needed care. Give me a heart that is open to all children and the compassion to nurture them.*

December 19

LISTEN: *"Mary!"*

JOHN 20:16

At first the risen Jesus called Mary Magdalene by the generic title "woman," and she thought he was the gardener. But as soon as he addressed her by name, she recognized him. No one else would say it quite that way.

Much thought goes into naming a baby. Some names have meaning. For example, God chose for his Son the name Jesus, which means "God saves." Presumably, the name parents choose will stand for their child forever. It gives him or her an identity and individuality. In the musical *West Side Story*, Tony is so smitten with Maria that he sings her name no less than twenty-six times in one song.

Calling someone by their name is a sign of respect, a way of recognizing their importance. It makes you feel valued. Dale Carnegie asserted that a person's name is to that person the sweetest and most important sound. It is pleasing to hear yourself addressed by name. How joyful to have a loved one pronounce your name! God says to you, "I have called you by name, you are mine" (Isaiah 43:1).

Imagine the love in Jesus's voice when he exclaimed, "Mary!" Imagine the love in his voice as he says your name. By what name does he call you? A nickname? A new name?

RESPOND: *Jesus, may your holy name often be on my lips. Help me make a conscious effort to address people by name.*

December 20

LISTEN: *"I am ascending to my Father and your Father,*
to my God and your God."

JOHN 20:17

In marriage a woman gains another mother and father, the parents of her spouse. In your union with Jesus, because of his reconciling sacrifice and because he cherishes you, you are an adopted daughter of God the Father. The omnipotent and compassionate Father of Jesus is also your Father.

Your heavenly Father loves you unconditionally; no sin or flaw will destroy his strong love for you. What's more, the Father delights in and cherishes you as though you were his only child. Although you are not always aware of him, he watches over you with tender care. He fulfills your needs and fills you with grace.

God the Father asked great things of Jesus and at times challenges you to accomplish what may seem impossible, or at least difficult. He did not spare his divine Son the agony of the Cross, and he allows crosses along your path too. These can build your character and, united with the suffering of Jesus, can further the redemption of the world.

In your conversations with God the Father, you might echo the psalmist and declare, "What god is so great as our God" (Psalm 77:13)? You might hear him say, "This is my beloved daughter in whom I am well pleased."

Just as your brother Jesus returned to heaven after he died and rose from the dead, someday you will ascend to the home of your Father and be wrapped in his divine embrace.

RESPOND: *Jesus, may I live as a worthy daughter of your Father.*
I want to please him in everything I do and shun anything that
would separate me from him.

December 21

LISTEN: *"Peace be with you."*

JOHN 20:19

S ome days your heart is in turmoil because of regrets; you feel bad because of the harsh words spoken to a family member, or because of your failure to act on the inspiration to visit a sick neighbor. And some days a cold fear grasps your heart: the fear of losing a job, the fear of getting sick, the vague fear of a random act of violence.

The apostles knew both regret and fear after Jesus was crucified. They had abandoned Jesus; one even denied knowing him. They were hiding behind locked doors for fear that they would be arrested next. But then the risen Lord appeared and his first words to them were "Peace be with you."

Jesus reads your heart and knows your weakness. He understands when you do not live up to the ideals he set before us, and he is quick to forgive. When you are sorry for something, he says, "Be at peace. I forgive you, now forgive yourself." Jesus also knows your fears. No matter what crisis you encounter, you can be at peace when you remember that he is with you, and nothing is impossible for God.

RESPOND: *Jesus, thank you for your love that encourages and sustains me whenever I feel bad about myself. Thank you too for your caring presence that calms all my fears.*

December 22

God the Father sent Jesus as an emissary on a mission to demonstrate his compassionate love in extraordinary ways and to teach us. Jesus revealed the Father. He also gave us a recipe for a good life: prayer, service, humility. Now Jesus commissions you to carry his message to the world. As his representative, you are to show his love, kindness, compassion, and forgiveness within your family and beyond. You are also responsible for spreading the Good News of our salvation.

An apostle is a messenger, one who is sent. Because you are a baptized Christian, you also can claim this title and aim to live up to it. The words "Mass," "emissary," and "mission" are rooted in the Latin word for "sent." At the conclusion of each Mass you are sent forth to be an emissary. The final words are "Go forth, the Mass is ended" or a similar directive. As a member of the Body of Christ, you are sent to evangelize.

You evangelize by boldly speaking about God, Jesus, Mary, the commandments, the Beatitudes, and the Church not only to children but to friends and colleagues. You also carry out this commission by your actions, such as working for justice, volunteering at a hunger center, comforting a crying child or friend, and visiting a sick person. Cardinal Emmanuel Suhard wrote that being a witness is living in a way that your life would not make sense if God did not exist.

RESPOND: *Jesus, at the end of the world when I report back to you, may I hear you say, "Well done, good and faithful servant. Welcome."*

December 23

Breathing on the apostles, Jesus gave them and the Church a parting gift: his own Spirit. Breath and life are related. Scripture tells us that at the creation of the cosmos *ruah*, which means the spirit or breath of God, swept over the waters. Then, when God breathed into the body of dust that was to be Adam, it came alive again. After giving birth, mothers anxiously await the first breath of their newborns. Dying persons sigh a last breath, and their spirit leaves their body.

The Holy Spirit animates Mother Church, empowering her and guiding her. As a member of the Church, you benefit from this awesome Person's help. The Holy Spirit inspires you to do good acts, fortifies you to stand strong during hardships, and floods you with the grace to refrain from sin.

Call on the Holy Spirit dwelling within you before you undertake a challenging task, when you need to find the right words to confront someone, and before you read the Bible so that you will be open to God's message for you. This Spirit, who is the love between the Father and Son, is eager to show love for you by being your best friend.

RESPOND: *Jesus, I thank you with all my heart for your constant presence in my life through your Holy Spirit.*

December 24

LISTEN: *"Let the children come to me; do not stop them; for it is to such as these that the kingdom of God belongs"*

MARK 10:14

One of the most charming scenes in the Gospels is when Jesus is surrounded by children, even holding some on his lap. The disciples, men of their times, considered children second-class citizens, unworthy of Jesus's time and attention. They tried to prevent the children from coming to Jesus. He, however, was no ordinary man. He valued children. After roundly scolding the disciples, he delighted in holding the little ones, embracing them, and blessing them. Having been a child once himself, he could identify with them, and he welcomed them as affectionately as a mother would.

The Church has a heart for children. She baptizes infants, lowered the age for receiving Communion to the age of reason, and instituted the Liturgy of the Word for Children during Mass. Smart Christian parents introduce their children to Jesus as soon as possible. They talk about him, teach their children to pray to him, and take them to church. And although you may be annoyed by crying babies or toddlers crawling under the pews at Mass, Jesus is pleased.

Jesus reached out to other little ones too: the weak and the helpless. He depends on his followers to do the same today, including showing love for adults who have the mentality of children.

RESPOND: *Jesus, you came to us as a baby. Bless the children of the world, especially the suffering ones. May I use every opportunity to bring children of all ages to you through my words and actions.*

December 25

LISTEN: *"Children, you have no fish, have you?"*
JOHN 21:5

The risen Jesus was aware that the apostles had no luck fishing all night. He told them to try the right side of the boat, and soon their net was weighed down with one hundred fifty-three large fish. They could hardly haul it in.

Jesus knows what you need too. When you are sad or worried, in the stillness of your prayer time you might hear him ask you, "Child, you have no _____, have you?" Fill in the blank: no job, friends, spouse, success, energy, . . . Then watch what happens.

Jesus loves you and cares about you as though you were the only one in the world. He wants nothing more than for you to have a happy, fruitful life. Just as you will do almost anything for your children or best friends, he will do anything for you—if, in the grand scheme of things, it is for your good. You may have to wait for a while. Remember, to God a thousand years are like a single day. Sooner or later, your divine friend may provide what you are searching for and sometimes in a marvelous way that takes you by surprise. So do not become discouraged. Trust in the Lord and his wisdom and goodness. He who can miraculously fill an empty net can easily arrange to fill your need.

RESPOND: *Jesus, thank you for supplying my needs in the past. I know I can count on you to continue doing so.*

December 26

LISTEN: *"Bring some of the fish that you have just caught."*
JOHN 21:10

When you're invited to a meal, you might contribute something for the feast, such as a bottle of wine or your signature dessert. You feel proud and happy when people consume and appreciate your gift. Similarly, children are delighted if you allow them to join you in baking holiday cookies, although working by yourself in the kitchen would be quicker and less messy. You understand, then, the risen Lord's motive for his considerate request after the miraculous catch of fish.

Jesus had fish cooking over a charcoal fire, yet he told the apostles to add to the breakfast some of their own fish. He could have provided enough for everyone; instead he chose to let the apostles share and enjoy the fruits of their labor.

Likewise, Jesus invites you to participate in his work of bringing people to the Father. He initiated this task of feeding those who are hungry for life and meaning long ago in Israel. Now he relies on you to use the nets he's supplied you with—talents, time, and treasure—to increase the number of faith-filled Christians. The "fish" you catch and add to the banquet of heaven will bring you much satisfaction and joy. You will not be alone as you work and witness. Jesus will be assisting you—perhaps in miraculous ways.

RESPOND: *Jesus, help me take advantage of opportunities to teach others about you and the kingdom of God.*

December 27

Listen: *"Do you love me?"* . . . *"Tend my sheep."*
John 21:16

You are fortunate if you know the love of parents, spouse, children, or friend. How wonderful it is when someone loves you! More than anything, Jesus desires your love. Sadly, he once bemoaned to St. Margaret Mary: "Behold this heart that loves so much but is so little loved in return." He, the all-powerful Creator of the cosmos, craves to be loved by you! Imagine Jesus asking you three times, "Do you love me?" as he asked Peter. What would you reply? Somewhat? A little? With my whole heart?

You can prove your love for Jesus, not by hugs and kisses, but by tending to his "sheep" who are placed in your care. The Holy Spirit, a current of divine love in your heart, empowers you to feed the hungry, clothe the naked, and comfort the sorrowful. The tender little services you extend to others are simultaneously acts of love for Jesus, who died for his love of you.

May this traditional act of love be frequently on your lips:

> O my God, I love you above all things, with my whole heart and soul, because you are all-good and worthy of all my love. For the love of you, I love my neighbor as myself. I forgive all who have injured me, and I ask pardon of all whom I have injured.

Respond: *Jesus, I want to profess my love for you over and over until I can declare it face-to-face.*

December 28

LISTEN: *"It is not for you to know the times or periods that the Father has set by his own authority."*

ACTS OF THE APOSTLES 1:7

When the apostles were eager to know when Israel's kingdom would be established, Jesus told them that this information was secret. You might wish to know any number of things: when the pain in your leg will stop, when you will meet the man of your dreams, when a war will cease, when you will conceive, when your immature teenager will grow up, when your house will sell. Such knowledge is withheld from you, sometimes leaving you frustrated.

Knowing the future would satisfy your curiosity and be reassuring. That is why people consult horoscopes and search out fortune tellers and prophets. But our wise God chose to blind you to the days ahead and keep you in suspense. You are to trust that the Father knows best and will eventually work everything out. His timing is impeccable.

After the universe was created, billions of years passed before the first humans came to be. And look how long it took for Abraham's promised Messiah to appear. At times you must exercise extreme patience. But as Jesus told the anchoress Julian of Norwich in 1373, "All will be well, and all manner of things will be well."

RESPOND: *Jesus, I trust that my future years are in your loving hands. Therefore, I face them not with fear but with hope.*

December 29

LISTEN: *"But you will receive power when the*
Holy Spirit comes upon you."
ACTS OF THE APOSTLES 1:8

When you lose electrical power, your lights, furnace, computer, television, refrigerator, microwave, and clocks shut down. You realize anew how much you rely on electricity as you bring out the candles and the board games.

Jesus promised you supernatural power through the indwelling of the Holy Spirit. This mighty Person infuses you with power to overcome the darkness of evil, sin, discouragement, and depression. When you are surrounded by lies, he enables you to discern the truth and act on it. He enlightens you to see clearly to make right decisions. He gives you energy to plough through difficult situations. And he fills you with the warmth to embrace others with love, even those who sorely try you. This Spirit of Jesus is your source of life who empowers you to function as you were designed to do.

The Spirit implanted the Messiah in Mary's womb. In a sense, he can make you pregnant with Christ so you can take him to others as Mary took him to Elizabeth. The Spirit transformed fishermen into evangelizers who spread a movement that has lasted two thousand years. That same Spirit animates you. Draw on his special power when you are faced with dilemmas, predicaments, or trials. It is one power that will not fail you.

RESPOND: *Jesus, I look to the Holy Spirit to give me wisdom,*
courage, and stamina. Thank you for this tremendous Gift.

December 30

LISTEN: *"And you will be my witnesses in Jerusalem, in all Judea and Samaria, and to the ends of the earth."*

ACTS OF THE APOSTLES 1:8

J esus depends on you to witness to him in your corner of the world. You learned about him from parents and grandparents. Now it is your turn to pass on the Good News to those in your house, in your neighborhood, your city or town, and beyond. Yes, you might teach the faith in your domestic church and in your parish. You might write articles and books and speak about the risen Christ and his teachings. But witnessing involves more than words.

You witness by exercising your faith: praying in front of your children, going to church, and displaying a crucifix and statue of Mary in your home. But you also witness by living as Jesus taught. When you comfort a friend, volunteer for a job no one likes, forgive a disobedient teenager, let someone go ahead of you at the store checkout, and accept criticism with a smile, you are living the Gospel and influencing people.

One way you can virtually witness "to the ends of the earth" is to support missionaries through your donations and prayers.

RESPOND: *Jesus, I accept my baptismal commission to spread the news about you and your teachings. May I live it out faithfully and creatively.*

December 31

LISTEN: *"My grace is sufficient for you,*
for power is made perfect in weakness."

2 CORINTHIANS 12:9

The Scripture above was Jesus's response when St. Paul was hoping to have an undefined "thorn" in his side. Jesus seems to favor weak people and in his eyes they accomplish mighty things. Moses has a speech defect but goes to make demands of the Pharaoh and becomes a towering leader. Jeremiah argues that he is too young, but he is known as one of the four major prophets. Mary is a lowly peasant girl but, as she acknowledges in the Magnificat, God did great things for her.

Don't ever underestimate the power of God's grace. Born two months premature, St. Frances Xavier Cabrini was barely five feet tall and coped with frail health all her life. Nevertheless, she founded a religious community in Italy, and then, with God's help, she surmounted tremendous difficulties and founded sixty-seven institutions for the sick and the poor in the United States. Although Mother Cabrini was afraid of water, she crossed the ocean twenty-seven times to do God's work.

Are you reluctant to take on a demanding task like organizing a neighborhood garage sale? Do you shrink back from a difficult situation such as living with an in-law or a needy foster child? You might think you are too weak, too untalented, or too impatient. God has more confidence in you than you do. His grace can work marvels through you.

RESPOND: *Jesus, may I remember that with you and your grace*
all things are possible.

My Reflections

_____

_____

_____

_____

_____

_____

_____

_____

_____

_____

_____

_____

_____

My Reflections

_____

_____

_____

_____

_____

_____

_____

_____

_____

_____

_____

_____

_____

_____

_____

My Reflections

_____

_____

_____

_____

_____

_____

_____

_____

_____

_____

_____

_____

_____

My Reflections

My Reflections

My Reflections

My Reflections

My Reflections

My Reflections

My Reflections

_____

_____

_____

_____

_____

_____

_____

_____

_____

_____

_____

_____

My Reflections

My Reflections

My Reflections